Betty Crocker

ANNUAL RECIPES

2·0·0·6

General Mills
Director, Book and Online Publishing: Kim Walter
Manager, Cookbook Publishing: Lois Tlusty
Recipe Development and Testing: Betty Crocker Kitchens
Photography and Food Styling: General Mills Photo Studio

Editor: Kimberly Tweed
Book Designer: Tracey J. Hambleton

ISBN-13 978–1–59486–241–0 hardcover
ISBN-10 1–59486–241–9 hardcover

Printed in the United States of America

2 4 6 8 10 9 7 5 3 1 hardcover

Cover: Peaches and Cream Cake (page 255)

For more great ideas, visit www.bettycrocker.com

C O N T E N T S

Turkey, Bacon and Avocado Wraps (page 93)

Introduction

Welcome to the fifth edition of *Betty Crocker Annual Recipes*. Once again this year, we've taken your favorite recipes from the past year of *Betty Crocker* magazine and combined them into one fantastic collection. Included are more than 240 mouthwatering recipes, each one destined to be a favorite among your friends and family.

Selections like Seafood and Spinach Enchiladas and Tuna with Three-Herb Pesto are sure to please your seafood fanatic, while hearty and delicious recipes like Barbecue Chicken and Bean Casserole and Cheesy Tomato-Beef Bake will warm the hearts of all who are lucky enough to grab a taste.

And just wait until you see the "Breakfasts and Breads" chapter! It is packed full of fantastic egg dishes like Bacon, Cheese and Tomato Strata and Canadian Bacon and Potato Quiche. Imagine how delighted your loved ones will be to wake up to the aroma of Cinnamon–Corn Bread Waffles with Apple-Cinnamon Syrup!

And then there are the desserts—two chapters full of the best Betty Crocker dessert recipes from the past year! Try the Truffle Lover's Cupcakes or the Praline Mini Bundt Cakes for the next bake sale. Make the Almond Baby Cakes as a surprise gift to take to the baby shower at work. Impress your friends and family with a lovely Lemon Cake with Raspberry Mousse or a Peaches and Cream Cake—both are almost too pretty to eat!

Aside from the hundreds of delicious recipes, you'll also find pages of new information on all the latest from Betty's kitchen. Check out "A New Take on Eggs" in the breakfast chapter to learn about the comeback of the egg and see how you can incorporate this healthful food into your diet. Before your next party, look up "The Fun of Fondue" in the appetizers chapter. Fondue is a fun way to entertain guests at your next gathering—with different varieties to choose from, this is sure to be the hit of the party!

Are you on a diet or in a rush? Betty helps out with her "Low Fat" label on any dish that has 6 grams or less of fat per serving—side dishes and desserts have 3 grams or less. The "Quick" label can be found on recipes that can be prepared in 30 minutes or less—leaving you time to serve a hearty meal while still completing all those errands on time!

To help you decide what to make first, we've included 12 "Inspired Entertaining" menu plans, created to make every meal easier from start to finish. Designed for holidays like Valentine's Day and Father's Day to occasions that should be celebrated, like the arrival of spring and the fun of summer—you'll find a menu to cater each day perfectly. And the "Seasonal Selections" recipe list arranges each recipe by season, helping you select the perfect dish, no matter what the weather is like outside. Full-color photos of each dish are also included, showing you the amazing dishes you can put on the table for your next meal!

We hope you enjoy this edition of *Betty Crocker Annual Recipes*. Thank you for joining us for another year!

Betty Crocker

Inspired Entertaining

MENU IDEAS TO MAKE EVERY OCCASION SPECIAL

Holidays and celebrations are great ways to bring your friends and family together to share a fantastic meal that you've prepared yourself. Try one of these inspired menus to help create a meal that will make your guests feel special no matter what the occasion. From snowy evenings by the fireplace to backyard fun warmed by the heat of summer, you're sure to find a great way to combine delicious recipes into a fabulous meal from drinks to dessert.

Fireside Favorites

Cheesy Olive Bread (page 24)
Slow-Cooker Steak and Black Bean Chili (page 70)
S'mores Chocolate Chip Ice-Cream Sandwiches (page 283)
Hot Chocolate

Monday Night Football Feast

Slow-Cooker Spiced Party Nut Mix (page 39)
Pepperoni Swirls (page 57)
Smoky Cranberry Chicken Wings (page 54)
Cheeseburger Calzones (page 110)
Cowboy BBQ Chicken Pizza (page 105)
Ball Game Cupcakes (page 240)
Assorted Beer and Soda

Be My Valentine

Feta-Topped Chicken (page 151)
New Potatoes and Spring Vegetables (page 216)
Peanut Butter Silk Cake (page 263)
Wine or Champagne

Spring Is in the Air

Light Lemon-Dijon Chicken Salad (page 78)
Grilled Pork Tenderloin with Firecracker Marinade (page 173)
Spring Rice Pilaf (page 224)
Ultimate Carrot Cake (page 264)
Spring Polka Dot Cupcakes (page 239)
Raspberry-Apricot Sangria (page 29)

Bridal Brunch

Bacon and Swiss Quiche (page 9)
Cinnamon–Corn Bread Waffles with Apple-Cinnamon Syrup (page 13)
Brunch Potatoes Alfredo with Roasted Peppers (page 10)
Morning Glory Muffin Squares (page 18)
Iced Hazelnut Coffee Coolers (page 36)
Coffee and Tea
Mimosas
Assorted Juices

Father's Day Lunch

Garden Harvest Chicken Soup (page 63)
Ham and Cheese Foldover Sandwiches (page 97)
Confetti Celebration Cake (page 258)
Assorted Sodas and Juices

Friday Night Cocktails

Summer Celebration

Backyard Barbecue

Giving Thanks

Welcome Winter

New Year's Eve Feast

Seasonal Selections

Need the perfect dessert for Thanksgiving dinner? A sensational salad to take to that Fourth of July picnic? Take your pick from this helpful recipe list, grouped by seasons, to help you select the perfect dish for any time of year!

Winter

Breakfasts and Breads

Rise and Shine with Something Special

Bacon, Cheese and Tomato Strata (page 4)

Sausage-Cheese Pancake Sandwiches (page 11)

Quick

Bacon and Tomato Frittata

Prep Time: 20 min Start to Finish: 20 min

1 carton (16 ounces) cholesterol-free fat-free egg product

$^1/_4$ teaspoon salt-free garlic-and-herb seasoning

$^1/_4$ teaspoon salt

2 teaspoons vegetable oil

4 medium green onions, sliced ($^1/_4$ cup)

2 large roma (plum) tomatoes, sliced

$^1/_2$ cup shredded sharp Cheddar cheese (2 ounces)

2 tablespoons real bacon pieces (from 2.8-ounce package)

2 tablespoons light sour cream

1. In medium bowl, mix egg product, garlic-and-herb seasoning and salt; set aside.

2. In 10-inch nonstick ovenproof skillet, heat oil over medium heat. Add onions; cook and stir 1 minute. Reduce heat to medium-low. Pour in egg mixture. Cook 6 to 9 minutes, gently lifting edges of cooked portions with spatula so that uncooked egg mixture can flow to bottom of skillet, until set.

3. Set oven control to broil. Top frittata with tomatoes, cheese and bacon. Broil with top 4 inches from heat 1 to 2 minutes or until cheese is melted. Top each serving with sour cream.

4 servings.
1 Serving: Calories 175 (Calories from Fat 80); Fat 9g (Saturated 4g); Cholesterol 20mg; Sodium 510mg; Carbohydrate 5g (Dietary Fiber 2g); Protein 18g
% Daily Value:Vitamin A 20%; Vitamin C 4%; Calcium 12%; Iron 14%
Exchanges: 1 Vegetable, 2$^1/_2$ Lean Meat
Carbohydrate Choices: 0

BETTY'S TIPS

⚙ **Kitchen Tip**

If you don't have an ovenproof skillet, just wrap the skillet handle in a double layer of heavy-duty foil.

Look for ready-to-use bacon pieces near the salad dressings in the grocery store. They are shelf stable until they are opened, then need to be refrigerated.

Bacon and Tomato Frittata

Eggs and Sausage Skillet

Prep Time: 35 min Start to Finish: 35 min

1 package (12 ounces) bulk reduced-fat pork sausage

4 ounces fresh mushrooms, sliced (1$\frac{1}{2}$ cups)

3 cups frozen potatoes O'Brien (from 1-pound 12-ounce bag), thawed

$\frac{1}{2}$ teaspoon salt

$\frac{1}{8}$ teaspoon pepper

6 eggs

1 cup shredded Swiss cheese (4 ounces)

1 large tomato, chopped (1 cup)

1. In 12-inch nonstick skillet, cook sausage over medium-high heat 5 to 7 minutes, stirring frequently, until no longer pink.

2. Stir mushrooms, potatoes, salt and pepper into sausage. Cook over medium heat about 8 minutes, stirring frequently, until potatoes begin to brown. Reduce heat to low.

3. Using back of spoon, make 6 indentations in mixture. Break 1 egg into each indentation. Cover and cook 8 to 10 minutes or until egg whites are set and yolks are beginning to thicken.

4. Sprinkle with cheese and tomato. Cover and cook 3 to 4 minutes or until cheese is melted.

Eggs and Sausage Skillet

6 servings (1 cup each).
1 Serving: Calories 330 (Calories from Fat 170); Fat 19g (Saturated 7g); Cholesterol 250mg; Sodium 700mg; Carbohydrate 21g (Dietary Fiber 2g); Protein 19g
% Daily Value: Vitamin A 16%; Vitamin C 18%; Calcium 18%; Iron 10%
Exchanges: 1 Starch, 1 Vegetable, 2 High-Fat Meat, $\frac{1}{2}$ Fat
Carbohydrate Choices: 1$\frac{1}{2}$

BETTY'S TIPS

⚙ **Kitchen Tip**
Reduced-fat sausage is less fatty, eliminating the need to drain the fat.

To capture the British tradition of this dish, serve it with toast and baked beans.

Bacon, Cheese and Tomato Strata

Prep Time: 15 min Start to Finish: 3 hr 15 min
(Photo on page 1)

   7   cups lightly packed 1-inch cubes French
       bread (8 ounces)
   2   cups shredded Cheddar cheese (8 ounces)
   2   cups chopped roma (plum) tomatoes
       (6 medium)
   6   eggs
1¹/₂   cups milk
   1   teaspoon Dijon mustard
   1   teaspoon dried basil leaves
 ¹/₂   teaspoon salt
   6   slices bacon

1. Spray 13 x 9-inch baking dish with cooking spray.
   Spread bread in baking dish. Sprinkle evenly with
   1¹/₂ cups cheese; mix lightly with bread. Sprinkle
   with tomatoes.

2. In medium bowl, beat eggs, milk, mustard, basil and
   salt with fork or wire whisk; pour over bread mixture.
   Cover tightly and refrigerate at least 2 hours but no
   longer than 24 hours.

3. Heat oven to 350°. Bake uncovered 40 to 45 minutes
   or until knife inserted in center comes out clean.
   Meanwhile, in 10-inch skillet, cook bacon over
   medium heat 8 to 10 minutes, turning occasionally,
   until crisp; drain on paper towel.

4. Crumble bacon. Sprinkle bacon and remaining
   ¹/₂ cup cheese over strata. Let stand 10 minutes
   before serving.

12 servings.
1 Serving: Calories 210 (Calories from Fat 110); Fat 12g (Saturated 6g);
Cholesterol 130mg; Sodium 440mg; Carbohydrate 13g (Dietary Fiber
1g); Protein 12g
% Daily Value: Vitamin A 12%; Vitamin C 4%; Calcium 16%; Iron 6%
Exchanges: 1 Starch, 1¹/₂ High-Fat Meat, ¹/₂ Fat
Carbohydrate Choices: 1

BETTY'S TIPS

⊛ **Success Hint**
Roma tomatoes aren't as juicy as regular slicing tomatoes, but they hold their shape better during baking and
cooking.

⊛ **Serve-With**
For a holiday brunch, serve this breakfast casserole with
sliced quick breads and a citrus fruit salad sprinkled
with pomegranate seeds.

⊛ **Special Touch**
Instead of sprinkling with shredded cheese, arrange
star-shaped cheese cutouts on top of the strata.

Tex-Mex Sausage and Egg Bake

Prep Time: 20 min Start to Finish: 9 hr 25 min

12 ounces bulk spicy pork sausage

5 cups frozen southern-style hash brown potatoes (from 32-ounce bag)

1 can (4.5 ounces) Old El Paso® chopped green chiles, undrained

3 cups shredded Colby-Monterey Jack cheese (12 ounces)

6 eggs

1 1/2 cups milk

1/4 teaspoon salt

1 cup Old El Paso Thick 'n Chunky salsa

1. Spray 13 x 9-inch baking dish with cooking spray. In 10-inch skillet, cook sausage over medium heat 8 to 10 minutes, stirring occasionally, until no longer pink. Drain on paper towel.

2. Spread frozen potatoes in baking dish. Sprinkle with sausage, green chiles and 1 1/2 cups cheese. In medium bowl, beat eggs, milk and salt with fork or wire whisk until well blended. Pour over potato mixture. Sprinkle with remaining 1 1/2 cups cheese. Cover and refrigerate at least 8 hours but no longer than 12 hours.

3. Heat oven to 350°. Bake uncovered 50 to 60 minutes or until knife inserted near center comes out clean. Let stand 10 minutes. Cut into squares. Serve with salsa.

10 servings.
1 Serving: Calories 355 (Calories from Fat 180); Fat 20g (Saturated 10g); Cholesterol 175mg; Sodium 1,120mg; Carbohydrate 25g (Dietary Fiber 3g); Protein 19g
% Daily Value: Vitamin A 18%; Vitamin C 10%; Calcium 32%; Iron 8%
Exchanges: 1 1/2 Starch, 2 High-Fat Meat, 1 Fat
Carbohydrate Choices: 1 1/2

BETTY'S TIPS

☺ **Substitution**
If you can't find a 12-ounce package of pork sausage, you can use a 16-ounce package.

☺ **Time-Saver**
No need to wait! You can bake this dish right away if you like.

☺ **Serve-With**
Warm corn bread with honey butter and a fruit salad of orange, grapefruit and mango pieces give your brunch a southwestern flair.

☺ **Did You Know?**
Cubed hash brown potatoes are called "southern-style," and shredded potatoes are called "country-style." Either one can be used in casseroles like this.

Tex-Mex Sausage and Egg Bake

Betty Crocker
ON HEALTH

Fitting Eggs into a Healthful Diet

One single egg serves up a fair amount of nutrition, yet bringing back eggs still calls for prudence. Here's how to make them part of a healthful diet:

▶ **Think averages.** If you want an egg a day or even two, choose fewer cholesterol-containing foods (that means meat, poultry and dairy foods) at other meals throughout the week.

▶ **Cook smart.** Skip frying. Use low-fat methods of egg preparation, such as scrambling, poaching or hard-cooking.

▶ **Pick wholesome partners.** Instead of opting for the traditional bacon and hash brown potatoes, choose vegetables, whole-grain bread and fruit as accompaniments.

For tips on egg safety, check out the FDA's Center for Food Safety and Applied Nutrition Web site: www.cfsan.fda.gov/~dms/fs-eggs.html.

A NEW TAKE ON EGGS
Things are looking sunny-side up

Eggs fell from favor 30 years ago when researchers linked the cholesterol in foods with an increased risk for heart disease. Back then, scientists thought the cholesterol in foods significantly influenced the amount of cholesterol in a person's blood. Because eggs are one of the richest sources of cholesterol in the diet, they were branded as "bad."

Today, eggs are back. A better understanding of how diet, including the cholesterol in food, affects heart health, plus a better idea of an egg's nutritional merits means eggs can have a place on the menu.

What's Inside the Shell?

NUTRIENT/SUBSTANCE	AMOUNT PER LARGE EGG	PERCENT OF DAILY VALUE
Calories	75	
Protein	6 grams	10
Fat (total)	4.5 grams	7
Saturated	1.5 grams	
Monounsaturated	2.0 grams	
Polyunsaturated	0.7 gram	
Cholesterol	213 milligrams	71
Vitamin A	318 IU	6
Vitamin B$_{12}$	0.5 microgram	8
Folate	23 micrograms	6
Vitamin D*	26 IU	6
Choline**	280 micrograms	No known value
Lutein***	150 to 250 micrograms	No known value
Zeaxanthin***	200 micrograms	No known value

*The vitamin D in eggs may be better absorbed in the body than vitamin D found in other foods.

**Choline has been linked to brain and memory development in babies.

***Lutein and zeaxanthin found in egg yolks may help maintain healthy eyes.

And there's more...

Eggs are an ideal source of protein; they contain all the amino acids your body needs to build bones, muscles, antibodies and more. They also contain other B vitamins plus iron, zinc and vitamin E.

The Cholesterol Controversy

For most adults, the cholesterol in food is not what really affects cholesterol levels in the blood. Other factors, such as saturated fat, have a greater impact.

Though cholesterol is still on the radar, the American Heart Association recommends people focus more on the amount and type of fat in their diet than on their egg consumption. Aim for less than 300 milligrams of dietary cholesterol a day.

Canadian Bacon and Potato Quiche

Prep Time: 20 min Start to Finish: 1 hr 5 min

1   refrigerated pie crust (from 15-ounce package)
1   cup frozen country-style shredded potatoes, thawed
1   cup $1/2$-inch pieces fresh asparagus
1   cup diced Canadian-style bacon
$1^1/2$ cups shredded Havarti cheese (6 ounces)
4   eggs
1   cup milk
$1/2$ teaspoon dried marjoram leaves
$1/4$ teaspoon salt

1. Heat oven to 375°. Place pie crust in 9-inch pie plate as directed on package for one-crust filled pie. Bake about 8 minutes or until light golden brown.

2. Layer potatoes, asparagus, bacon and cheese in partially baked crust. In medium bowl, beat eggs, milk, marjoram and salt with wire whisk until well blended. Pour over mixture in pie plate.

3. Bake 45 to 50 minutes or until knife inserted in center comes out clean. Let stand 5 minutes before cutting.

8 servings.
1 Serving: Calories 295 (Calories from Fat 170); Fat 19g (Saturated 8g); Cholesterol 140mg; Sodium 640mg; Carbohydrate 16g (Dietary Fiber 1g); Protein 15g
% Daily Value: Vitamin A 12%; Vitamin C 4%; Calcium 18%; Iron 6%
Exchanges: 1 Starch, 2 High-Fat Meat, $1/2$ Fat
Carbohydrate Choices: 1

BETTY'S TIPS

✿ **Success Hint**
Partially baking the pie crust before adding the filling prevents the crust from getting soggy.

✿ **Serve-With**
Greet your guests with mimosas and serve the quiche with Overnight Lemon Country Coffee Cake (page 20) and a fruit cup of fresh berries.

✿ **Do-Ahead**
You can prepare all of the parts of this quiche ahead of time. Shape the crust in the pie plate; cover and refrigerate. Cut the asparagus, dice the bacon, shred the cheese and place each in an individual plastic food-storage bag; refrigerate. Beat egg-milk mixture; cover and refrigerate. Just before serving, prebake the crust, assemble the quiche and bake as directed.

Canadian Bacon and Potato Quiche

Bacon and Swiss Quiche

Prep Time: 15 min Start to Finish: 55 min

1¼ cups Original Bisquick® mix

¼ cup butter or margarine, softened

2 tablespoons boiling water

1 package (6 ounces) sliced Canadian-style bacon, chopped

1 cup shredded Swiss cheese (4 ounces)

4 medium green onions, thinly sliced (¼ cup)

1½ cups half-and-half

3 eggs

½ teaspoon salt

¼ teaspoon ground red pepper (cayenne)

1. Heat oven to 375°. Spray 9-inch pie plate with cooking spray. In medium bowl, stir Bisquick mix and butter until mixed. Add boiling water; stir vigorously until soft dough forms. Press in bottom and up side of pie plate, forming edge on rim of pie plate.

2. Sprinkle bacon, cheese and onions over crust. In medium bowl, beat half-and-half, eggs, salt and pepper with wire whisk until well mixed. Pour into crust.

3. Bake 35 to 40 minutes or until edge is brown and knife inserted in center comes out clean.

8 servings.
1 Serving: Calories 300 (Calories from Fat 190); Fat 21g (Saturated 11g); Cholesterol 135mg; Sodium 800mg; Carbohydrate 15g (Dietary Fiber 0g); Protein 13g
% Daily Value: Vitamin A 14%; Vitamin C 0%; Calcium 22%; Iron 6%
Exchanges: 1 Starch, ½ High-Fat Meat, 1½ Fat
Carbohydrate Choices: 1

BETTY'S TIPS

⊛ **Substitution**
Shredded Monterey Jack or Pepper Jack cheese can be used instead of the Swiss.

⊛ **Do-Ahead**
Break out of the sandwich rut and try a slice of this cheesy quiche for lunch. Make it a day ahead, then pull it out of the refrigerator and warm it up in the microwave. It even tastes great cold!

⊛ **Special Touch**
Dress up this baked egg dish with tomato wedges arranged in a pinwheel pattern on top of the quiche.

Bacon and Swiss Quiche

Brunch Potatoes Alfredo with Roasted Peppers

Prep Time: 10 min Start to Finish: 50 min

7 cups frozen country-style shredded hash brown potatoes (from 30-ounce bag), thawed

³/₄ cup chopped drained roasted red bell peppers (from 7-ounce jar)

4 medium green onions, sliced (¹/₄ cup)

1 container (10 ounces) refrigerated Alfredo pasta sauce

1¹/₂ cups shredded Swiss cheese (6 ounces)

Additional sliced green onion tops, if desired

1. Heat oven to 350°. Spray 11 x 7-inch or 12 x 8-inch baking dish with cooking spray. Place potatoes, peppers and onions in baking dish; mix lightly. Top with Alfredo sauce; sprinkle with cheese.

2. Bake uncovered 40 to 45 minutes or until golden brown. Sprinkle with additional green onion tops and chopped roasted bell peppers just before serving.

10 servings.
1 Serving: Calories 295 (Calories from Fat 125); Fat 14g (Saturated 9g); Cholesterol 45mg; Sodium 570mg; Carbohydrate 32g (Dietary Fiber 3g); Protein 10g
% Daily Value: Vitamin A 26%; Vitamin C 28%; Calcium 26%; Iron 4%
Exchanges: 2 Starch, ¹/₂ High-Fat Meat, 2 Fat
Carbohydrate Choices: 2

BETTY'S TIPS

⊙ **Time-Saver**
Quickly thaw the potatoes by microwaving them in a microwavable bowl, uncovered, on High 3 to 5 minutes, stirring once.

⊙ **Serve-With**
This potato casserole goes well with egg dishes, ham and other breakfast main dishes. Round out the brunch with sliced fresh winter fruits and a coffee cake.

⊙ **Do-Ahead**
Assemble all the ingredients in the baking dish, and cover and refrigerate up to 12 hours ahead. You don't need to thaw the potatoes, because they'll thaw while in the fridge.

Brunch Potatoes Alfredo with Roasted Peppers

Sausage-Cheese Pancake Sandwiches

Prep Time: 20 min   Start to Finish: 20 min
(Photo on page 1)

1	cup Original Bisquick mix
$^1/_2$	cup milk
3	eggs
2	tablespoons maple-flavored syrup
4	fully cooked pork sausage patties
1	tablespoon milk
1	teaspoon butter or margarine
4	slices ($^2/_3$ ounce each) processed American cheese

1. Heat griddle or skillet over medium heat or to 375°. Grease griddle with vegetable oil if necessary (or spray with cooking spray before heating).

2. In small bowl, stir Bisquick mix, $^1/_2$ cup milk, 1 egg and maple syrup with spoon until blended. For each pancake, pour 2 tablespoons batter onto hot griddle (make 8 pancakes total). Cook until edges are dry. Turn; cook other sides until golden.

3. Meanwhile, heat sausage patties as directed on package. In small bowl, beat remaining 2 eggs and 1 tablespoon milk. In 8-inch nonstick skillet, melt butter over medium heat. Cook eggs in butter, stirring occasionally, until set.

4. For each sandwich, place 1 sausage patty on 1 pancake; top with one-quarter of the eggs, 1 slice cheese and another pancake.

4 sandwiches.

1 Sandwich: Calories 440 (Calories from Fat 260); Fat 29g (Saturated 13g); Cholesterol 215mg; Sodium 1,050mg; Carbohydrate 28g (Dietary Fiber 0g); Protein 17g
% Daily Value: Vitamin A 12%; Vitamin C 0%; Calcium 22%; Iron 10%
Exchanges: 2 Starch, $1^1/_2$ High-Fat Meat, 3 Fat
Carbohydrate Choices: 2

BETTY'S TIPS

⚙ **Substitution**
Try slices of Canadian-style bacon or fully cooked ham instead of the sausage patties, if you like..

⚙ **Serve-With**
Start your day off right with these morning sandwiches. Add a piece of fresh fruit and a glass of milk for a great breakfast.

⚙ **Do-Ahead**
You can make the pancakes ahead, stack them with waxed paper between each pancake and then wrap and freeze until you need them.

Overnight Filled French Toast with Raspberry Sauce

Prep Time: 25 min Start to Finish: 9 hr 5 min

French Toast

- 12 slices French bread, 1$\frac{1}{2}$ inches thick
- 2 packages (3 ounces each) cream cheese, softened
- 2 tablespoons sugar
- 2 tablespoons orange marmalade
- $\frac{1}{2}$ cup dried cranberries
- 8 eggs
- 2 cups milk
- $\frac{1}{4}$ cup sugar
- $\frac{1}{4}$ teaspoon salt
- 3 tablespoons butter or margarine, melted

Raspberry Sauce

- 1 package (10 ounces) frozen sweetened raspberries, thawed
- 2 teaspoons cornstarch
- 2 tablespoons sugar
- 2 tablespoons orange marmalade

Overnight Filled French Toast with Raspberry Sauce

1. Spray 13 x 9-inch baking dish with cooking spray. Cut almost through each bread slice, cutting from top crust to—but not through—bottom crust. In small bowl, stir together cream cheese, 2 tablespoons sugar, 2 tablespoons marmalade and cranberries. Open bread slices enough to spread 1 heaping tablespoon cheese mixture evenly on 1 cut surface of each slice. Press bread slices together. Place in baking dish.

2. In medium bowl, beat eggs, milk, $\frac{1}{4}$ cup sugar and salt with wire whisk until well blended. Pour over bread; turn slices carefully to coat. Cover and refrigerate at least 8 hours or overnight.

3. Heat oven to 425°. Drizzle melted butter over bread. Bake uncovered 20 to 25 minutes or until golden brown.

4. Meanwhile, drain juice from raspberries into 1-cup glass measuring cup; add enough water to measure $\frac{3}{4}$ cup. In 1-quart saucepan, stir together juice mixture, cornstarch, 2 tablespoons sugar and 2 tablespoons marmalade. Heat to boiling, stirring occasionally; remove from heat. Cool 15 minutes. Stir in raspberries. Serve sauce with French toast.

6 servings.
1 Serving: Calories 795 (Calories from Fat 260); Fat 29g (Saturated 14g); Cholesterol 335mg; Sodium 1,100mg; Carbohydrate 108g (Dietary Fiber 6g); Protein 25g
% Daily Value: Vitamin A 22%; Vitamin C 8%; Calcium 26%; Iron 30%
Exchanges: 3 Starch, 1 Fruit, 3 Other Carbohydrates, 2 Medium-Fat Meat, 3 Fat
Carbohydrate Choices: 7

BETTY'S TIPS

✪ **Success Hint**
Arrange the bread slices so they fit in a single layer in the pan. Once you pour the milk mixture over them, you'll be more flexible.

✪ **Time-Saver**
Quickly thaw raspberries by removing the lid of the package and microwaving on High 1 minute 30 seconds to 2 minutes, stirring once.

✪ **Serve-With**
Enjoy with bacon and/or sausage links and fresh fruit.

✪ **Do-Ahead**
Assemble the French toast the night before. Prepare the sauce and put it in a microwavable serving dish; cover and refrigerate. Warm the sauce by microwaving on High 1 minute 30 seconds to 2 minutes.

Cinnamon–Corn Bread Waffles with Apple-Cinnamon Syrup

Prep Time: 30 min Start to Finish: 30 min

Apple-Cinnamon Syrup

- 1 cup cinnamon apple pie filling (from 21-ounce can)
- 1 cup maple-flavored syrup

Waffles

- 1$^1/_2$ cups Original Bisquick mix
- $^1/_2$ cup cornmeal
- 1$^1/_3$ cups milk
- 2 tablespoons vegetable oil
- 1 teaspoon ground cinnamon
- 1 egg

1. In medium microwavable bowl, mix pie filling and maple syrup. Microwave uncovered on High 1 to 2 minutes or until warm; set aside.

2. Heat waffle iron. (Waffle irons without a nonstick coating may need to be brushed with vegetable oil or sprayed with cooking spray before you add batter for each waffle.)

3. In medium bowl, stir all waffle ingredients with spoon until blended. Pour batter onto hot waffle iron. (Check manufacturer's directions for recommended amount of batter.) Close lid of waffle iron.

4. Bake 4 to 5 minutes or until steaming stops. Carefully remove waffle. Serve with syrup.

7 servings (two 3$^1/_2$-inch waffles each).
1 Serving: Calories 380 (Calories from Fat 80); Fat 9g (Saturated 2g); Cholesterol 35mg; Sodium 450mg; Carbohydrate 70g (Dietary Fiber 2g); Protein 5g
% Daily Value: Vitamin A 4%; Vitamin C 0%; Calcium 10%; Iron 8%
Exchanges: 2 Starch, $^1/_2$ Fruit, 2 Other Carbohydrate, 1$^1/_2$ Fat
Carbohydrate Choices: 4$^1/_2$

Cinnamon–Corn Bread Waffles with Apple-Cinnamon Syrup

BETTY'S TIPS

✺ **Success Hint**

Leftovers? Stack cooled waffles between sheets of waxed paper. Wrap in foil and freeze. To reheat, unwrap waffles and remove waxed paper. Microwave uncovered on High, or heat them in the oven for a few minutes until hot.

Any extra pie filling makes a terrific ice cream topper, or try it spooned over slices of angel food or pound cake. Tightly covered, the pie filling should keep up to a week in the refrigerator.

✺ **Serve-With**

Warm up a cool fall morning with these toasty waffles and hot apple cider. Add an extra sprinkle of cinnamon to the waffles, if you like.

Blueberry-Orange Pancakes with Blueberry-Orange Sauce

Prep Time: 35 min Start to Finish: 35 min

Blueberry-Orange Sauce

- 1/4 cup sugar
- 1 1/2 teaspoons cornstarch
- 2 tablespoons orange juice
- 1/4 teaspoon grated orange peel
- 2 cups fresh or frozen unsweetened blueberries

Pancakes

- 2 cups Original Bisquick mix
- 1 cup milk
- 2 eggs
- 1 teaspoon grated orange peel
- 1/4 teaspoon ground nutmeg
- 1 cup fresh or frozen unsweetened blueberries

1. In 1 1/2-quart saucepan, mix sugar and cornstarch. Stir in orange juice and 1/4 teaspoon orange peel until smooth. Stir in 2 cups blueberries. Heat to boiling over medium heat, stirring constantly. Boil about 2 minutes, stirring occasionally, until thickened. Keep warm.

2. Heat griddle or skillet over medium heat or to 375°. Grease griddle with vegetable oil if necessary. In medium bowl, stir all pancake ingredients except blueberries with spoon until blended. Fold in 1 cup blueberries with spoon until blended. For each pancake, pour slightly less than 1/4 cup batter onto hot griddle. Cook until edges are dry. Turn; cook other sides until golden. Serve with warm sauce.

7 servings.
1 Serving: Calories 215 (Calories from Fat 65); Fat 7g (Saturated 2g); Cholesterol 65mg; Sodium 530mg; Carbohydrate 32g (Dietary Fiber 2g); Protein 6g
% Daily Value: Vitamin A 4%; Vitamin C 8%; Calcium 10%; Iron 8%
Exchanges: 1 Starch, 1 Fruit, 1/2 Medium-Fat Meat, 1 Fat
Carbohydrate Choices: 2

BETTY'S TIPS

⚙ **Success Hint**
When using frozen blueberries in the pancakes, be sure to blot them with paper towels to keep the juice from staining the batter.

⚙ **Do-Ahead**
Save yourself some time in the morning by making the sauce the night before. When the pancakes are ready, simply warm the sauce in the microwave, and breakfast is served.

⚙ **Special Touch**
For a restaurant-style touch, top each serving with sweetened whipped cream, a few fresh berries and additional grated orange peel.

Blueberry-Orange Pancakes with Blueberry-Orange Sauce

Quick

Oatmeal–Brown Sugar Pancakes with Banana-Walnut Syrup

Prep Time: 30 min Start to Finish: 30 min

Banana-Walnut Syrup

- 2 tablespoons butter or margarine
- $1/4$ cup chopped walnuts
- 2 bananas, sliced
- 1 cup maple-flavored syrup

Pancakes

- 2 cups Original Bisquick mix
- $1/2$ cup old-fashioned or quick-cooking oats
- 2 tablespoons packed brown sugar
- $1^1/4$ cups milk
- 2 eggs

1. In $1^1/2$-quart saucepan, melt butter over medium heat. Cook walnuts in butter, stirring occasionally, until walnuts and butter just begin to brown. Add bananas; stir to coat with butter. Stir in syrup; reduce heat to low. Cook until warm. Keep warm while making pancakes.

2. Heat griddle or skillet over medium heat or to 375°. Grease griddle with vegetable oil if necessary (or spray with cooking spray before heating).

3. In medium bowl, stir all pancake ingredients with spoon until blended. For each pancake, pour $1/4$ cup batter onto hot griddle. Cook until edges are dry. Turn; cook other sides until golden. Serve with warm syrup.

6 servings.
1 Serving: Calories 520 (Calories from Fat 145); Fat 16g (Saturated 5g); Cholesterol 85mg; Sodium 710mg; Carbohydrate 85g (Dietary Fiber 2g); Protein 9g
% Daily Value: Vitamin A 6%; Vitamin C 2%; Calcium 16%; Iron 12%
Exchanges: $2^1/2$ Starch, 1 Fruit, 2 Other Carbohydrate, 3 Fat
Carbohydrate Choices: $5^1/2$

BETTY'S TIPS

⊗ **Substitution**
Instead of walnuts, you can used chopped pecans in the syrup.

⊗ **Success Hint**
Watch the butter carefully when it's browning, so it turns an even golden brown color that just begins to smell toasty.

⊗ **Variation**
For a Bananas Foster–style treat, make extra syrup to serve over bowlfuls of vanilla ice cream.

Oatmeal–Brown Sugar Pancakes with Banana-Walnut Syrup

Nutty Whole-Grain Silver Dollar Pancakes

Prep Time: 25 min Start to Finish: 25 min

3/4 cup Wheaties® cereal, slightly crushed (1/2 cup)

1/4 cup raisins

1/4 cup dry-roasted sunflower nuts

2 cups Original Bisquick mix

1 1/2 cups Wheaties cereal, crushed (3/4 cup)

1 1/4 cups milk

2 eggs

1/3 cup vanilla yogurt

3/4 cup honey

1. In small bowl, toss 1/2 cup slightly crushed cereal, the raisins and nuts; set aside.

2. Heat griddle or skillet over medium heat or to 375°. Grease griddle with vegetable oil if necessary (or spray with cooking spray before heating).

3. In medium bowl, stir Bisquick mix, 3/4 cup crushed cereal, milk and eggs with fork until blended. For each pancake, pour 1 measuring tablespoon batter onto hot griddle. Cook until edges are dry. Turn; cook other sides until golden.

4. For each serving, arrange 6 pancakes on plate. Top with 1 tablespoon yogurt and about 2 1/2 tablespoons cereal mixture. Drizzle 2 tablespoons honey over all.

6 servings.
1 Serving: Calories 460 (Calories from Fat 100); Fat 11g (Saturated 3g); Cholesterol 75mg; Sodium 750mg; Carbohydrate 80g (Dietary Fiber 2g); Protein 10g
% Daily Value: Vitamin A 8%; Vitamin C 2%; Calcium 18%; Iron 28%
Exchanges: 3 Starch, 2 Other Carbohydrate, 2 Fat
Carbohydrate Choices: 5

BETTY'S TIPS

✿ **Substitution**
Take your pick of yogurt flavors to use on these good-for-you breakfast cakes.

✿ **Variation**
Make peanut butter and jelly pancake-wiches with these little gems. Leave off the toppings and instead spread with peanut butter and jelly.

Instead of topping with the cereal mixture, try these mini pancakes with yogurt, honey, sliced strawberries and bananas.

Nutty Whole-Grain Silver Dollar Pancakes

Morning Glory Muffin Squares

Prep Time: 15 min Start to Finish: 1 hr 20 min

Brown Sugar Streusel

$^1/_2$ cup Original Bisquick mix

$^1/_3$ cup packed brown sugar

2 tablespoons firm butter or margarine

Muffins

2 cups Original Bisquick mix

$1^1/_2$ teaspoons pumpkin pie spice

$^1/_2$ cup chopped walnuts

$^1/_2$ cup shredded carrots

$^1/_2$ cup raisins

2 tablespoons granulated sugar

$^2/_3$ cup milk

2 tablespoons vegetable oil

1 egg

1. Heat oven to 375°. In small bowl, mix $^1/_2$ cup Bisquick mix and brown sugar until well blended. Cut in butter, using fork or pastry blender, until mixture is crumbly; set aside.

2. In large bowl, stir 2 cups Bisquick mix, pumpkin pie spice, walnuts, carrots, raisins and granulated sugar. Stir in milk, oil and egg. Pour into ungreased 8-inch-square pan. Sprinkle with streusel.

3. Bake 30 to 35 minutes or until toothpick inserted in center comes out clean. Cool 30 minutes before serving. Serve warm.

9 servings.

1 Serving: Calories 325 (Calories from Fat 145); Fat 16g (Saturated 4g); Cholesterol 30mg; Sodium 510mg; Carbohydrate 40g (Dietary Fiber 1g); Protein 5g
% Daily Value: Vitamin A 26%; Vitamin C 0%; Calcium 10%; Iron 8%
Exchanges: 2 Starch, $^1/_2$ Other Carbohydrate, 3 Fat
Carbohydrate Choices: $2^1/_2$

BETTY'S TIPS

⊙ **Variation**
Stir $^1/_2$ cup miniature chocolate chips into the batter for a fun chocolaty twist to this quick morning bread.

⊙ **Do-Ahead**
Go ahead and make this recipe ahead of time, but be sure to warm each piece before serving to enjoy these squares at their very best.

⊙ **Special Touch**
Mmm, spread a little honey or honey butter over split muffin squares for a melt-in-your-mouth treat.

Morning Glory Muffin Squares

Quick
Almond–Poppy Seed Muffins
Prep Time: 10 min Start to Finish: 30 min

$1/2$ cup sugar

$1/3$ cup vegetable oil

1 egg

$1/2$ teaspoon almond extract

$1/2$ cup sour cream

$1/4$ cup milk

$1^1/3$ cups Gold Medal® all-purpose flour

$1/2$ teaspoon baking powder

$1/2$ teaspoon salt

$1/4$ teaspoon baking soda

2 tablespoons poppy seed

3 teaspoons sugar

2 tablespoons sliced almonds

1. Heat oven to 375°. Line 12 medium muffin cups with paper baking cups (or spray cups with cooking spray or grease with shortening).

2. In large bowl, stir together $1/2$ cup sugar, oil, egg and almond extract. Beat in sour cream and milk with spoon until blended. Stir in flour, baking powder, salt, baking soda and poppy seed until well blended. Divide batter evenly among muffin cups. Sprinkle batter with 3 teaspoons sugar and almonds.

3. Bake 14 to 17 minutes or until toothpick inserted in center comes out clean. Remove from pan to wire rack. Serve warm or cool.

12 muffins.
1 Muffin: Calories 185 (Calories from Fat 90); Fat 10g (Saturated 2g); Cholesterol 25mg; Sodium 160mg; Carbohydrate 21g (Dietary Fiber 1g); Protein 3g
% Daily Value: Vitamin A 2%; Vitamin C 0%; Calcium 4%; Iron 4%
Exchanges: 1 Starch, $1/2$ Other Carbohydrate, $1^1/2$ Fat
Carbohydrate Choices: $1^1/2$

BETTY'S TIPS

❂ **Do-Ahead**
You can make the batter the night before, cover the bowl and put it in the fridge. Pop the muffins in the oven to bake just as your guests arrive. Bake at 375° for 16 to 18 minutes or until golden brown.

❂ **Special Touch**
Add a gourmet touch by making a glaze with $1/2$ cup powdered sugar and 2 to 3 teaspoons milk. Use a spoon to drizzle the glaze over the muffins.

Almond–Poppy Seed Muffins

Overnight Lemon Country Coffee Cake

Prep Time: 15 min Start to Finish: 9 hr 10 min

¹/₂ cup butter or margarine, softened

1 cup granulated sugar

2 eggs

2 containers (6 ounces each) Yoplait® Original lemon burst yogurt

2 teaspoons grated lemon peel

2¹/₃ cups Gold Medal all-purpose flour

1¹/₂ teaspoons baking powder

¹/₂ teaspoon salt

¹/₄ teaspoon baking soda

³/₄ cup packed brown sugar

³/₄ cup chopped pecans

¹/₂ teaspoon ground nutmeg

Overnight Lemon Country Coffee Cake

1. Spray bottom only of 13 x 9-inch pan with cooking spray. Beat butter and granulated sugar with electric mixer on low speed until light and fluffy. Add eggs, one at a time, beating well after each addition. Add yogurt, lemon peel, flour, baking powder, salt and baking soda; beat on low speed until smooth. Spread batter in pan. Cover and refrigerate at least 8 hours but no longer than 16 hours.

2. In small resealable plastic bag, mix brown sugar, pecans and nutmeg. Refrigerate.

3. When ready to bake, let coffee cake stand at room temperature while heating oven to 350°. Uncover coffee cake; sprinkle with brown sugar mixture.

4. Bake 30 to 40 minutes or until toothpick inserted in center comes out clean. Cool 15 minutes. Serve warm.

15 servings.
1 Serving: Calories 250 (Calories from Fat 110); Fat 12g (Saturated 5g); Cholesterol 45mg; Sodium 220mg; Carbohydrate 31g (Dietary Fiber 1g); Protein 5g
% Daily Value: Vitamin A 6%; Vitamin C 0%; Calcium 8%; Iron 8%
Exchanges: 2 Starch, 2 Fat
Carbohydrate Choices: 2

BETTY'S TIPS

✪ **Time-Saver**
You can bake the coffee cake right away. Just sprinkle it with the topping and reduce the baking time to 25 to 30 minutes.

✪ **Serve-With**
The sweet-tart flavor of this coffee cake is great with a Tex-Mex Sausage and Egg Bake (page 5). Serve with sliced honeydew and cantaloupe.

✪ **Variation**
Make an orange version of this coffee cake with orange yogurt and grated orange peel.

Cranberry-Apple-Nut Bread

Prep Time: 15 min Start to Finish: 2 hr 50 min

$^3/_4$ cup sugar

$^1/_2$ cup vegetable oil

1 egg

1 cup shredded peeled apple (about 1 medium)

$1^1/_2$ cups Gold Medal all-purpose flour

$^1/_2$ teaspoon baking soda

$^1/_2$ teaspoon baking powder

$^1/_2$ teaspoon salt

$^3/_4$ cup chopped walnuts

$^1/_2$ cup dried cranberries

1 tablespoon sugar

$^1/_2$ teaspoon ground cinnamon

1. Heat oven to 350°. Grease bottom only of 8 x 4- or 9 x 5-inch loaf pan with shortening.

2. In large bowl, mix $^3/_4$ cup sugar, oil and egg. Stir in apple, flour, baking soda, baking powder and salt. Stir in walnuts and cranberries. Pour batter into pan. In small bowl, mix 1 tablespoon sugar and cinnamon; sprinkle over batter.

3. Bake 45 to 55 minutes or until toothpick inserted in center comes out clean. Cool 10 minutes. Loosen sides of loaf from pan; remove from pan to wire rack. Cool completely, about $1^1/_2$ hours, before slicing.

1 loaf (12 slices).
1 Serving: Calories 275 (Calories from Fat 135); Fat 15g (Saturated 2g); Cholesterol 20mg; Sodium 180mg; Carbohydrate 32g (Dietary Fiber 1g); Protein 3g
% Daily Value: Vitamin A 0%; Vitamin C 0%; Calcium 2%; Iron 6%
Exchanges: 1 Starch, 1 Fruit, 3 Fat
Carbohydrate Choices: 2

BETTY'S TIPS

⊛ **Success Hint**
To easily shred the apple, use a medium-size grater.

⊛ **Health Twist**
For added fiber, leave the peel on the apple.

⊛ **Do-Ahead**
Make the bread ahead and refrigerate or freeze. The bread will actually become moister and easier to slice after storage.

⊛ **Special Touch**
This is a perfect bread for gift giving! Bake it in a disposable aluminum foil pan. When cool, wrap in foil or colored plastic wrap and tie with a ribbon.

Cranberry-Apple-Nut Bread

Quick
Double-Cheese and Herb Bread

PrepTime: 10 min Start to Finish: 15 min

- 4 slices Italian bread, $1/2$ inch thick
- 1 tablespoon chopped fresh or $1/2$ teaspoon dried basil leaves
- 1 tablespoon chopped fresh or $1/2$ teaspoon dried oregano leaves
- $1/4$ teaspoon garlic powder
- $1/2$ cup shredded Colby or mild Cheddar cheese (2 ounces)
- $1/2$ cup shredded Havarti cheese (2 ounces)

1. Heat coals or gas grill for direct heat. Spray both sides of each bread slice with cooking spray. Sprinkle one side with basil, oregano and garlic powder. Top with cheeses.

2. Cover and grill bread 4 to 6 inches from medium heat 2 to 3 minutes or until bread is toasted and cheese is melted.

4 servings.
1 Serving: Calories 170 (Calories from Fat 100); Fat 11g (Saturated 6g); Cholesterol 30mg; Sodium 310mg; Carbohydrate 10g (Dietary Fiber 1g); Protein 8g
% Daily Value: Vitamin A 8%; Vitamin C 0%; Calcium 20%; Iron 4%
Exchanges: $1/2$ Starch, 1 High-Fat Meat, $1/2$ Fat
Carbohydrate Choices: $1/2$

BETTY'S TIPS

⊕ **Substitution**
Use sourdough instead of the Italian bread.

In place of the Colby and Havarti, experiment with your own cheese combo.

⊕ **Time-Saver**
Prepare the bread up to 1 hour ahead of time. Place the slices in a shallow pan, and cover with plastic wrap until it's time to pop them on the grill.

Quick
Focaccia with Brie

Prep Time: 15 min Start to Finish: 30 min

- 1 cup Grilled Tricolored Bell Peppers (page 102) or purchased roasted bell peppers
- 1 round focaccia bread, 8 to 11 inches in diameter (8.8 to 16 ounces)
- 4 ounces Brie cheese, thinly sliced
- 2 tablespoons chopped fresh basil leaves

1. If using charcoal grill, place drip pan directly under grilling area, and arrange coals around edge of firebox. Heat coals or gas grill for indirect heat. Coarsely chop grilled peppers. Top focaccia with peppers, cheese and basil.

2. Cover and grill over drip pan or over unheated side of gas grill and 4 to 6 inches from high heat 10 to 15 minutes or until heated and cheese is melted. Cut into wedges to serve.

6 servings.
1 Serving: Calories 215 (Calories from Fat 100); Fat 11g (Saturated 4g); Cholesterol 20mg; Sodium 530mg; Carbohydrate 22g (Dietary Fiber 1g); Protein 7g
% Daily Value: Vitamin A 4%; Vitamin C 8%; Calcium 10%; Iron 8%
Exchanges: 1 Starch, 1 Fruit, $1/2$ Medium-Fat Meat, 1 Fat
Carbohydrate Choices: $1 1/2$

BETTY'S TIPS

⊕ **Substitution**
If you don't have focaccia, top French bread slices with the grilled peppers, cheese and basil.

⊕ **Serve-With**
A hearty accompaniment to any meal, this bread also can be cut into smaller wedges or squares and served as an appetizer.

⊕ **Did You Know?**
Brie is a soft, delicious French cheese known for its downy white rind and creamy, buttery interior. To thinly slice Brie, use a sharp knife.

Double-Cheese and Herb Bread

Focaccia with Brie

Quick
Cheesy Olive Bread
Prep Time: 10 min Start to Finish: 20 min

Cheesy Olive Bread

2 cups American and Cheddar cheese blend (8 ounces)

1 jar (5 ounces) olive-pimiento cheese spread

1 can (4.5 ounces) Old El Paso chopped green chiles

1/4 cup mayonnaise or salad dressing

1/2 teaspoon onion powder

1 loaf (1 pound) unsliced French bread, cut horizontally in half

Sliced pimiento-stuffed olives, if desired

1. If using charcoal grill, arrange coals around edge of firebox. Heat coals or gas grill for indirect heat. Mix all ingredients except bread and olives in medium bowl.

2. Place bread, cut sides down, over center of charcoal grill or over unheated side of gas grill and 4 to 6 inches from medium-low heat. Cover and grill 4 to 5 minutes or until toasted.

3. Remove bread to cookie sheet; spread toasted sides with cheese mixture. Cover and grill bread, cheese sides up, 5 to 7 minutes or until cheese is hot and melted. Garnish with olives. Cut bread into slices to serve.

16 servings.
1 Serving: Calories 175 (Calories from Fat 90); Fat 10g (Saturated 5g); Cholesterol 20mg; Sodium 470mg; Carbohydrate 16g (Dietary Fiber 1g); Protein 7g
% Daily Value: Vitamin A 6%; Vitamin C 0%; Calcium 10%; Iron 6%
Exchanges: 1 Starch, 1/2 High-Fat Meat, 1 Fat
Carbohydrate Choices: 1

BETTY'S TIPS

✪ **Success Hint**
If your grill is full or you don't want to light it up, just broil the bread in the oven instead. Before adding the cheese mixture, broil bread, cut sides up, 2 to 3 minutes or until golden brown. Spread with the cheese mixture, then broil 2 to 3 minutes longer until cheese is hot and melted.

✪ **Variation**
Kids love cheesy bread, but if they don't care for olives and green chiles, leave them off and use plain cheese spread.

✪ **Do-Ahead**
The toasted bread can be topped, covered and refrigerated for up to 2 hours before heating it on the grill.

Low-Fat
Pumpkin Dinner Crescents

Prep Time: 25 min Start to Finish: 2 hr 40 min

3¹/₂ to 4   cups Gold Medal all-purpose flour
      1   package regular active dry yeast
    ¹/₄   cup packed brown sugar
      1   teaspoon salt
  2 to 3   teaspoons pumpkin pie spice
    ³/₄   cup water
    ¹/₂   cup canned pumpkin (not pumpkin pie mix)
      4   tablespoons butter or margarine, softened
      1   egg

1. In large bowl, mix 1 cup flour, yeast, brown sugar, salt and pumpkin pie spice; set aside.

2. In 1-quart saucepan, heat water, pumpkin and 3 tablespoons butter over medium heat to 120° to 130°F, stirring occasionally. Add pumpkin mixture and egg to flour mixture. Beat with electric mixer on medium speed 3 minutes, scraping bowl occasionally. By hand, stir in just enough of the remaining 2¹/₂ to 3 cups flour to make a soft dough that leaves sides of bowl. Place dough on floured surface. Knead 3 to 5 minutes or until dough is smooth and springy.

3. Place dough in large bowl greased with shortening, turning dough to grease all sides. Cover and let rise in warm place about 1 hour or until double in size.

4. Place dough on lightly floured surface. Knead a few times. Shape dough into ball, then flatten. Roll into 15-inch circle. Spread with remaining 1 tablespoon butter. Cut into 16 wedges. Roll up each wedge, starting at wide end. On ungreased cookie sheet, place rolls with points underneath and curve slightly. Cover and let rise in warm place 20 to 30 minutes or until double in size.

5. Heat oven to 400°. Bake uncovered 12 to 15 minutes or until golden brown. Serve warm.

16 rolls.
1 Roll: Calories 150 (Calories from Fat 35); Fat 3g (Saturated 2g); Cholesterol 20mg; Sodium 170mg; Carbohydrate 25g (Dietary Fiber 1g); Protein 4g
% Daily Value: Vitamin A 26%; Vitamin C 0%; Calcium 0%; Iron 8%
Exchanges: 1¹/₂ Starch, ¹/₂ Fat
Carbohydrate Choices: 1¹/₂

BETTY'S TIPS

⊛ **Do-Ahead**
Prepare the rolls up to 12 hours ahead, then cover and refrigerate. About 1¹/₂ hours before serving, remove rolls to a warm place to rise until double in size. Bake at 400° for 9 to 11 minutes or until golden brown.

⊛ **Special Touch**
Enhance the sweet flavor of these rolls with cinnamon-walnut cream cheese or honey butter.

Pumpkin Dinner Crescents

Herb Pull-Apart Bread

Prep Time: 10 min Start to Finish: 4 hr 45 min

3 tablespoons butter or margarine
1 teaspoon dried basil leaves
1 teaspoon parsley flakes
$^1/_2$ teaspoon dried thyme leaves
2 cloves garlic, finely chopped
24 balls frozen white dinner roll dough
   (from 3-pound package)

12 servings.
1 Serving: Calories 225 (Calories from Fat 100); Fat 11g (Saturated 4g); Cholesterol 10mg; Sodium 690mg; Carbohydrate 27g (Dietary Fiber 1g); Protein 4g
% Daily Value: Vitamin A 2%; Vitamin C 0%; Calcium 0%; Iron 8%
Exchanges: 2 Starch, $1^1/_2$ Fat
Carbohydrate Choices: 2

BETTY'S TIPS

⊙ **Success Hint**
If you're serving this bread warm, use a fork to pull the rolls apart. If you're serving it cool, cut it into slices with a serrated knife.

⊙ **Time-Saver**
You can cut the rising time of the bread to about 1 hour if you follow the frozen dough package directions for the "speed method."

Cut down on chopping time by using already-chopped garlic from a jar. You'll find it in the produce section near the fresh garlic.

1. Spray 12-cup fluted tube cake pan (do not use 10-cup) with cooking spray. In 1-quart saucepan, heat all ingredients except roll dough over low heat, stirring occasionally, until butter is melted.

2. Place half of the frozen dough balls in pan. Generously brush butter mixture over dough in pan. Layer remaining dough balls in pan. Brush with remaining butter mixture. Cover and let stand in warm place about 4 hours or until double in size.

3. Heat oven to 350°. Bake 22 to 27 minutes or until bread sounds hollow when tapped and top is deep golden brown. Cool 5 minutes; turn upside down onto serving plate.

Herb Pull-Apart Bread

Beverages and Appetizers

Make Every Party Perfect

Warm Chicken Spread (page 55)

Dreamy Tropical Cream Fizz (page 30)

Quick & Low Fat
Mangoritas

Prep Time: 10 min Start to Finish: 10 min

1   can (10 ounces) frozen margarita drink mix
1   cup mango nectar
¹⁄₂   cup tequila or mango nectar
2   cups cracked ice

1. Place all ingredients except ice in blender. Cover and blend on high speed until blended.

2. Add ice. Cover and blend until smooth and slushy.

4 servings (1 cup each).
1 Serving: Calories 265 (Calories from Fat 0); Fat 0g (Saturated 0g); Cholesterol 0mg; Sodium 5mg; Carbohydrate 53g (Dietary Fiber 1g); Protein 0g
% Daily Value: Vitamin A 4%; Vitamin C 44%; Calcium 0%; Iron 4%
Exchanges: 3¹⁄₂ Fruit, 1 Fat
Carbohydrate Choices: 3¹⁄₂

BETTY'S TIPS

❂ **Substitution**
If you are having trouble finding mango nectar, use a tropical fruit juice blend that includes mango as one of the ingredients.

❂ **Special Touch**
This lovely golden-colored beverage would look nice garnished with lime wedges or fresh strawberries.

When serving margaritas, the rims of the glasses are typically coated with lime juice and dipped in coarse salt. For these sweeter "mangoritas," coat the rim with lime juice and dip in coarse sugar.

Mangoritas

Quick & Low-Fat

Raspberry-Apricot Sangria

Prep Time: 15 min Start to Finish: 15 min

1 package (10 ounces) frozen sweetened raspberries, thawed

2 cups apricot nectar

1 bottle (750 ml) white wine or nonalcoholic white wine, chilled

1/4 cup apricot brandy, if desired

2 cans (12 ounces each) lemon-lime carbonated beverage, chilled

1/2 pint (1 cup) fresh raspberries
   Lemon and/or orange slices, if desired

1. Place thawed raspberries in blender. Cover and blend on high speed until pureed. Press blended raspberries through a strainer into small bowl, using wooden spoon; discard seeds.

2. Mix raspberry puree, nectar, wine and brandy in 2-quart nonmetal pitcher or container. Just before serving, add carbonated beverage, fresh raspberries and lemon slices. Serve over ice.

9 servings (1 cup each).
1 Serving: Calories 165 (Calories from Fat 0); Fat 0g (Saturated 0g); Cholesterol 0mg; Sodium 20mg; Carbohydrate 29g (Dietary Fiber 3g); Protein 1g
% Daily Value: Vitamin A 12%; Vitamin C 14%; Calcium 2%; Iron 4%
Exchanges: 2 Fruit, 1 Fat
Carbohydrate Choices: 2

Raspberry-Apricot Sangria

BETTY'S TIPS

✪ **Do-Ahead**
You can make this recipe several hours ahead and refrigerate it, except don't add the carbonated beverage or the fresh raspberries. Add these ingredients just before serving.

✪ **Special Touch**
Thread a couple of fresh raspberries on a toothpick for a quick and easy garnish.

✪ **Did You Know?**
Sangria was originally made with red wine and fruit juices. The Spanish word *sangria* refers to the blood red color of the beverage. White or blush wines offer a lighter version of this summer drink.

Quick & Low-Fat
Frosty Guava-Peach Sippers

Prep Time: 10 min Start to Finish: 10 min
(Photo on page iii)

- 1 can (10 ounces) frozen fuzzy navel drink mix
- 1 cup guava juice or guava blend juice
- $1/4$ cup dark rum or guava juice
- 2 cups cracked ice

1. Place all ingredients except ice in blender. Cover and blend on high speed until blended.

2. Add ice. Cover and blend until smooth and slushy.

4 servings (1 cup each).
1 Serving: Calories 185 (Calories from Fat 0); Fat 0g (Saturated 0g); Cholesterol 0mg; Sodium 0mg; Carbohydrate 46g (Dietary Fiber 0g); Protein 0g
% Daily Value: Vitamin A 0%; Vitamin C 36%; Calcium 0%; Iron 0%
Exchanges: 3 Fruit
Carbohydrate Choices: 3

BETTY'S TIPS

⚙ **Success Hint**
Some blenders are powerful enough to handle large ice cubes, while others work best with smaller chunks of ice. To quickly crack ice into small pieces, put cubes in a heavy plastic food-storage bag and tap gently with a meat mallet or rolling pin.

Like orange juice, guava juice often settles to the bottom of the bottle and needs to be shaken well before using.

⚙ **Did You Know?**
Fuzzy navel drinks combine the summer-fresh flavors of peach and orange. The drink mix used in this recipe can be found near the other frozen juices and beverages.

Dreamy Tropical Cream Fizz

Prep Time: 10 min Start to Finish: 1 hr 10 min
(Photo on page 27)

- $1/4$ cup shredded coconut
- 2 cups tropical juice blend
- $1/2$ cup sugar
- $1/4$ cup lime juice
- 12 to 14 ice cubes
- $1^1/2$ cups club soda
- 1 pint coconut ice cream, coconut sorbet or vanilla ice cream

1. Place coconut in food processor or blender. Cover and process until coconut is in small pieces. Place coconut in shallow dish. Dip rims of six 12-ounce stemmed glasses into water, then dip into coconut to coat. Chill glasses in freezer at least 1 hour before serving.

2. Place tropical juice blend, sugar, lime juice and ice cubes in blender. Cover and blend on high speed about 45 seconds or until smooth. Pour mixture into glasses.

3. Pour $1/4$ cup club soda into juice mixture in each glass. Add 1 large scoop ice cream to each glass. Garnish with remaining coconut if desired.

6 servings (1 cup each).
1 Serving: Calories 220 (Calories from Fat 55); Fat 6g (Saturated 4g); Cholesterol 20mg; Sodium 50mg; Carbohydrate 40g (Dietary Fiber 1g); Protein 2g
% Daily Value: Vitamin A 4%; Vitamin C 34%; Calcium 6%; Iron 2%
Exchanges: $1/2$ Starch, 2 Fruit, 1 Fat
Carbohydrate Choices: $2^1/2$

BETTY'S TIPS

⚙ **Substitution**
If you like coconut but can't find coconut ice cream, use vanilla ice cream and add $1/4$ teaspoon coconut extract to the juice mixture.

⚙ **Did You Know?**
Endless varieties of fruit juice blends are available on supermarket shelves. The tropical blends usually include flavors of pineapple, banana, mango, coconut and papaya.

Quick & Low-Fat
Cranberry-Mint Iced Tea

Prep Time: 15 min Start to Finish: 15 min

6 cups cranberry juice cocktail
4 tea bags black tea
10 mint leaves (1 inch each)
2 tablespoons sugar

1. Heat cranberry juice cocktail to boiling in 2-quart saucepan. Pour over tea bags and mint in 2-quart glass measuring cup or heatproof pitcher. Let steep 5 to 10 minutes.

2. Strain tea mixture. Stir in sugar. Serve tea over ice. Add more sugar if desired.

6 servings (1 cup each).
1 Serving: Calories 165 (Calories from Fat 0); Fat 0g (Saturated 0g); Cholesterol 0mg; Sodium 5mg; Carbohydrate 41g (Dietary Fiber 0g); Protein 0g
% Daily Value: Vitamin A 2%; Vitamin C 100%; Calcium 0%; Iron 2%
Exchanges: 3 Fruit
Carbohydrate Choices: 3

BETTY'S TIPS

⊗ **Success Hint**
Be sure to use cranberry juice "cocktail," which contains added sugar, for this refreshing iced tea. Regular cranberry juice is not as sweet and would make this summer sipper much too tart tasting.

To keep tea from becoming cloudy, heat the liquid and steep the tea in nonreactive utensils, such as glass or stainless steel.

⊗ **Special Touch**
Make this tea extra minty by adding a small sprig of fresh mint to each glass.

Cranberry-Mint Iced Tea

Low Fat

Raspberry Lemonade

Prep Time: 20 min Start to Finish: 2 hr 20 min

$^3/_4$ cup sugar

4   cups water

1   cup fresh lemon juice (about 4 lemons)

1   container (10 ounces) frozen raspberries in syrup, thawed

Raspberry Ice Cubes (below)

1. Mix sugar and $^1/_2$ cup of the water in 1-quart saucepan. Cook over medium heat, stirring once, until sugar is dissolved. Cool to room temperature.

2. Mix cooled sugar syrup, lemon juice and remaining $3^1/_2$ cups water in 2-quart nonmetal pitcher. Place raspberries in strainer over small bowl to drain (do not press berries through strainer). Reserve berries for Raspberry Ice Cubes. Stir raspberry liquid into lemon mixture; refrigerate.

3. Make Raspberry Ice Cubes. Serve lemonade over ice cubes.

6 servings (about 1 cup each).

Raspberry Ice Cubes

Reserved raspberries

$^3/_4$ cup water

Spoon raspberries evenly into 12 sections of ice-cube tray. Divide water evenly among sections with raspberries. Freeze about 2 hours or until firm.

1 Serving: Calories 160 (Calories from Fat 0); Fat 0g (Saturated 0g); Cholesterol 0mg; Sodium 10mg; Carbohydrate 40g (Dietary Fiber 2g); Protein 0g
% Daily Value: Vitamin A 0%; Vitamin C 30%; Calcium 0%; Iron 2%
Exchanges: $2^1/_2$ Fruit
Carbohydrate Choices: $2^1/_2$

Raspberry Lemonade

BETTY'S TIPS

✪ **Substitution**
Frozen lemon juice from concentrate, thawed, can be used in place of the fresh lemon juice.

✪ **Success Hint**
Heating the sugar with a little water makes a syrup that is easily dissolved in the lemonade.

✪ **Special Touch**
Before juicing the lemons, use a citrus zester to cut thin strips of peel to add to each glass of lemonade.

32   **www.bettycrocker.com**

Strawberry-Rhubarb Slush

Prep Time: 20 min Start to Finish: 8 hr 20 min

1   bag (16 ounces) frozen rhubarb or 3 cups chopped fresh rhubarb

1   cup sugar

2   packages (10 ounces each) frozen sweetened strawberries, slightly thawed

1 1/2   cups vodka

1   can (12 ounces) lemon-lime carbonated beverage

1   bottle (2 liters) lemon-lime carbonated beverage, chilled

Sliced fresh strawberries, if desired

1. Heat rhubarb and sugar to boiling in 3-quart saucepan over medium heat, stirring occasionally. Cook 8 to 10 minutes, stirring occasionally, until rhubarb is very tender. Stir in strawberries.

2. Spoon half of strawberry mixture into blender. Cover and blend on high speed until smooth. Pour into large nonmetal container. Cover and blend remaining strawberry mixture; add to container. Stir in vodka and 12-ounce can of carbonated beverage. Freeze at least 8 hours until frozen and slushy.

3. For each serving, stir together 1/2 cup frozen mixture and 1/2 cup chilled carbonated beverage in tall glass until slushy. Garnish with strawberry slices.

16 servings (1 cup each).
1 Serving: Calories 165 (Calories from Fat 0); Fat 0g (Saturated 0g); Cholesterol 0mg; Sodium 20mg; Carbohydrate 41g (Dietary Fiber 0g); Protein 0g
% Daily Value: Vitamin A 0%; Vitamin C 26%; Calcium 6%; Iron 2%
Exchanges: 3 Fruit, 1 Fat
Carbohydrate Choices: 3

BETTY'S TIPS

⊙ **Variation**
This whole recipe can be served as a slushy punch. Spoon the slush mixture into a large punch bowl, then stir in the carbonated beverage. This is handy if you are serving a large number of people all at once.

⊙ **Do-Ahead**
This is a perfect do-ahead recipe because it makes a big batch and can be kept in the freezer for several weeks. Scoop out just the amount you need at one time.

⊙ **Did You Know?**
Slush beverage recipes rely on the alcohol to keep them from freezing solid. Because they remain slushy in the freezer, portions can be scooped out at a moment's notice.

Strawberry-Rhubarb Slush

Key Lime–Banana Smoothies

Creamy Peachsicle Smoothies

Creamy Peachsicle Smoothies

Prep Time: 5 min Start to Finish: 5 min

    1   cup frozen sliced peaches
    1   banana, thickly sliced
 $1/2$ cup vanilla low-fat yogurt
$1^1/2$ cups orange juice
    1   tablespoon honey

1. Place all ingredients in food processor or blender.

2. Cover and blend on high speed about 1 minute or until smooth and creamy.

3 servings (1 cup each).
1 Serving: Calories 320 (Calories from Fat 10); Fat 1g (Saturated 0g); Cholesterol 0mg; Sodium 30mg; Carbohydrate 52g (Dietary Fiber 2g); Protein 3g
% Daily Value: Vitamin A 14%; Vitamin C 100%; Calcium 8%; Iron 4%
Exchanges: $3^1/2$ Fruit
Carbohydrate Choices: $3^1/2$

BETTY'S TIPS

⚙ **Success Hint**
If your blender doesn't handle frozen fruit very well, thaw the peaches slightly before adding them to the blender.

⚙ **Variation**
Choose a fruit-flavored yogurt, such as strawberry or raspberry, instead of the vanilla.

For a frosty version of this creamy smoothie, use vanilla frozen yogurt instead of the regular yogurt.

⚙ **Special Touch**
Poke toothpicks or little drink umbrellas through fresh peach slices to serve with these smoothies.

Key Lime–Banana Smoothies

Prep Time: 10 min Start to Finish: 10 min

    1   container (6 ounces) Yoplait Original key lime pie low-fat yogurt
    1   ripe banana, sliced
 $1/2$ cup milk
    1   tablespoon lime juice
 $1/4$ teaspoon dry lemon-lime soft drink mix (from 0.13-ounce package)
    1   cup vanilla frozen yogurt

1. Place all ingredients except frozen yogurt in blender. Cover and blend on high speed until smooth.

2. Add frozen yogurt. Cover and blend until smooth.

2 servings (1 cup each).
1 Serving: Calories 295 (Calories from Fat 35); Fat 4g (Saturated 2g); Cholesterol 10mg; Sodium 140mg; Carbohydrate 54g (Dietary Fiber 2g); Protein 11g
% Daily Value: Vitamin A 6%; Vitamin C 14%; Calcium 36%; Iron 2%
Exchanges: $2^1/2$ Fruit, 1 Milk, 1 Fat
Carbohydrate Choices: $3^1/2$

BETTY'S TIPS

⚙ **Success Hint**
For the best banana flavor, choose bananas that have flecks of brown on the skin. Bananas that are too green will not be as sweet or flavorful.

⚙ **Special Touch**
Decorate the rim of each glass with a fresh slice of lime.

Iced Hazelnut Coffee Coolers

Prep Time: 10 min Start to Finish: 3 hr 10 min

2/3 cup instant coffee (dry)

3/4 cup hazelnut-flavored nondairy liquid creamer

1 cup sugar

1 cup water

1/4 teaspoon ground cinnamon

8 cups milk

48 water ice cubes

12 servings (1½ cups each).
1 Serving: Calories 170 (Calories from Fat 35); Fat 4g (Saturated 2g); Cholesterol 10mg; Sodium 85mg; Carbohydrate 28g (Dietary Fiber 0g); Protein 6g
% Daily Value: Vitamin A 6%; Vitamin C 2%; Calcium 20%; Iron 0%
Exchanges: 1 Milk, 1 Other Carbohydrate, ½ Fat
Carbohydrate Choices: 2

BETTY'S TIPS

1. Stir coffee, creamer, sugar, water and cinnamon in medium bowl until coffee is dissolved.

2. Pour coffee mixture into 2 ice-cube trays. Freeze at least 3 hours until hardened. Transfer frozen coffee cubes to plastic storage container or freezer bag.

3. For each serving, place 2 coffee cubes, 2/3 cup milk and 4 water ice cubes in blender. Cover and blend on high speed about 20 minutes or until blended and slightly slushy. Pour into glass.

⊘ **Success Hint**
Look for the nondairy liquid creamer in the dairy case next to the whipping cream.

⊘ **Variation**
Pick your favorite flavor for this cool coffee drink. Try Irish cream-, amaretto- or French vanilla-flavored nondairy liquid creamer.

⊘ **Special Touch**
Top this coffee cooler with a dollop of whipped cream, a dash of ground cinnamon and a couple of hazelnuts (filberts).

Iced Hazelnut Coffee Coolers

Ginger-Spiced Almonds

Prep Time: 30 min Start to Finish: 2 hr 5 min

  5 cups blanched whole almonds
  1 cup sugar
  1 tablespoon grated fresh ginger
$1^1/_2$ teaspoon garlic salt
$^1/_2$ teaspoon dry mustard
$^1/_2$ teaspoon onion powder
  2 egg whites
$^1/_3$ cup butter or margarine, cut into pieces

1. Heat oven to 325°. In 15 x 10 x 1-inch pan, spread almonds. Bake 25 to 30 minutes, stirring occasionally, until lightly toasted.

2. Meanwhile, in small bowl, mix remaining ingredients except egg whites and butter; set aside. In large bowl, beat egg whites with electric mixer on high speed until soft peaks form. Continue beating, gradually adding sugar mixture. Fold in almonds.

3. Place butter in same pan. Place in oven 3 to 5 minutes or until butter is melted. Spread almond mixture over butter. Bake 30 to 35 minutes, stirring every 10 minutes, until almonds are brown and no butter remains. Cool completely, about 1 hour. Store in airtight container.

32 servings ($^1/_4$ cup each).
1 Serving: Calories 180 (Calories from Fat 115); Fat 13g (Saturated 2g); Cholesterol 5mg; Sodium 60mg; Carbohydrate 11g (Dietary Fiber 3g); Protein 5g
% Daily Value: Vitamin A 0%; Vitamin C 0%; Calcium 6%; Iron 4%
Exchanges: 1 Other Carbohydrate, $^1/_2$ High-Fat Meat, $1^1/_2$ Fat
Carbohydrate Choices: 1

BETTY'S TIPS

⚙ **Kitchen Tip**
Any mix of nuts equaling 5 cups can be substituted for the almonds.

These almonds can be made up to a week before the party. Store in an airtight container.

Ginger-Spiced Almonds

Slow-Cooker Spiced Party Nut Mix

Prep Time: 20 min Start to Finish: 4 hr 20 min

6 tablespoons butter or margarine, melted

1 envelope (1.25 ounces) Old El Paso taco seasoning mix

1 teaspoon ground cinnamon

1/4 teaspoon ground red pepper (cayenne)

2 cups pecan halves

2 cups roasted unsalted cashews

2 cups walnut halves

2 cups unblanched whole almonds

3 cups bite-size cheese crackers

2 cups sourdough pretzel nuggets

1. In 4- to 5-quart slow cooker, mix butter, taco seasoning mix, cinnamon and red pepper. Add remaining ingredients; toss gently.

2. Cook uncovered on Low heat setting 3 to 4 hours, stirring every 30 minutes, until nuts are toasted. Turn off slow cooker. Serve with large serving spoon.

26 servings (1/2 cup each).
1 Serving: Calories 320 (Calories from Fat 235); Fat 26g (Saturated 4g); Cholesterol 5mg; Sodium 210mg; Carbohydrate 14g (Dietary Fiber 3g); Protein 7g
% Daily Value: Vitamin A 4%; Vitamin C 0%; Calcium 4%; Iron 10%
Exchanges: 1 Starch, 1/2 High-Fat Meat, 4 Fat
Carbohydrate Choices: 1

BETTY'S TIPS

⚙ **Kitchen Tip**
Make this nut mix the day before the party. Serve it in a pretty bowl with a serving spoon.

Slow-Cooker Spiced Party Nut Mix

Quick

Guacamole-Cheese Crisps

Prep Time: 25 min Start to Finish: 25 min

1 cup finely shredded Mexican-style Cheddar
    Jack cheese with jalapeño peppers
    (4 ounces)
1 ripe avocado, pitted, peeled and chopped
1 tablespoon lime juice
1 clove garlic, finely chopped
3 tablespoons sour cream
3 tablespoons Old El Paso Thick 'n Chunky
    salsa

1. Heat oven to 400°. Line cookie sheet with parchment
paper. For each cheese crisp, spoon 2 teaspoons
cheese onto paper-lined cookie sheet; pat into
2-inch round. Bake 6 to 8 minutes or until edges are
light golden brown. Immediately remove from
cookie sheet to wire rack. Cool 5 minutes or until
crisp.

2. Mix avocado, lime juice and garlic in small bowl;
mash avocado with fork and mix with ingredients.
Spoon 1¹/₂ teaspoons avocado mixture on each

cheese crisp; top with about ¹/₂ teaspoon each sour
cream and salsa.

16 appetizers.
1 Appetizer: Calories 50 (Calories from Fat 35); Fat 4g (Saturated 2g);
Cholesterol 10mg; Sodium 55mg; Carbohydrate 1g (Dietary Fiber 1g);
Protein 2g
% Daily Value: Vitamin A 2%; Vitamin C 2%; Calcium 4%; Iron 0%
Exchanges: 1 Fat
Carbohydrate Choices: 0

BETTY'S TIPS

⊛ **Time-Saver**
    In a pinch, pick up a container of guacamole from the
    store to top the crisps.

⊛ **Do-Ahead**
    Prepare the crisps up to 4 hours ahead. Store them
    tightly covered at room temperature, and top them
    just before serving.

⊛ **Special Touch**
    Add a tiny sprig of fresh cilantro to each appetizer.

Guacamole-Cheese Crisps

Italian Sautéed Olives

Prep Time: 5 min Start to Finish: 15 min

- 2 tablespoons olive or vegetable oil
- 2 tablespoons chopped parsley
- 1 medium green onion, chopped (1 tablespoon)
- 1 teaspoon crushed red pepper
- 2 cloves garlic, finely chopped
- 1 cup imported Kalamata olives (8 ounces), drained and pitted
- 1 cup imported Greek green olives (8 ounces), drained and pitted
- 1 cup imported Gaeta olives (8 ounces), drained and pitted

1. In 10-inch skillet, heat oil over medium heat. Cook parsley, onion, red pepper and garlic in oil about 4 minutes, stirring frequently, until garlic just begins to become golden brown.

2. Stir in olives. Cover and cook about 5 minutes, stirring occasionally, until olives are tender and skins begin to wrinkle.

20 servings (6 olives each).
1 Serving: Calories 40 (Calories from Fat 35); Fat 4g (Saturated 0.5g); Cholesterol 0mg; Sodium 220mg; Carbohydrate 1g (Dietary Fiber less than 1g); Protein 0g
% Daily Value: Vitamin A 4%; Vitamin C 2%; Calcium 2%; Iron 2%
Exchanges: 1 Fat
Carbohydrate Choices: 0

BETTY'S TIPS

⚙ **Kitchen Tip**
You can use any combination of imported olives that you like for this recipe.

Pineapple-Lime Fruit Dip

Prep Time: 15 min Start to Finish: 15 min

- 1 can (8 ounces) crushed pineapple, well drained
- 1 cup sour cream
- 1 tablespoon packed brown sugar
- 1 teaspoon grated fresh lime peel
- 2 apples, each cut into 12 slices
  Strawberry halves, if desired

1. In small bowl, mix all ingredients except apples and strawberries.

2. Cover and refrigerate dip until serving. Serve with apple slices and strawberry halves.

12 servings (2 tablespoons dip and 2 apple slices each).
1 Serving: Calories 70 (Calories from Fat 35); Fat 4g (Saturated 2g); Cholesterol 15mg; Sodium 10mg; Carbohydrate 8g (Dietary Fiber 1g); Protein 1g
% Daily Value: Vitamin A 2%; Vitamin C 4%; Calcium 2%; Iron 0%
Exchanges: 1/2 Fruit, 1 Fat
Carbohydrate Choices: 1/2

BETTY'S TIPS

⚙ **Kitchen Tip**
Serve in a hollowed-out fresh pineapple. Just cut a fresh pineapple in half lengthwise; cut and remove center of pineapple.

Pineapple-Lime Fruit Dip

Italian Sautéed Olives

Apricot Baked Brie

Prep Time: 20 min Start to Finish: 45 min

¹/₃ cup apricot preserves

¹/₄ cup chopped pecans

2 tablespoons finely chopped red onion

1 sheet puff pastry (from 17.3-ounce package), thawed

1 round (8 ounces) Brie cheese, cut horizontally in half

1 tablespoon whipping (heavy) cream or half-and-half

1. Heat oven to 400°. Line cookie sheet with aluminum foil or cooking parchment paper; lightly spray foil or paper with cooking spray. In small bowl, mix preserves, pecans and onions; set aside.

2. On lightly floured surface, roll pastry into 10 x 14-inch rectangle. Using the round of cheese as a pattern, cut a pastry circle 3 to 4 inches larger than the cheese. Set aside excess pastry.

3. Spread half of the preserves mixture in center of pastry circle, leaving 3-inch edge. Place 1 cheese round (in rind) on preserves. Spoon remaining preserves over cheese. Top with remaining cheese round.

4. Gently fold edges of pastry up and over cheese to cover, folding and pinching edges to seal. Place seam side down on cookie sheet. Cut out decorative pieces from excess pastry. Brush pastry with whipping cream; place pastry cutouts on top.

5. Bake 20 to 25 minutes or until golden brown. Serve warm.

12 servings
1 Serving: Calories 175 (Calories from Fat 100); Fat 11g (Saturated 4g); Cholesterol 30mg; Sodium 105mg; Carbohydrate 15g (Dietary Fiber 1g); Protein 4g
% Daily Value: Vitamin A 2%; Vitamin C 0%; Calcium 2%; Iron 4%
Exchanges: 1 Starch, 2 Fat
Carbohydrate Choices: 1

BETTY'S TIPS

✿ Kitchen Tip
Sourdough bread slices, crispy crackers or apple and pear slices go well with this dressed-up cheese appetizer.

Assemble the Brie the day before, cover tightly and refrigerate. Just before serving, bake as directed.

Apricot Baked Brie

Quick & Low Fat
Mushroom-Olive Bruschetta

Prep Time: 20 min Start to Finish: 20 min

1 can (4 ounces) Green Giant® mushroom pieces and stems, drained
$^1/_2$ cup pitted Kalamata or ripe olives
2 tablespoons capers, drained
1 clove garlic, sliced
2 tablespoons extra-virgin olive oil
1 tablespoon balsamic vinegar
10 slices French bread, toasted

1. Mix mushrooms, olives, capers and garlic in food processor bowl. Cover and process by using quick on-and-off motions until finely chopped. Add oil and vinegar; process just until mixed (do not over-process).

2. Spread mushroom mixture on toasted bread. Cut slices in half.

20 appetizers.
1 Appetizer: Calories 105 (Calories from Fat 25); Fat 3g (Saturated 1g); Cholesterol 0mg; Sodium 260mg; Carbohydrate 17g (Dietary Fiber 1g); Protein 3g
% Daily Value: Vitamin A 0%; Vitamin C 0%; Calcium 2%; Iron 6%
Exchanges: 1 Starch, $^1/_2$ Fat
Carbohydrate Choices: 1

BETTY'S TIPS

⚙ **Success Hint**
If you already have your grill going, use it to toast the bread for this recipe too.

⚙ **Variation**
For a warm appetizer, place the topped bread on the grill for 1 to 2 minutes. Cut the slices in half after heating them.

⚙ **Do-Ahead**
Make the mushroom mixture several hours ahead, cover and refrigerate. Toast the bread in advance, and top it off just before serving.

⚙ **Special Touch**
Add small curls of fresh Parmesan cheese and fresh marjoram leaves to the tops of these tangy treats.

Mushroom-Olive Bruschetta

Tangy Hot Cheese and Caper Spread

Tangy Hot Cheese and Caper Spread

Prep Time: 10 min Start to Finish: 10 min

1 package (6 ounces) chevre (goat) cheese with peppercorns, softened
1 cup shredded fresh Parmesan cheese (4 ounces)
1/4 cup mayonnaise or salad dressing
1/4 cup diced red bell pepper
2 tablespoons small capers, drained
Toasted baguette slices

1. Mix all ingredients except baguette slices in shallow 6-inch microwavable quiche or au gratin dish. Microwave uncovered on High 2 minutes, stirring every 30 seconds.

2. Serve cheese spread with baguette slices.

24 servings (1 tablespoon spread and 1 baguette slice each).
1 Serving: Calories 100 (Calories from Fat 65); Fat 7g (Saturated 3g); Cholesterol 10mg; Sodium 260mg; Carbohydrate 6g (Dietary Fiber 0g); Protein 3g
% Daily Value: Vitamin A 2%; Vitamin C 4%; Calcium 8%; Iron 2%
Exchanges: 1/2 Fruit, 1 1/2 Fat
Carbohydrate Choices: 1/2

BETTY'S TIPS

⊕ **Substitution**
Plain chevre and a dash of black pepper make a great stand-in for the goat cheese with peppercorns.

⊕ **Do-Ahead**
Prepare the spread a few hours ahead. Cover and refrigerate until serving time, then heat in the microwave.

⊕ **Special Touch**
Sprinkle a few extra capers on top of the dip just before serving.

⊕ **Did You Know?**
Capers have a flavor similar to olives. The buds vary in size. For this recipe, purchase capers that are very small, called nonpareil, so the flavor will be better distributed throughout the spread. Look for capers near the pickles and olives in the grocery store.

Antipasto Pizzettes

Prep Time: 30 min Start to Finish: 40 min

2 cups Original Bisquick mix
$1/2$ cup water
2 tablespoons olive or vegetable oil
2 teaspoons dried basil leaves
$1/2$ cup shredded mozzarella cheese (2 ounces)
$1/4$ cup basil pesto
24 slices roma (plum) tomatoes (about 3 small)
24 slices pepperoni
24 slices banana peppers or sliced pepperoncini peppers (bottled Italian peppers), if desired

1. Heat oven to 450°. Lightly spray cookie sheet with cooking spray. In medium bowl, stir Bisquick mix, water, oil and 1 teaspoon basil with fork or wire whisk until soft dough forms. On lightly floured surface, knead dough 10 times.

2. Roll dough into 12-inch circle, about $1/4$ inch thick. Using 2-inch round cutter, cut out dough rounds; reroll dough once to get 24 rounds. Place on cookie sheet.

3. Bake 8 to 10 minutes or until light golden brown. Cool completely, about 15 minutes. Store in airtight container until serving.

4. Meanwhile, in small bowl, mix cheese and remaining 1 teaspoon basil. To serve, spread about $1/2$ teaspoon pesto on each biscuit round. Top each with 1 slice tomato, 1 slice pepperoni and cheese mixture. Top with sliced pepper. Serve at room temperature.

24 appetizers.
1 Appetizer: Calories 105 (Calories from Fat 65); Fat 7g (Saturated 2g); Cholesterol 5mg; Sodium 290mg; Carbohydrate 7g (Dietary Fiber 0g); Protein 3g
% Daily Value: Vitamin A 2%; Vitamin C 0%; Calcium 4%; Iron 2%
Exchanges: $1/2$ Starch, $1 1/2$ Fat
Carbohydrate Choices: $1/2$

BETTY'S TIPS

⚙ **Kitchen Tip**
Bake and freeze the biscuit rounds up to a week ahead. Warm thawed rounds on a cookie sheet at 450° for 2 to 4 minutes.

Antipasto Pizzettes

Quick & Low-Fat
Mini Barbecue Pizza Wedges

Prep Time: 10 min Start to Finish: 20 min
(Photo on page viii)

1   package (8 ounces) ready-to-serve Italian pizza crusts (2 crusts)
1/4   cup barbecue sauce
1/2   cup chopped cooked chicken
1   tablespoon chopped red onion
1   cup finely shredded mozzarella cheese (4 ounces)
6   cherry tomatoes, cut in half (1/3 cup)

1. If using charcoal grill, arrange coals around edge of firebox. Heat coals or gas grill for indirect heat. Top pizza crusts with remaining ingredients in order listed.

2. Place pizzas over center of charcoal grill or over unheated side of gas grill and 4 to 6 inches from medium heat. Cover and grill 8 to 10 minutes, rotating pizzas occasionally, until cheese is melted and pizzas are hot. Cut each into 6 wedges.

12 servings.
1 Serving: Calories 100 (Calories from Fat 25); Fat 3g (Saturated 1g); Cholesterol 10mg; Sodium 200mg; Carbohydrate 12g (Dietary Fiber 1g); Protein 6g
% Daily Value: Vitamin A 2%; Vitamin C 0%; Calcium 6%; Iron 4%
Exchanges: 1 Starch, 1/2 Lean Meat
Carbohydrate Choices: 1

BETTY'S TIPS

⊙ **Success Hint**
To make these pizzas easy to transport to the grill, assemble them on a cookie sheet.

Instead of grilling, you can also bake these pizzas in a 450° oven for 6 minutes.

⊙ **Do-Ahead**
You can put together the pizzas 1 to 2 hours ahead. Cover and refrigerate them until it's time to grill.

Low-Fat
Vegetable–Blue Cheese Rounds

Prep Time: 15 min Start to Finish: 35 min
(Photo on page iii)

1   tablespoon olive or vegetable oil
1/3   cup chopped green onions (about 5 medium)
1/3   cup chopped red bell pepper
1/2   cup crumbled blue cheese
30   melba toast rounds

1. In 10-inch skillet, heat oil over medium heat. Cook onions and bell pepper in oil 4 to 5 minutes, stirring frequently, until crisp-tender. Cool until lukewarm, about 10 minutes. Stir in cheese.

2. Heat oven to 350°. Spoon slightly less than 2 teaspoons of the cheese mixture onto each melba toast. Place on ungreased cookie sheet.

3. Bake 1 to 2 minutes or until cheese just begins to melt.

30 appetizers.
1 Appetizer: Calories 25 (Calories from Fat 10); Fat 1g (Saturated 0g); Cholesterol 0mg; Sodium 50mg; Carbohydrate 3g (Dietary Fiber 0g); Protein 1g
% Daily Value: Vitamin A 2%; Vitamin C 6%; Calcium 0%; Iron 2%
Exchanges: 1 Serving Free
Carbohydrate Choices: 0

BETTY'S TIPS

⊙ **Kitchen Tip**
You can make the cheese mixture a day ahead, then warm it up in the microwave just before assembling the appetizers. Bake as directed.

Betty Crocker
ON WHAT'S NEW

The Fun of Fondue

Feeling groovy? Then fondue is the thing to do! This popular '70s trend is back—and with good reason. The simple, easygoing cooking style makes it fun for families and terrific for entertaining. Cooking around a big table, creating your own unique meal, fondue is the ideal blend of food, friendship and fun.

Equipment Essentials

Fondue pots come in a variety of shapes and sizes. Most fondue sets consist of a fondue pot, a burner and four or six long-handled forks. The burner can be fueled with canned cooking fuel, alcohol or even small candles. You can also purchase electric fondue pots. Deluxe fondue sets will include two pots or a metal pot and a ceramic insert. Most fondue sets have four or six forks, although you may find a set that includes eight. If you plan to share fondue with more than six, you'll probably need more than one fondue set.

CHEESE FONDUE

Fondue pots used for cheese fondue tend to be shallow and wide. Good choices are ceramic and earthenware because they spread out the heat. These types of pots are less suitable for meat fondues, which require large amounts of hot oil or broth to cook in.

SAVORY FONDUE

A taller, narrower fondue pot works best for meat fondue or other foods you want to cook in oil or broth. Cast iron, copper and metal-lined pots are good choices because metal absorbs the heat and keeps the oil or broth hot.

DESSERT FONDUE

Pots for chocolate and dessert fondues can easily be interchanged with cheese fondue pots. Like pots used for cheese fondue, ceramic and earthenware are the best for temperature-sensitive chocolate fondue. These fondue pots may even be heated by a small candle, which can better maintain the low temperature needed for chocolate.

Foods to Dip and Dunk

	CHEESE FONDUE	SAVORY FONDUE	DESSERT FONDUE
BREADS (CUT INTO 1-INCH CUBES OR PIECES)	Bagels; biscuits; soft breadsticks; croissants; English muffins; focaccia; French bread; pita bread; rye bread	None	Cinnamon bread or rolls; chocolate bread; scones
MEATS	Cubed cooked beef; cubed cooked chicken or turkey; cubed cooked ham; pepperoni or smoked salami slices	Cubes or thin slices of uncooked beef, pork, or lamb; cubes or thin slices of boneless, skinless chicken or turkey breasts; uncooked scallops or shrimp; uncooked fish fillet pieces	
VEGETABLES	*Lightly cooked:* Asparagus; broccoli; carrots; cauliflower; new potatoes *Uncooked:* Bell pepper strips; cherry tomatoes; cucumber slices; whole mushrooms	*Uncooked:* Bell pepper strips; broccoli; carrot slices or baby-cut carrots; cauliflower; whole mushrooms; quartered or cubed new potatoes; sliced water chestnuts; zucchini slices	

Fondue Tips and Tricks

CHEESE FONDUE

▸ Let the cheese melt slowly. Make sure it doesn't boil or the cheese will get stringy.

▸ As you add liquids, the cheese may look like it's separating. Just give it a stir until the mixture becomes smooth.

▸ If the cheese starts to lump, increase the heat and continue stirring until smooth.

▸ If the fondue is too thin, mix equal amounts of cornstarch and water or cooking liquid and stir into cheese mixture. If the fondue is too thick, stir in a small amount of warmed cooking liquid.

▸ If the cheese appears to curdle, stir in 1 teaspoon lemon juice and stir well.

▸ If you don't want to cook the fondue in the pot, prepare it on the stove top and then transfer to the fondue pot to serve.

	CHEESE FONDUE	SAVORY FONDUE	DESSERT FONDUE
FRUITS	Apple and pear wedges	None	Apple and pear wedges; banana; kiwifruit; peach and plum slices; mango, melon, papaya and pineapple cubes; orange and tangerine segments; whole strawberries, cherries and grapes; dried figs, dates and apricots
OTHER	Pretzel rods, tortilla chips	None	Angel food or pound cake pieces; biscotti; brownie pieces; small cookies; graham crackers; ladyfingers; marshmallows; pretzel rods

SAVORY FONDUE

▸ If you're cooking with oil, keep the temperature between 350° and 375°. Use a thermometer to make sure the temperature stays consistent. Be careful not to add too much food at one time, or the temperature may drop and the meat won't cook properly.

▸ If a recipe doesn't call for a particular type of oil, use one you would normally use for cooking.

▸ To prevent the hot oil from spattering, pat meats dry with a paper towel before placing them out for cooking.

DESSERT FONDUE

▸ Keep dessert and chocolate fondues warm, but don't let them boil.

▸ Fondue coating sticks best when the fruit is cold, so keep your platter of fruit in the fridge until just before serving.

▸ Many chocolate and dessert fondues are best prepared on the stove top and then transferred to the fondue pot to serve.

Pesto-Cheese Cups

Pepperoni Swirls

Pesto-Cheese Cups

Prep Time: 20 min Start to Finish: 45 min

- 1 package (8 ounces) cream cheese, softened
- 1 egg
- $1/2$ cup shredded Swiss cheese (2 ounces)
- $1/4$ cup basil pesto
- 2 medium green onions, chopped (2 tablespoons)
- 2 packages (2.1 ounces each) frozen mini phyllo dough shells (15 shells each)
- $1/3$ cup shredded Swiss cheese ($1/2$ ounces)

1. Heat oven to 375°. Line cookie sheet with foil or cooking parchment paper. In medium bowl, beat cream cheese and egg with wire whisk. Stir in $1/2$ cup cheese, pesto and onions.

2. Place phyllo shells on cookie sheet. Fill each shell with slightly less than 1 tablespoon cheese mixture. Sprinkle each with $1/2$ teaspoon Swiss cheese.

3. Bake 20 to 25 minutes or until cups begin to turn golden brown and are puffed. Serve warm.

30 appetizers.
1 Appetizer: Calories 65 (Calories from Fat 45); Fat 5g (Saturated 3g); Cholesterol 20mg; Sodium 65mg; Carbohydrate 3g (Dietary Fiber 0g); Protein 2g
% Daily Value: Vitamin A 2%; Vitamin C 0%; Calcium 4%; Iron 2%
Exchanges: 1 Fat
Carbohydrate Choices: 0

BETTY'S TIPS

✿ **Kitchen Tip**
Look for mini phyllo dough shells in the frozen pastry section of most large supermarkets.

Pepperoni Swirls

Prep Time: 20 min Start to Finish: 3 hr 40 min

- 1 sheet frozen puff pastry (from 17.3-ounce package), thawed
- 3 tablespoons country-style Dijon mustard
- 4 ounces pepperoni, chopped
- 1 cup shredded mozzarella cheese (4 ounces)
- 2 teaspoons dried oregano leaves

1. On lightly floured surface, roll puff pastry into 16 x 14-inch rectangle. Spread mustard over all of pastry. Sprinkle pepperoni evenly over mustard. Sprinkle cheese and oregano over pepperoni.

2. Starting at 16-inch side, tightly roll up pastry; gently pinch edge into roll to seal. Wrap in plastic wrap and refrigerate 2 to 3 hours.

3. Heat oven to 425°. Line cookie sheet with aluminum foil; lightly spray foil with cooking spray. Cut pastry into $1/2$-inch slices. Place on cookie sheet.

4. Bake 15 to 20 minutes or until golden brown and slightly puffed. Serve warm.

32 appetizers.
1 Appetizer: Calories 65 (Calories from Fat 45); Fat 5g (Saturated 2g); Cholesterol 10mg; Sodium 140mg; Carbohydrate 3g (Dietary Fiber 0g); Protein 2g
% Daily Value: Vitamin A 0%; Vitamin C 0%; Calcium 2%; Iron 2%
Exchanges: $1/2$ Fat
Carbohydrate Choices: 0

BETTY'S TIPS

✿ **Kitchen Tip**
A serrated knife works well for slicing these pastry swirl treats.

Smoky Cranberry Chicken Wings

Prep Time: 15 min Start to Finish: 3 hr 5 min

 2 pounds chicken wings
 1 can (16 ounces) jellied cranberry sauce
 $^1/_2$ cup mesquite smoke marinade or hickory smoke barbecue sauce
 $^1/_3$ cup chopped onion

1. Cut each chicken wing at joints to make 3 pieces; discard tip. Cut off and discard excess skin.

2. In large bowl, mix remaining ingredients. Add chicken; stir to coat well. Cover and refrigerate 2 to 3 hours, stirring occasionally.

3. Heat oven to 375°. Line 15 x 10 x 1-inch pan with aluminum foil or cooking parchment paper; lightly spray foil or paper with cooking spray. Remove chicken from marinade; reserve marinade. Place chicken in pan.

4. Bake 50 to 60 minutes or until well browned and no longer pink in center. Meanwhile, in 1-quart saucepan, heat marinade to boiling over medium-high heat. Reduce heat to medium; cook 3 to 4 minutes longer, stirring occasionally, until slightly thickened. Brush chicken with sauce halfway through baking.

16 servings.
1 Serving: Calories 155 (Calories from Fat 55); Fat 6g (Saturated 2g); Cholesterol 35mg; Sodium 115mg; Carbohydrate 14g (Dietary Fiber 0g); Protein 11g
% Daily Value: Vitamin A 0%; Vitamin C 0%; Calcium 0%; Iron 2%
Exchanges: 1 Other Carbohydrate, 1$^1/_2$ Lean Meat, $^1/_2$ Fat
Carbohydrate Choices: 1

BETTY'S TIPS

⚙ **Kitchen Tip**
Using regular barbecue sauce for these wings is also okay. They'll just be a little sweeter and not as smoky flavored.

Cut-up appetizer-style chicken wings can be found in the frozen-foods section of most grocery stores.

Smoky Cranberry Chicken Wings

Warm Chicken Spread

Prep Time: 15 min Start to Finish: 45 min
(Photo on page 27)

3 cans (9.75 to 10 ounces each) chunk chicken, drained

$^1/_2$ cup mayonnaise or salad dressing

2 tablespoons Dijon mustard with horseradish (from 7.2-ounce jar)

$^1/_2$ cup frozen stir-fry bell peppers and onions (from 1-pound bag), thawed and drained

3 tablespoons mayonnaise or salad dressing

$^3/_4$ cup Progresso® plain bread crumbs

$1^1/_2$ loaves (12-ounce size) French baguette bread, cut into $^1/_4$-inch slices

1. Heat oven to 375°. Spray 9-inch pie plate with cooking spray. In large bowl, mix chicken, $^1/_2$ cup mayonnaise, mustard and stir-fry vegetables. Spread in pie plate.

2. In small bowl, mix 3 tablespoons mayonnaise and bread crumbs. Sprinkle evenly over top of chicken mixture.

3. Bake 20 to 30 minutes or until light golden brown and hot. Serve with bread.

28 servings (2 tablespoons spread and 2 bread slices each).
1 Serving: Calories 130 (Calories from Fat 55); Fat 6g (Saturated 1g); Cholesterol 15mg; Sodium 290mg; Carbohydrate 12g (Dietary Fiber 1g); Protein 7g
% Daily Value: Vitamin A 0%; Vitamin C 0%; Calcium 2%; Iron 4%
Exchanges: 1 Starch, $^1/_2$ High-Fat Meat
Carbohydrate Choices: 1

BETTY'S TIPS

⚙ **Kitchen Tip**
Get a head start by making the spread 3 to 4 hours ahead, then covering and refrigerating. Bake as directed.

Southwest Chicken Nachos

Prep Time: 15 min Start to Finish: 4 hr 45 min

1 package (16 ounces) mild Mexican pasteurized prepared cheese product with jalapeño peppers, cut into cubes

$3/4$ cup old El Paso Thick 'n Chunky salsa

1 can (15 ounces) black beans, rinsed and drained

1 package (9 ounces) frozen cooked Southwest-seasoned chicken breast strips, thawed and cubed

1 container (8 ounces) Southwest ranch sour cream dip

1 medium green bell pepper, chopped (1 cup)

1 medium red bell pepper, chopped (1 cup)

12 ounces large tortilla chips

1. Place cheese, salsa, beans and chicken in 3- to 4-quart slow cooker.

2. Cover and cook on Low heat setting 3 to 4 hours, stirring halfway through cooking, until cheese is melted and mixture is hot.

3. Stir in sour cream dip and bell peppers. Increase heat setting to High. Cover and cook about 30 minutes or until mixture is hot. Serve over tortilla chips. Topping will hold on Low heat setting up to 2 hours; stir occasionally.

21 servings ($1/4$ cup topping and 5 chips each).
1 Serving: Calories 230 (Calories from Fat 110); Fat 12g (Saturated 5g); Cholesterol 30mg; Sodium 600mg; Carbohydrate 20g (Dietary Fiber 3g); Protein 11g
% Daily Value: Vitamin A 14%; Vitamin C 14%; Calcium 16%; Iron 8%
Exchanges: 1 Starch, 1 Vegetable, 1 Medium-Fat Meat
Carbohydrate Choices: 1

Southwest Chicken Nachos

BETTY'S TIPS

⚙ **Success Hint**
Be sure to cut the cheese into chunks that are about the same size, so they'll melt evenly during cooking.

⚙ **Time-Saver**
To cut down on some of the chopping, thaw 2 cups from a bag of frozen stir-fry bell pepper blend and stir into the nacho topping instead of using the fresh peppers.

⚙ **Special Touch**
Multicolored tortilla chips jazz up these nachos with a splash of Southwest color.

Greek Beef Bites

Prep Time: 40 min Start to Finish: 5 hr 40 min

2 tablespoons olive or vegetable oil

3 pounds beef boneless chuck roast, trimmed of fat and cut into 1- to 1^1/$_2$-inch pieces

4 cloves garlic, finely chopped

1 tablespoon dried oregano leaves

1^1/$_2$ teaspoons salt

^{1}/$_2$ teaspoon coarsely ground pepper

4 tablespoons grated lemon peel

1 cup yogurt

^{1}/$_2$ small cucumber, peeled, cored and finely chopped (^{1}/$_3$ cup)

^{1}/$_2$ teaspoon salt

1. Heat oil in 12-inch skillet over medium-high heat. Cook beef in oil, in batches if necessary, 8 to 10 minutes, turning occasionally, until brown on all sides.

2. Place beef in 3- to 4-quart slow cooker. Sprinkle with garlic, oregano, 1^1/$_2$ teaspoons salt, pepper and 3 tablespoons lemon peel; toss to mix.

3. Cover and cook on Low heat setting 4 to 5 hours.

4. Stir together yogurt, cucumber, ^{1}/$_2$ teaspoon salt and remaining 1 tablespoon lemon peel in small bowl. Serve beef with toothpicks for dipping into yogurt sauce. Beef bites will hold on Low heat setting up to 2 hours; stir occasionally.

20 servings (3 beef bites and 1 tablespoon sauce each).
1 Serving: Calories 145 (Calories from Fat 80); Fat 9g (Saturated 3g);
Cholesterol 45mg; Sodium 280mg; Carbohydrate 1g (Dietary Fiber 0g);
Protein 15g
% Daily Value: Vitamin A 0%; Vitamin C 0%; Calcium 2%; Iron 8%
Exchanges: 2 Medium-Fat Meat
Carbohydrate Choices: 0

Greek Beef Bites

BETTY'S TIPS

⊛ **Success Hint**
For the best flavor and to reduce the amount of liquid during cooking, trim any excess fat from the beef before browning it.

⊛ **Time-Saver**
Look for beef stew meat—already trimmed and cut into 1- and 1^1/$_2$-inch pieces—in the meat department.

⊛ **Variation**
For a gyro-type sandwich, spoon this beef onto pita bread, top with sliced onions and tomatoes and drizzle with the cucumber sauce.

Quick & Low Fat
Tropical Prosciutto Bites

Prep Time: 20 min Start to Finish: 20 min

¹/₄ pound thinly sliced prosciutto or fully cooked ham, cut into 1-inch-wide strips

1 large mango or papaya, peeled, pitted or seeded and cut into 12 pieces

12 medium strawberries

1. Wrap strips of prosciutto around mango pieces and strawberries. Secure with toothpicks.

24 appetizers.
1 Appetizer: Calories 10 (Calories from Fat 0); Fat 0g (Saturated 0g);
Cholesterol 5mg; Sodium 70mg; Carbohydrate 2g (Dietary Fiber 0g);
Protein 1g
% Daily Value: Vitamin A 2%; Vitamin C 10%; Calcium 0%; Iron 0%
Exchanges: 1 Serving Free
Carbohydrate Choices: 9

BETTY'S TIPS

✪ **Success Hint**
Strawberries can become mushy once they have been in water, so wash them just before you are going to use them.

✪ **Do-Ahead**
Cut the strips of prosciutto and peel and cut the mango several hours ahead. Cover and refrigerate them separately. Shortly before serving, wrap the fruit in the prosciutto.

✪ **Did You Know?**
A popular Italian appetizer is melon wrapped with strips of prosciutto. Wrapping the prosciutto around mango and strawberries is a nice flavor twist to this classic recipe.

Tropical Prosciutto Bites

Grilled Salmon with Wasabi Mayonnaise

Prep Time: 20 min Start to Finish: 40 min

2 tablespoons soy sauce

2 teaspoons white wine vinegar

1 teaspoon vegetable oil

1/2 teaspoon grated fresh ginger

1/2 pound salmon fillet

1/2 cup wasabi mayonnaise (from 11-ounce bottle)

16 round wheat crackers

1 medium green onion, thinly sliced (1 tablespoon)

1. Heat coals or gas grill for direct heat. Mix soy sauce, vinegar, oil and ginger in small shallow container. Place salmon in mixture, skin side up. Let stand 10 minutes.

2. Cover and grill salmon, skin side down, 4 to 6 inches from medium heat 10 to 12 minutes, brushing once with marinade, until salmon flakes easily with fork.

3. To serve, spread mayonnaise on crackers; top each with about 1 tablespoon flaked salmon, additional mayonnaise and green onion.

16 appetizers.

1 Appetizer: Calories 85 (Calories from Fat 65); Fat 7g (Saturated 1g); Cholesterol 15mg; Sodium 180mg; Carbohydrate 3g (Dietary Fiber 0g); Protein 3g
% Daily Value: Vitamin A 0%; Vitamin C 0%; Calcium 0%; Iron 2%
Exchanges: 1/2 Medium-Fat Meat, 1 Fat
Carbohydrate Choices: 0

BETTY'S TIPS

⊙ **Substitution**

If you can't find wasabi mayonnaise, mix 1 tablespoon horseradish into 1/2 cup plain mayonnaise.

Instead of crackers, you may want to try this Asian-style salmon on toasted baguette slices.

⊙ **Variation**

To make Grilled Salmon with Dill Mayonnaise, mix 1 tablespoon chopped fresh dillweed with 1/2 cup plain mayonnaise, and use in place of the wasabi mayonnaise.

Grilled Salmon with Wasabi Mayonnaise

Crab Fondue

Prep Time: 30 min Start to Finish: 30 min

2 cups shredded Gruyère or Swiss cheese (8 ounces)

2 packages (8 ounces each) cream cheese, softened

$1/4$ cup frozen stir-fry bell peppers and onions (from 1-pound bag)

$1/2$ cup dry white wine or milk

$1/8$ teaspoon ground red pepper (cayenne)

3 cans (6 ounces each) crabmeat, drained and cartilage removed

1 loaf (14 to 16 ounces) French bread, cut into 1-inch cubes

1. In 2-quart saucepan or chafing dish, heat all ingredients except crabmeat and bread over medium heat, stirring constantly, until cheese is melted. Stir in crabmeat. Pour into fondue pot or chafing dish to keep warm. Dip will hold for 2 hours.

2. Spear bread cubes with fondue forks; dip into fondue. (If fondue becomes too thick, stir in a small amount of dry white wine or milk.)

28 servings ($2^1/_2$ tablespoons fondue and 4 bread cubes each).
1 Serving: Calories 150 (Calories from Fat 80); Fat 9g (Saturated 5g); Cholesterol 45mg; Sodium 220mg; Carbohydrate 8g (Dietary Fiber 0g); Protein 9g
% Daily Value: Vitamin A 6%; Vitamin C 0%; Calcium 12%; Iron 4%
Exchanges: $1/2$ Starch, 1 High-Fat Meat
Carbohydrate Choices: $1/2$

BETTY'S TIPS

⊙ **Kitchen Tip**
This sensational seafood dip is also great served with raw zucchini sticks, red bell pepper strips or blanched pea pods.

Crab Fondue

Soups, Salads and Other Light Meals

Great for Lunch or a Light Supper

California Citrus Broccoli Slaw (page 79)

Taco-Corn Chili (page 65)

Southwest Chicken Soup with Baked Tortilla Strips

Prep Time: 15 min Start to Finish: 7 hr 45 min

1 pound boneless skinless chicken thighs, cut into 1-inch pieces

2 medium sweet potatoes, peeled, cut into 1-inch pieces (2 cups)

1 large onion, chopped (1 cup)

2 cans (14.5 ounces each) diced tomatoes with green chilies, undrained

1 can (14 ounces) chicken broth

1 teaspoon dried oregano leaves

$^1/_2$ teaspoon ground cumin

1 cup Green Giant® Niblets® frozen whole kernel corn (from 1-pound bag)

$^1/_2$ cup chopped green bell pepper

8 yellow or blue corn tortillas (5 to 6 inches)

2 tablespoons chopped fresh cilantro

1. In 3$^1/_2$- to 4-quart slow cooker, mix chicken, sweet potatoes, onion, tomatoes, broth, oregano and cumin.

2. Cover and cook on Low heat setting 7 to 8 hours.

3. Stir corn and bell pepper into soup. Increase heat setting to High. Cover and cook about 30 minutes or until chicken is no longer pink in center and vegetables are tender.

4. Meanwhile, heat oven to 450°. Spray 2 cookie sheets with cooking spray. Cut each tortilla into strips; place in single layer on cookie sheets. Bake about 6 minutes or until crisp but not brown; cool. Spoon soup into bowls. Top with tortilla strips. Sprinkle with cilantro.

6 servings.

1 Serving: Calories 310 (Calories from Fat 70); Fat 8g (Saturated 2g); Cholesterol 45mg; Sodium 760mg; Carbohydrate 42g (Dietary Fiber 5g); Protein 22g
% Daily Value: Vitamin A 110%; Vitamin C 30%; Calcium 15%; Iron 15%
Exchanges: 2$^1/_2$ Starch, 1 Vegetable, 2 Lean Meat
Carbohydrate Choices: 2$^1/_2$

BETTY'S TIPS

⚙ **Kitchen Tip**

You can use two cans regular diced tomatoes and 1 can of Old El Paso chopped green chilies instead of the tomatoes with green chilies.

Sweet potatoes and other bright orange vegetables contain beta-carotene, which your body converts to vitamin A.

Southwest Chicken Soup with Baked Tortilla Strips

Golden Harvest Chicken Soup

Prep Time: 25 min Start to Finish: 8 hr 45 min

1 pound boneless, skinless chicken thighs, cut into ³/₄-inch pieces

1 teaspoon peppered seasoned salt

2 medium unpeeled red potatoes, cut into ¹/₂-inch pieces (2 cups)

2 medium carrots, sliced (1 cup)

1 medium onion, coarsely chopped (¹/₂ cup)

2 cans (14 ounces each) chicken broth

2 cups small broccoli flowerets

1 medium yellow summer squash, coarsely chopped (1¹/₂ cups)

2 tablespoons chopped fresh basil leaves

1. Spray 10-inch nonstick skillet with cooking spray; heat over medium-high heat. Add chicken to skillet; sprinkle with peppered seasoned salt. Cook 6 to 8 minutes, stirring occasionally, until brown.

2. Mix chicken and remaining ingredients except broccoli, squash and basil in 3¹/₂- to 4-quart slow cooker.

3. Cover and cook on Low heat setting 7 to 8 hours.

4. Stir in broccoli, squash and basil. Increase heat setting to High. Cover and cook 15 to 20 minutes or until vegetables are tender.

6 servings (1¹/₃ cups each).
1 Serving: Calories 210 (Calories from Fat 65); Fat 7g (Saturated 2g); Cholesterol 45mg; Sodium 890mg; Carbohydrate 16g (Dietary Fiber 3g); Protein 21g
% Daily Value: Vitamin A 86%; Vitamin C 34%; Calcium 6%; Iron 16%
Exchanges: ¹/₂ Starch, 2 Vegetable, 2 Lean Meat
Carbohydrate Choices: 1

BETTY'S TIPS

⊗ **Substitution**
In place of fresh broccoli, you can use 2 cups Green Giant Select frozen broccoli flowerets. Thaw them before adding to the slow cooker.

⊗ **Success Hint**
Chicken thigh meat is ideal for long, slow cooking, because the rich dark meat doesn't dry out in the slow cooker as would leaner light meat such as chicken breasts.

For food-safety reasons, any leftover soup should be cooled in a shallow container in the refrigerator, rather than at room temperature.

Golden Harvest Chicken Soup

Chicken Enchilada Chili

Prep Time: 10 min Start to Finish: 8 hr 10 min

1¼ pounds boneless, skinless chicken thighs

1 medium onion, chopped (½ cup)

1 medium yellow or green bell pepper, chopped (1 cup)

2 cans (14.5 ounces each) stewed tomatoes with garlic and onion, undrained

2 cans (15 to 16 ounces each) chili beans in sauce, undrained

1 can (10 ounces) Old El Paso enchilada sauce

⅓ cup sour cream

2 tablespoons chopped fresh cilantro

1. Spray 4- to 5-quart slow cooker with cooking spray. Mix all ingredients except sour cream and cilantro in cooker.

2. Cover and cook on Low heat setting 7 to 8 hours.

3. Stir mixture to break up chicken. Top each serving with sour cream and cilantro.

6 servings (1²/₃ cups each).
1 Serving: Calories 340 (Calories from Fat 100); Fat 11g (Saturated 4g); Cholesterol 65mg; Sodium 1,700mg; Carbohydrate 38g (Dietary Fiber 8g); Protein 30g

% Daily Value: Vitamin A 28%; Vitamin C 62%; Calcium 12%; Iron 30%
Exchanges: 2 Starch, 2 Vegetable, 3 Very Lean Meat, ½ Fat
Carbohydrate Choices: 2½

BETTY'S TIPS

✪ **Substitution**
Regular stewed tomatoes, along with some chopped onion and a dash of garlic powder or finely chopped fresh garlic, can be used in place of the flavored stewed tomatoes.

✪ **Success Hint**
Lifting the lid of your slow cooker can add up to 20 minutes of cooking time. Instead, spin the lid to clear it of condensation, so you can check the food.

✪ **Do-Ahead**
For super-quick dinners and portable lunches, freeze the chili in single-serving freezer containers. Thaw, then heat in the microwave on High for 4 to 5 minutes, stirring once or twice, until hot.

Chicken Enchilada Chili

Taco-Corn Chili

Prep Time: 30 min Start to Finish: 30 min
(Photo on page 61)

1 pound extra-lean (at least 90%) ground beef

1 can (15 to 16 ounces) kidney beans, rinsed, drained

1 envelope (1.25 ounces) Old El Paso taco seasoning mix

1 can (10 ounces) diced tomatoes and green chilies, undrained

1 package (9 ounces) Green Giant Niblets frozen corn, thawed, drained

2 cups water

2 teaspoons sugar

1. Spray 4-quart Dutch oven with cooking spray; heat over medium-high heat. Cook beef in Dutch oven 5 to 7 minutes, stirring occasionally, until brown; drain.

2. Stir in remaining ingredients. Heat to boiling, reduce heat. Simmer uncovered about 18 minutes, stirring occasionally.

5 servings.
1 Serving: Calories 300 (Calories from Fat 70); Fat 8g (Saturated 3g); Cholesterol 55mg; Sodium 1,030mg; Carbohydrate 36g (Dietary Fiber 6g); Protein 25g
% Daily Value: Vitamin A 8%; Vitamin C 10%; Calcium 6%; Iron 30%
Exchanges: $2^1/_2$ Starch, $1^1/_2$ Lean Meat
Carbohydrate Choices: 2

BETTY'S TIPS

⚙ **Kitchen Tip**
When you can't find extra-lean beef, substitute extra-lean pork, turkey or chicken.

Burger Beef Soup

Prep Time: 30 min Start to Finish: 30 min

1 pound lean (at least 80%) ground beef

1 small onion, chopped ($^1/_4$ cup)

1 can ($10^3/_4$ ounces) condensed cream of celery soup

$^1/_2$ cup Green Giant frozen sweet peas (from 1-pound bag)

2 cups tomato juice

$1^1/_4$ cups water

$^3/_4$ teaspoon chopped fresh or $^1/_4$ teaspoon dried basil leaves

$^3/_4$ teaspoon chopped fresh or $^1/_4$ teaspoon dried marjoram leaves

$^1/_8$ teaspoon pepper

1 dried bay leaf

1 cup uncooked egg noodles (2 ounces)

1. In 4-quart Dutch oven, cook beef and onion over medium heat 8 to 10 minutes, stirring occasionally, until beef is browned; drain.

2. Stir in remaining ingredients except noodles. Heat to boiling. Stir in noodles, reduce heat. Simmer uncovered about 10 minutes, stirring occasionally, until noodles are tender. Remove bay leaf.

4 servings ($1^1/_4$ cups each).
1 Serving: Calories 390 (Calories from Fat 190); Fat 21g (Saturated 8g); Cholesterol 80mg; Sodium 1,060mg; Carbohydrate 24g (Dietary Fiber 3g); Protein 26g
% Daily Value: Vitamin A 26%; Vitamin C 22%; Calcium 8%; Iron 20%
Exchanges: 1 Starch, 2 Vegetable, $2^1/_2$ Medium-Fat Meat, $1^1/_2$ Fat
Carbohydrate Choices: $1^1/_2$

BETTY'S TIPS

⊗ **Kitchen Tip**
Make this simple soup fun by stirring in pasta such as rotini, radiatore or wagon wheels instead of the egg noodles.

Burger Beef Soup

Beef Barley Soup

Prep Time: 10 min Start to Finish: 8 hr 20 min

1$\frac{1}{2}$ pounds beef stew meat

2 medium carrots, sliced (1 cup)

1 medium onion, chopped ($\frac{1}{2}$ cup)

1 cup sliced fresh mushrooms

4 cans (10.5 ounces each) condensed beef consommé

$\frac{1}{2}$ cup uncooked pearled barley

2 dried bay leaves

1 cup Green Giant Select® LeSueur® frozen baby sweet peas (from 1-pound bag)

1. In 4- to 5-quart slow cooker, mix all ingredients except peas.

2. Cover and cook on Low heat setting 8 to 9 hours.

3. About 10 minutes before serving, stir in peas. Increase heat setting to High. Cover and cook about 10 minutes or until peas are cooked through. Remove bay leaves.

6 servings (1$\frac{1}{3}$ cups each).
1 Serving: Calories 350 (Calories from Fat 115); Fat 13g (Saturated 5g); Cholesterol 70mg; Sodium 1,120mg; Carbohydrate 23g (Dietary Fiber 5g); Protein 35g
% Daily Value: Vitamin A 78%; Vitamin C 4%; Calcium 4%; Iron 24%
Exchanges: 1 Starch, 2 Vegetable, 4 Lean Meat
Carbohydrate Choices: 1$\frac{1}{2}$

BETTY'S TIPS

⚙ **Kitchen Tip**
Add the peas at the end to preserve their fresh flavor and bright green color.

Beef Barley Soup

Old-Fashioned Oven Beef Stew

Prep Time: 15 min Start to Finish: 4 hr 15 min

1½ pounds beef stew meat

3 tablespoons Gold Medal all-purpose flour

2 bags (1 pound each) frozen vegetables for stew

1 can (14.5 ounces) diced tomatoes, undrained

2 cans (10 ounces each) condensed beef consommé

1 tablespoon sugar

⅛ teaspoon pepper

2 dried bay leaves

1. Heat oven to 325°. In 4-quart Dutch oven or 13 x 9-inch (3-quart) baking dish, toss beef with flour. Add frozen vegetables.

2. In large bowl, stir tomatoes, beef consommé, sugar, pepper and bay leaves. Pour over beef and vegetables; gently stir until mixed.

3. Cover and bake 3 hours 30 minutes to 4 hours or until beef is tender. Remove bay leaves.

6 servings (1½ cups each).
1 Serving: Calories 350 (Calories from Fat 115); Fat 13g (Saturated 5g); Cholesterol 70mg; Sodium 730mg; Carbohydrate 28g (Dietary Fiber 4g); Protein 31g
% Daily Value: Vitamin A 100%; Vitamin C 16%; Calcium 6%; Iron 22%
Exchanges: 1 Starch, 3 Vegetable, 3 Lean Meat, ½ Fat
Carbohydrate Choices: 2

BETTY'S TIPS

⚙ **Kitchen Tip**
A loaf of crusty French bread and a tossed salad complete this hearty meal. For a quick shepherd's pie, reheat single servings of leftover stew in soup bowls. Top with prepared mashed potatoes.

Old-Fashioned Oven Beef Stew

Low Fat

Minestrone Soup

Prep Time: 20 min Start to Finish: 40 min

1 can (28 ounces) whole tomatoes, undrained

1 can (15 to 16 ounces) great northern beans, undrained

1 can (15 to 16 ounces) kidney beans, undrained

1 can (15.25) Green Giant whole kernel corn, undrained

2 medium ribs celery, thinly sliced (1 cup)

1 small zucchini, sliced (1 cup)

1 medium onion, chopped ($^1/_2$ cup)

1 cup shredded cabbage

$^1/_2$ cup uncooked elbow macaroni or broken spaghetti

$1^1/_4$ cups water

1 teaspoon Italian seasoning

2 vegetable bouillon cubes

1 clove garlic, finely chopped

Grated Parmesan cheese, if desired

1. In 4-quart Dutch oven, heat all ingredients except cheese to boiling, breaking up tomatoes; reduce heat to low.

2. Cover and simmer 15 to 20 minutes, stirring occasionally, until macaroni and vegetables are tender. Serve with cheese.

6 servings ($1^2/_3$ cups each).
1 Serving: Calories 305 (Calories from Fat 20); Fat 2g (Saturated 0g); Cholesterol 0mg; Sodium 920mg; Carbohydrate 65g (Dietary Fiber 13g); Protein 19g
% Daily Value: Vitamin A 14%; Vitamin C 28%; Calcium 14%; Iron 38%
Exchanges: 4 Starch, 1 Vegetable
Carbohydrate Choices: 4

BETTY'S TIPS

⊕ Kitchen Tip
For a delicious vegetarian meal, sprinkle the hot soup with chopped parsley instead of the cheese. All this meal needs is multigrain bread slices spread with garlic butter and a spinach salad tossed with poppy seed dressing.

Minestrone Soup

Slow-Cooker Steak and Black Bean Chili

Prep Time: 10 min Start to Finish: 8 hr 10 min

2 pounds beef top round steak, trimmed and cut into $^3/_4$-inch cubes

1 envelope (1 ounce) onion soup mix (from 2-ounce package)

2 cans (15 ounces each) black beans, rinsed and drained

1 can (28 ounces) diced tomatoes, undrained

1 can (8 ounces) tomato sauce

1 can (4.5 ounces) Old El Paso chopped green chilies, undrained

3 teaspoons chili powder

1 teaspoon ground cumin

1. In $3^1/_2$- to 4-quart slow cooker, mix beef and soup mix (dry). Stir in remaining ingredients.

2. Cover and cook on Low heat setting 8 to 10 hours.

6 servings.
1 Serving: Calories 390 (Calories from Fat 55); Fat 6g (Saturated 2g); Cholesterol 80mg; Sodium 1,810mg; Carbohydrate 51g (Dietary Fiber 12g); Protein 45g
% Daily Value: Vitamin A 28%; Vitamin C 24%; Calcium 16%; Iron 44%
Exchanges: 3 Starch, 1 Vegetable, 4 Very Lean Meat
Carbohydrate Choices: $3^1/_2$

BETTY'S TIPS

⊛ **Health Twist**
If you're watching your sodium intake, rinse the beans well to remove excess sodium before adding them to the slow cooker.

⊛ **Serve-With**
Cool down the spicy flavor of this chili with warm corn bread and assorted crunchy fresh veggies with ranch dip.

⊛ **Special Touch**
Top each serving with a dollop of sour cream, then sprinkle with shredded Cheddar cheese and sliced green onions.

Slow-Cooker Steak and Black Bean Chili

Ham and Wild Rice Soup

Southwestern Pork Soup

Ham and Wild Rice Soup

Prep Time: 10 min Start to Finish: 9 hr 25 min

- 2 cups diced cooked ham
- ³/₄ cup uncooked wild rice
- 1 medium onion, chopped (¹/₂ cup)
- 1 bag (1 pound) Green Giant frozen mixed vegetables, thawed
- 1 can (14 ounces) chicken broth
- 1 can (10.75 ounces) reduced-sodium cream of celery soup
- ¹/₄ teaspoon pepper
- 3 cups water
- ¹/₂ cup half-and-half

1. Mix all ingredients except half-and-half in 3¹/₂- to 4-quart slow cooker.

2. Cover and cook on Low heat setting 8 to 9 hours.

3. Stir in half-and-half. Increase heat setting to High. Cover and cook 10 to 15 minutes or until hot.

8 servings (1 cup each).
1 Serving: Calories 205 (Calories from Fat 70); Fat 8g (Saturated 3g); Cholesterol 25mg; Sodium 1,030mg; Carbohydrate 20g (Dietary Fiber 3g); Protein 13g
% Daily Value: Vitamin A 34%; Vitamin C 16%; Calcium 6%; Iron 8%
Exchanges: 1 Starch, 1 Vegetable, 1 Lean Meat, 1 Fat
Carbohydrate Choices: 1

BETTY'S TIPS

⚙ **Substitution**
Cream of mushroom or chicken soup can be used instead of the cream of celery.

⚙ **Success Hint**
To quickly thaw frozen vegetables, rinse them under cold running water. All frozen veggies should be thawed before using them in a slow-cooker recipe.

⚙ **Did You Know?**
One cup of uncooked wild rice cooked in three cups of water yields 4 cups of cooked rice. It can take up to an hour to cook wild rice on the stove.

Southwestern Pork Soup

Prep Time: 25 min Start to Finish: 35 min

- 2 teaspoons vegetable oil
- 1 pound boneless pork loin, trimmed of fat, cut into ¹/₂-inch cubes
- 4 medium green onions, sliced (¹/₄ cup)
- 1 small jalapeño chili, seeded, finely chopped
- 1 clove garlic, finely chopped
- 2 cans (14 ounces each) 33%-less-sodium chicken broth
- 2 cans (15 to 16 ounces each) great northern beans, rinsed, drained
- ¹/₂ cup loosely packed chopped fresh cilantro
- ¹/₄ cup loosely packed chopped parsley

1. In 3-quart nonstick saucepan, heat oil over medium-high heat. Add pork; cook 3 to 5 minutes, stirring occasionally, until browned. Add onions, chili and garlic; cook and stir 1 minute.

2. Add broth and beans. Heat to boiling; reduce heat. Cover and simmer about 10 minutes or until pork is no longer pink in center. Stir in cilantro and parsley; cook until heated through.

5 servings (1¹/₄ cups each).
1 Serving: Calories 400 (Calories from Fat 100); Fat 11g (Saturated 3g); Cholesterol 60mg; Sodium 380mg; Carbohydrate 45g (Dietary Fiber 11g); Protein 40g
% Daily Value: Vitamin A 8%; Vitamin C 6%; Calcium 18%; Iron 42%
Exchanges: 3 Starch, 1 Very Lean Meat, ¹/₂ Fat
Carbhydrate Choices: 3

BETTY'S TIPS

⚙ **Kitchen Tip**
One pound of boneless pork loin chops, cut into cubes, would also work well for this recipe.

A squeeze of fresh lime juice over servings of this Mexican-inspired soup adds a wonderful fresh flavor. It also blends well with the chili and cilantro.

Seafood Bisque

Fish Chowder

Quick

Seafood Bisque

Prep Time: 15 min Start to finish: 25 min

$1/3$ cup butter or margarine

$1/3$ cup Gold Medal all-purpose flour

2 cans (14 ounces each) chicken broth

4 cups (1 quart) half-and-half

$1/2$ cup dry white wine or water

$1/2$ cup chopped drained roasted red bell peppers (from 7-ounce jar)

12 ounces cod fillet, cut into 1-inch pieces

12 ounces uncooked peeled deveined medium shrimp, thawed if frozen and tails peeled

$1/2$ cup basil pesto

$1/4$ teaspoon salt

$1/8$ teaspoon freshly ground pepper

1. In 4-quart Dutch oven, melt butter over medium-high heat. Stir in flour. Gradually stir in broth, half-and-half and wine. Stir in bell peppers and cod. Heat to boiling, stirring occasionally.

2. Stir in shrimp. Simmer uncovered 2 to 3 minutes or until shrimp are pink and firm. Stir in pesto, salt and pepper.

8 servings.
1 Serving: Calories 410 (Calories from Fat 280); Fat 31g (Saturated 15g); Cholesterol 150mg; Sodium 860mg; Carbohydrate 11g (Dietary Fiber 1g); Protein 22g
% Daily Value: Vitamin A 22%; Vitamin C 16%; Calcium 22%; Iron 12%
Exchanges: 1 Milk, 2 Medium-Fat Meat, 4 Fat
Carbohydrate Choices: 1

BETTY'S TIPS

❂ **Substitution**
Cooked shrimp works great in this recipe too. Just add the shrimp to the bisque and simmer until heated through.

If you use cooked shrimp, reserve 8 shrimp, and tie a chive around each shrimp for an extra-special garnish.

❂ **Special Touch**
As you dish up the soup, sprinkle chopped fresh basil leaves and a little freshly shredded Parmesan cheese on each serving.

Quick

Fish Chowder

Prep Time: 30 min Start to Finish: 30 min

2 teaspoons vegetable oil

1 small onion, chopped ($1/4$ cup)

1 medium rib celery, chopped ($1/2$ cup)

2 cups frozen potatoes O'Brien with onions and peppers

1 can (14.75 ounces) Green Giant® cream-style sweet corn

1 can (14 ounces) 33%-less-sodium chicken broth

$1/2$ teaspoon salt

$1 1/4$ pounds firm white fish fillets, such as cod or pollock, skin removed

1 cup fat-free (skim) milk

2 teaspoons cornstarch

1. In 3-quart saucepan, heat oil over medium heat. Add onion and celery; cook 2 to 3 minutes, stirring occasionally, until tender.

2. Stir in potatoes, corn, broth and salt. Heat to boiling; reduce heat. Simmer uncovered about 5 minutes or until potatoes are tender.

3. Add whole fish fillets. Cover and cook 5 to 7 minutes or until fish flakes easily with fork. In measuring cup, mix milk and cornstarch; stir into chowder. Heat just to boiling.

5 servings (1$1/2$ cups each).
1 Serving: Calories 325 (Calories from Fat 80); Fat 9g (Saturated 2g); Cholesterol 65mg; Sodium 1,000mg; Carbohydrate 32g (Dietary Fiber 3g); Protein 29g
% Daily Value: Vitamin A 12%; Vitamin C 12%; Calcium 14%; Iron 6%
Exchanges: 2 Starch, 3 Lean Meat
Carbohydrate Choices: 2

BETTY'S TIPS

❂ **Kitchen Tip**
Halibut is a bit more expensive than some fish, but it provides a wonderful flavor and texture to this chowder. If you like, any firm fish can be used. It's best to leave the fish fillets whole when you cook them. If you cut up the fish, it will flake into tiny pieces instead of staying in nice chunks.

Chicken and Squash Salad with Lime-Taco Dressing

Prep Time: 20 min Start to Finish: 40 min

Lime-Taco Dressing (right)

1 small butternut squash, peeled and cut into 1- to 1½-inch pieces (about 3 cups)

1 medium red onion, sliced

4 boneless, skinless chicken breast halves (1¼ pounds)

1 bag (10 ounces) torn mixed salad greens (romaine, iceberg and leaf lettuce or another mix)

1 medium avocado, pitted, peeled and diced

2 tablespoons chopped fresh cilantro

1. Heat coals or gas grill for direct heat. Make Lime-Taco Dressing. Use about ¼ cup dressing for grilling; reserve remaining dressing to drizzle on salad. Toss squash and onion with about 2 tablespoons dressing for grilling in large bowl. Place squash and onion in grill basket (grill "wok").

2. Place chicken and grill basket on grill. Cover and grill 4 to 6 inches from medium heat 15 to 20 minutes, turning chicken once and shaking grill basket or stirring vegetables occasionally, until juice of chicken is no longer pink when centers of thickest pieces are cut and vegetables are tender. Brush chicken and vegetables with remaining dressing for grilling during last 5 minutes of grilling.

3. Arrange salad greens on large platter. Top with avocado, squash and onion. Cut each chicken breast into slices; fan over vegetables. Drizzle with reserved dressing. Sprinkle with cilantro.

4 servings.

Lime-Taco Dressing

¾ cup frozen limeade concentrate, thawed

⅓ cup olive or vegetable oil

2 tablespoons honey

¼ teaspoon ground ginger

1 envelope (1.25 ounces) Old El Paso taco seasoning mix

Stir all ingredients in small bowl until well blended.

1 Serving: Calories 625 (Calories from Fat 260); Fat 29g (Saturated 5g); Cholesterol 75mg; Sodium 450mg; Carbohydrate 60g (Dietary Fiber 7g); Protein 31g
% Daily Value: Vitamin A 100%; Vitamin C 70%; Calcium 12%; Iron 18%
Exchanges: 2 Starch, 2 Vegetable, 1 Other Carbohydrate, 3 Lean Meat, 4 Fat
Carbohydrate Choices: 4

BETTY'S TIPS

✪ **Success Hint**
Choose avocados that are firm but give slightly to gentle pressure. Because avocados begin to turn brown after being cut, wait to add them to recipes until just before serving so that they retain their bright color.

Grill baskets are perfect for cut-up vegetables. A hinged basket can be flipped easily to turn everything at once and ensure even cooking.

✪ **Did You Know?**
Butternut squash is peanut shaped with a peel that ranges in color from cream to yellow. Inside, the flesh is bright orange and very sweet. For the best flavor, choose a firm, unblemished squash.

Chicken and Squash Salad with Lime-Taco Dressing

Quick

Light Lemon-Dijon Chicken Salad

Prep Time: 20 min Start to Finish: 20 min

Lemon-Dijon Dressing (below)
4 cups shredded romaine lettuce
2 cups shredded cooked chicken breasts
1/4 cup sliced drained oil-packed sun-dried tomatoes
1 hard-cooked egg, chopped
2 medium green onions, sliced (2 tablespoons)
1/4 cup shredded Parmesan cheese, if desired

1. Make Lemon-Dijon Dressing.

2. Arrange lettuce, chicken, tomatoes and egg on individual serving plates. Spoon dressing over top. Sprinkle with onions and cheese.

4 servings.

Lemon-Dijon Dressing
1/4 cup reduced-fat mayonnaise or salad dressing
2 tablespoons lemon juice
2 teaspoons Dijon mustard
1 clove garlic, finely chopped

Beat all ingredients in small bowl with wire whisk.

1 Serving: Calories 220 (Calories from Fat 100); Fat 11g (Saturated 2g); Cholesterol 115mg; Sodium 240mg; Carbohydrate 6g (Dietary Fiber 2g); Protein 24g
% Daily Value: Vitamin A 10%; Vitamin C 14%; Calcium 4%; Iron 8%
Exchanges: 1 Vegetable, 3 Lean Meat, 1 Fat
Carbohydrate Choices: 1/2

BETTY'S TIPS

⚙ **Success Hint**
To easily remove the skin from a garlic clove, press the clove firmly with the broad side of a chef's knife, then slice off the ends and the skin will pop right off.

⚙ **Health Twist**
Slash the fat to just 4 grams per serving by using fat-free mayonnaise instead of reduced-fat.

Light Lemon-Dijon Chicken Salad

California Citrus Broccoli Slaw

Prep Time: 20 min Start to Finish: 20 min

1 bag (16 ounces) broccoli slaw
1 small jicama, peeled and cut into julienne strips (2 cups)
3 medium oranges
1 small red onion, cut in half and thinly sliced (1 cup)
$^2/_3$ cup chopped fresh cilantro
   Citrus Dressing (below)

1. Mix broccoli slaw and jicama in large bowl. Peel oranges with sharp paring knife; cut into $^1/_4$-inch slices. Cut each slice into quarters. Add oranges, onion and cilantro to broccoli mixture.

2. Make Citrus Dressing; pour over salad and toss. Serve immediately, or cover and refrigerate up to 24 hours.

12 servings.

Citrus Dressing

3 tablespoons olive or vegetable oil
3 tablespoons lemon juice
4 teaspoons sugar
$1^1/_2$ teaspoons grated orange peel
$^1/_8$ teaspoon salt

Shake all ingredients in tightly covered container.

1 Serving: Calories 85 (Calories from Fat 35); Fat 4g (Saturated 0g); Cholesterol 0mg; Sodium 35mg; Carbohydrate 10g (Dietary Fiber 3g); Protein 2g
% Daily Value: Vitamin A 12%; Vitamin C 100%; Calcium 4%; Iron 2%
Exchanges: 1 Vegetable, $^1/_2$ Fruit, $^1/_2$ Fat
Carbohydrate Choices: $^1/_2$

BETTY'S TIPS

✿ **Success Hint**
Before peeling the orange, grate the orange peel for the dressing.

✿ **Health Twist**
The delicious combination in this recipe gives you 100% of the daily requirement of vitamin C. Wow!

✿ **Did You Know?**
Jicama is a crunchy root vegetable with a sweet, nutty flavor that's popular in Mexican cuisine. Its pretty ivory color does not become discolored, which makes it a natural to use in salads like this one.

Potato Salad with Chili Vinaigrette

Prep Time: 20 min Start to Finish: 50 min

1   can (4.5 ounces) Old El Paso chopped green chiles

Chili Vinaigrette (below)

4   unpeeled small red potatoes, cut into $1/2$-inch pieces ($1^1/_2$ cups)

2   unpeeled Yukon gold potatoes, cut into $1/2$-inch pieces ($2^1/_2$ cups)

2   tablespoons olive or vegetable oil

$1/_2$ teaspoon salt

1   medium yellow bell pepper, cut into $1/2$-inch pieces

3   medium roma (plum) tomatoes, coarsely chopped (1 cup)

Potato Salad with Chili Vinaigrette

1. Heat coals or gas grill for direct heat. Reserve 2 table-spoons of the chiles for Chili Vinaigrette; reserve remaining chiles for salad. Make Chili Vinaigrette.

2. Place potatoes in grill basket (grill "wok"). Drizzle with oil; sprinkle with salt. Shake basket to mix and turn potatoes.

3. Cover and grill potatoes 4 to 6 inches from medium heat 25 to 30 minutes, shaking basket or stirring potatoes occasionally, until tender. Add bell pepper to basket for last 5 minutes of grilling.

4. Place Chili Vinaigrette in large bowl; stir in tomatoes and remaining green chiles. Add potatoes and bell pepper to tomato mixture in bowl; toss to mix.

4 servings.

Chili Vinaigrette

$1/_4$ cup white balsamic vinegar

Reserved 2 tablespoons Old El Paso chopped green chiles

2   tablespoons olive or vegetable oil

$1/_4$ teaspoon black and red pepper blend

$1/_4$ teaspoon salt

Place all ingredients in blender. Cover and blend about 10 seconds or until smooth.

1 Serving: Calories 290 (Calories from Fat 125); Fat 14g (Saturated 2g); Cholesterol 0mg; Sodium 990mg; Carbohydrate 42g (Dietary Fiber 5g); Protein 4g
% Daily Value: Vitamin A 14%; Vitamin C 70%; Calcium 2%; Iron 16%
Exchanges: 1 Starch, $1^1/_2$ Other Carbohydrate, 1 Vegetable, 2 Fat
Carbohydrate Choices: 3

BETTY'S TIPS

⊗ **Substitution**
You can use red, yellow or green bell peppers in this yummy potato salad.

If you want to make this recipe with just one variety of potato, use a total of 4 cups of potatoes.

Low Fat

Lime-Mint Melon Salad

Prep Time: 20 min Start to Finish: 2 hr 20 min

1¹/₂ cups ¹/₂-inch cubes honeydew melon
(¹/₂ medium)

1¹/₂ cups ¹/₂-inch cubes cantaloupe (¹/₂ medium)

1 teaspoon grated lime peel

3 tablespoons lime juice

2 tablespoons chopped fresh or 1 tablespoon dried mint leaves

1 teaspoon honey

¹/₄ teaspoon salt

1. Toss all ingredients in medium glass or plastic bowl.

2. Cover and refrigerate about 2 hours or until chilled.

6 servings.
1 Serving: Calories 40 (Calories from Fat 0); Fat 0g (Saturated 0g);
Cholesterol 0mg; Sodium 110mg; Carbohydrate 9g (Dietary Fiber 1g);
Protein 1g
% Daily Value: Vitamin A 26%; Vitamin C 52%; Calcium 0%; Iron 0%
Exchanges: ¹/₂ Fruit
Carbohydrate Choices: ¹/₂

BETTY'S TIPS

⚙ **Success Hint**
Select cantaloupe and honeydew melon by smelling the soft stem end. A sweet fruity fragrance means ripeness. Store both varieties of melon at room temperature until they are ripe, then keep them in the refrigerator.

⚙ **Variation**
Instead of cubing the melons, cut into balls with a melon baller.

Lime-Mint Melon Salad

Betty Crocker ON WHAT'S NEW

Easy Party Platters

Think summer. Think casual entertaining. Think platters!
Platters are pretty, impressive and practical—one-dish appetizers! Take a look at the ideas on the following pages, and imagine how easy it will be to assemble an assortment of enticing appetizers for your next summer get-together.

Shrimp Cocktail Platter

Shrimp doesn't need a lot of dressing up to be beautiful, plus using cooked, peeled shrimp pares down the prep time.

INGREDIENT IDEAS

- 1½ to 2 pounds (26 to 30 count) cooked peeled medium to large shrimp with tails
- Watercress or parsley sprigs
- Lemon slices
- Purchased cocktail sauce or a creamy Spanish dip

PUTTING THE PLATTER TOGETHER

- Thaw and rinse shrimp; pat dry.
- Line a 3- or 4-cup bowl with enough plastic wrap so that it hangs over edge of bowl.
- Arrange a layer of shrimp in a spiral pattern in bottom of bowl. Add additional layers, filling all spaces and pressing down, until bowl is full.
- Fold the plastic wrap over shrimp. Place two 1-pound cans on top of shrimp and refrigerate 1 hour.
- Unwrap bowl. Pull plastic wrap away from top of bowl. To unmold, place a large platter upside down over bowl, then turn platter and bowl over; remove plastic wrap. Garnish the shrimp spiral with watercress and lemon slices. Serve with sauce or dip.

Garden Vegetable Platter

Mix and match veggies fresh from the garden or farmers' market to create a platter bursting with color, texture and flavor.

PUTTING THE PLATTER TOGETHER

▸ Choose new clay flowerpots and saucers in a variety of sizes.

▸ Line pots with plastic wrap and loosely fill with greens. Line saucers with a lettuce or cabbage leaf.

▸ Place jicama, carrot and celery sticks and radishes in taller pots.

▸ Fill saucers with cauliflowerets, broccoli flowerets and dip.

▸ Arrange pots and saucers on a wooden serving tray.

INGREDIENT IDEAS

▸ Greens such as curly endive, mustard, napa cabbage, leaf lettuce, radicchio

▸ Jicama sticks

▸ Carrot sticks

▸ Celery sticks

▸ Radishes

▸ Cauliflowerets

▸ Broccoli flowerets

▸ Spinach dip or your favorite dip

Fruit and Cheese Platter

For a guest-pleasing platter, choose a variety of cheeses, then pair them with an assortment of fresh fruit.

INGREDIENT IDEAS

- Blue cheese wedge
- Brie or Camembert wedge
- Log of goat cheese rolled in chopped fresh herbs such as chives, parsley or basil
- Pineapple wedges or slices
- Melon—cantaloupe, honeydew or watermelon—cut into cubes
- Berries—raspberries, blueberries, blackberries, strawberries (whole or halved)
- Grape clusters—red, green or purple
- Bay leaves or fresh herb sprigs such as mint, basil or parsley, if desired

PUTTING THE PLATTER TOGETHER

- Choose a large round or rectangular tray, along with a small round cutting board or ceramic tile.
- Set the cutting board or tile on the tray for the cheese wedges.
- Quarter the pineapple, cut out the fruit and use the rind as a "basket" for the fruit wedges.
- Place the melon cubes on bay leaves. Arrange grape clusters on the tray.

Antipasto Platter

What's antipasto? It's the appetizer platter of Italy that's filled with little bites of savory foods to spark the appetite before a meal. Look for ingredients to make your own antipasto platter in the condiment and deli sections of your supermarket.

INGREDIENT IDEAS

- Olives—ripe, green or Kalamata
- Pickled vegetables (Giardiniera mixture)
- Fresh mozzarella—plain or herb—shaped into balls
- Radicchio leaves
- Prosciutto (Italian ham)—sliced wafer thin and folded into accordion pleats
- Provolone cheese—thinly sliced rounds, cut in half
- Fresh basil sprigs
- Thin slices of baguette—whole wheat, sesame or sourdough

PUTTING THE PLATTER TOGETHER

- Pick up a granite or marble slab from a tile or home improvement store, or use a marble cutting board. Put it in the refrigerator to chill, which will keep the food cold longer.
- Serve the olives, pickled vegetables and mozzarella in cupped radicchio leaves. Arrange them on the slab or cutting board.
- Arrange the proscuitto and provolone cheese on the slab or cutting board. Or you can do this step before chilling the slab; just cover with plastic wrap, then chill.
- Garnish the platter with basil sprigs.
- Serve with baguette slices.

Orange, Kiwifruit and Poppy Seed Salad

Prep Time: 15 min   Start to Finish: 15 min

Poppy Seed Dressing

- ¹/₂ cup regular or reduced-fat mayonnaise or salad dressing
- ¹/₃ cup sugar
- ¹/₄ cup milk
- 2 tablespoons white vinegar
- 1 tablespoon poppy seeds

Salad

- 1 bunch romaine lettuce, torn into bite-size pieces (6 cups)
- 2 kiwifruit, peeled and cut into slices
- 2 oranges, peeled and cut into sections
- ¹/₂ medium red onion, sliced

1. In small bowl, beat all dressing ingredients with wire whisk.

2. In large bowl, toss dressing and salad ingredients. Serve immediately.

6 servings.

1 Serving: Calories 225 (Calories from Fat 145); Fat 16g (Saturated 2g); Cholesterol 10mg; Sodium 115mg; Carbohydrate 18g (Dietary Fiber 1g); Protein 2g
% Daily Value: Vitamin A 24%; Vitamin C 24%; Calcium 6%; Iron 4%
Exchanges: ¹/₂ Fruit, 2 Vegetable, 3 Fat
Carbohydrate Choices: 1

BETTY'S TIPS

⊙ **Substitution**
You can use 1 cup pomegranate seeds instead of the kiwifruit and oranges.

⊙ **Do-Ahead**
Make the dressing; cover and refrigerate. Up to 6 hours ahead, put the greens, fruit and onion in the serving bowl, cover with a damp paper towel and plastic wrap and refrigerate. Just before serving, shake the dressing well and toss it with the salad.

Orange, Kiwifruit and Poppy Seed Salad

Quick & Low Fat

Dilled Cucumber-Tomato Salad

Prep Time: 15 min Start to Finish: 15 min

1/4 cup plain yogurt

1 small clove garlic, finely chopped

1/2 teaspoon dried dillweed

1/4 teaspoon sugar

1/8 teaspoon salt

3 large roma (plum) tomatoes, seeded, diced (1 1/2 cups)

1 medium cucumber, peeled, seeded and cubed (1 cup)

1. In medium bowl, mix yogurt, garlic, dillweed, sugar and salt.

2. Fold in tomatoes and cucumber. Serve immediately.

5 servings (1/2 cup each).
1 Serving: Calories 25 (Calories from Fat 0); Fat 0g (Saturated 0g); Cholesterol 0mg; Sodium 75mg; Carbohydrate 4g (Dietary Fiber 1g); Protein 1g
% Daily Value: Vitamin A 8%; Vitamin C 18%; Calcium 2%; Iron 2%
Exchanges: 1 Vegetable
Carbohydrate Choices: 0

BETTY'S TIPS

✿ **Kitchen Tip**
Use about 1 1/2 teaspoons of chopped fresh dillweed instead of the dried dill, and garnish the salad with a sprig of fresh dill.

Roma (plum) tomatoes work well in this type of salad because they contain less moisture than regular slicing tomatoes.

Dilled Cucumber-Tomato Salad

Pasta and Grilled Vegetable Salad

Prep Time: 25 min   Start to Finish: 50 min

2 cups uncooked gemelli or rotini pasta (8 ounces)

1 small red onion, cut into thin wedges

1¹/₂ cups baby-cut carrots

¹/₂ cup balsamic vinaigrette dressing

¹/₂ teaspoon seasoned salt

8 ounces fresh asparagus spears, cut into 2-inch pieces

1 jar (6 ounces) marinated artichoke hearts, drained and liquid reserved

2 slices bacon, crisply cooked and crumbled

1. Heat coals or gas grill for direct heat. Cook and drain pasta as directed on package.

2. Place onion and carrots in large bowl; drizzle with about ¹/₄ cup dressing. Sprinkle with seasoned salt; toss to coat. Place in grill basket (grill "wok"), using slotted spoon; reserve dressing in bowl.

3. Cover and grill onion and carrots 4 to 6 inches from medium heat 15 minutes, shaking basket or stirring vegetables occasionally. Add asparagus to dressing in bowl; toss to coat. Add asparagus to onion and carrots in grill basket. Cover and grill 8 to 10 minutes longer or until vegetables are crisp-tender.

4. Add cooked pasta, grilled vegetables and artichoke liquid to remaining dressing in bowl. Drizzle with remaining ¹/₄ cup dressing; toss to mix. Stir in artichokes. Sprinkle with bacon.

4 servings.
1 Serving: Calories 405 (Calories from Fat 145); Fat 16g (Saturated 2g); Cholesterol 5mg; Sodium 640mg; Carbohydrate 59g (Dietary Fiber 6g); Protein 12g
% Daily Value: Vitamin A 100%; Vitamin C 12%; Calcium 8%; Iron 18%
Exchanges: 3¹/₂ Starch, 1 Vegetable, 1 Fat
Carbohydrate Choices: 4

BETTY'S TIPS

⊛ **Success Hint**
Before cutting the asparagus into pieces, wash it under cool running water to remove any sand. Then snap off the end of each stalk where it breaks naturally.

⊛ **Time-Saver**
If you don't feel like cooking bacon, buy a package of precooked bacon in the deli or meat department of your supermarket.

⊛ **Serve-With**
Pair this deli-style salad with pork, chicken or steak. Or if you're in the mood for a lighter meal, serve it as a main-dish salad along with sliced French bread.

Pasta and Grilled Vegetable Salad

Hot Sandwiches, Burgers and Pizzas

A Twist on the Traditional

Chicken and Veggie Pizza (page 104)

Veggie Burger and Grilled Pepper Sandwiches (page 102)

Alfredo Chicken Folds

Prep Time: 20 min Start to Finish: 7 hr 55 min

2 pounds boneless, skinless chicken thighs

1/2 teaspoon crushed red pepper

1 jar (16 ounces) Alfredo pasta sauce

8 ounces thinly sliced fully cooked ham, cut into julienne (matchstick-size) strips

15 pita breads

2 large tomatoes, chopped (2 cups)

1/2 cup shredded Parmesan cheese

1. Place chicken in 3- to 4-quart slow cooker. Sprinkle with red pepper.

2. Cover and cook on Low heat setting 6 to 7 hours.

3. Remove chicken from cooker, using slotted spoon; place on cutting board. Shred chicken, using 2 forks. Return chicken to cooker. Stir Alfredo sauce and ham into chicken. Increase heat setting to High. Cover and cook 30 to 35 minutes or until mixture is hot.

4. Meanwhile, heat oven to 350°. Wrap pita breads in aluminum foil; place in oven 7 to 10 minutes or until warm. To serve, spoon 1/3 cup chicken mixture into each warm pita bread; sprinkle with tomatoes and cheese. Chicken mixture will hold on Low heat setting up to 2 hours; stir occasionally.

15 sandwiches.
1 Sandwich: Calories 370 (Calories from Fat 160); Fat 18g (Saturated 9g); Cholesterol 80mg; Sodium 700mg; Carbohydrate 28g (Dietary Fiber 1g); Protein 24g
% Daily Value: Vitamin A 12%; Vitamin C 8%; Calcium 18%; Iron 14%
Exchanges: 1 1/2 Starch, 3 Lean Meat, 2 Fat
Carbohydrate Choices: 2

BETTY'S TIPS

⊛ **Substitution**
Instead of the ham, try thinly sliced and julienned prosciutto or crumbled cooked bacon in this recipe.

⊛ **Serve-With**
Fresh fruit kabobs and an assortment of olives—green, black, garlic-stuffed and herbed—would complement the Italian flavors in these sandwiches.

⊛ **Variation**
For a party entrée with Italian flair, serve this sandwich filling over pasta such as angel hair or linguine.

Alfredo Chicken Folds

Italian Turkey Sandwiches with Garlic Cheese Spread

Prep Time: 20 min Start to Finish: 8 hr 20 min

3 pounds turkey thighs, skin removed

1/3 cup Italian dressing

12 small French sandwich rolls (3 inches long)

1 container (6.5 ounces) garlic-and-herb spreadable cheese

1 jar (7.25 ounces) roasted red bell peppers, drained and cut into strips

1. Place turkey in 3- to 4-quart slow cooker.

2. Cover and cook on Low heat setting 7 to 8 hours.

3. Remove turkey from cooker, using slotted spoon; place on cutting board. Discard liquid in cooker. Remove bones from turkey and discard. Shred turkey, using 2 forks. Return turkey to cooker. Stir in Italian dressing.

4. Cut rolls horizontally in half. To serve, spread bottom half of each roll with 1 rounded tablespoon spreadable cheese; top with 1/3 cup turkey and bell peppers. Turkey mixture will hold on Low heat setting up to 2 hours; stir occasionally.

12 sandwiches.
1 Sandwich: Calories 305 (Calories from Fat 110); Fat 12g (Saturated 5g); Cholesterol 90mg; Sodium 420mg; Carbohydrate 25g (Dietary Fiber 1g); Protein 24g
% Daily Value: Vitamin A 24%; Vitamin C 24%; Calcium 6%; Iron 16%
Exchanges: 1 1/2 Starch, 3 Lean Meat, 1/2 Fat
Carbohydrate Choices: 1 1/2

BETTY'S TIPS

✿ **Success Hint**
Look for garlic-and-herb spreadable cheese in the dairy case. It's available in several flavor variations, so experiment to discover which one you like best in this recipe.

✿ **Serve-With**
Garlic- or Parmesan-flavored kettle chips and clusters of red and green grapes round out this casual get-together meal.

✿ **Special Touch**
Add a New Orleans twist by sprinkling sliced pimiento-stuffed green olives over the sandwiches to give them the taste of the Crescent City's famous Muffuletta sandwich.

Italian Turkey Sandwiches with Garlic Cheese Spread

Turkey Cacciatore Sandwiches

Prep Time: 20 min Start to Finish: 8 hr 20 min

- 1 medium yellow bell pepper, sliced
- 1 medium onion, sliced
- 4 bone-in turkey thighs (about 3 pounds), skin removed
- 1 can (8 ounces) tomato sauce
- 2 tablespoons balsamic vinegar
- 1 teaspoon Italian seasoning
- 8 Italian or French rolls, split
- 1/2 cup basil pesto
- 8 slices (1 ounce each) mozzarella cheese

1. Spray 3¹/₂- to 4-quart slow cooker with cooking spray. Place bell pepper and onion in cooker; top with turkey. Mix tomato sauce, vinegar and Italian seasoning in small bowl; pour over turkey and vegetables.

2. Cover and cook on Low heat setting 7 to 8 hours.

3. Place turkey on cutting board. Use 2 forks to cut or break up turkey into thin pieces; discard bones. Return turkey to cooker. To serve, spread cut sides of rolls with pesto. Fill with turkey mixture, using slotted spoon; top with cheese.

8 sandwiches.
1 Sandwich: Calories 450 (Calories from Fat 170); Fat 19g (Saturated 7g); Cholesterol 125mg; Sodium 810mg; Carbohydrate 29g (Dietary Fiber 2g); Protein 41g
% Daily Value: Vitamin A 12%; Vitamin C 26%; Calcium 34%; Iron 24%
Exchanges: 2 Starch, 5 Lean Meat, ¹/₂ Fat
Carbohydrate Choices: 2

BETTY'S TIPS

⚙ **Variation**
A few drops of red pepper sauce would add zing to this sandwich meat.

⚙ **Did You Know?**
Basil pesto, a traditional Italian sauce, is made from fresh basil, garlic, Parmesan cheese and pine nuts. Look for it in the dairy section or near the pasta sauces. You also can make it from scratch.

Turkey Cacciatore Sandwiches

Turkey, Bacon and Avocado Wraps

Prep Time: 20 min Start to Finish: 6 hr 20 min

 4 slices bacon, cut into $^1/_2$-inch pieces

 2 pounds turkey breast tenderloins, cut crosswise into 1-inch slices

 $^3/_4$ cup barbecue sauce

 2 tablespoons Old El Paso taco seasoning mix (from 1.25-ounce envelope)

 1 medium ripe avocado, pitted, peeled and mashed

 2 cups shredded lettuce

 $^1/_2$ cup drained roasted red or yellow bell peppers (from 7-ounce jar), large pieces cut up

 8 flour tortillas (6 to 8 inches in diameter), heated

1. Cook bacon in 12-inch nonstick skillet over medium heat 4 to 6 minutes, stirring occasionally, until almost crisp. Add turkey slices to skillet. Cook 4 to 6 minutes, stirring occasionally, until turkey is brown on all sides.

2. Spray 3- to 4-quart slow cooker with cooking spray. Place turkey mixture in cooker. Top with barbecue sauce and taco seasoning mix; stir to mix well.

3. Cover and cook on Low heat setting 5 to 6 hours.

4. Place turkey on cutting board; use 2 forks to break up turkey. Return turkey to cooker. Layer avocado, lettuce, turkey mixture and bell peppers on tortillas; roll up.

8 wraps.

1 Wrap: Calories 295 (Calories from Fat 70); Fat 8g (Saturated 2g); Cholesterol 80mg; Sodium 570mg; Carbohydrate 26g (Dietary Fiber 3g); Protein 30g
% Daily Value: Vitamin A 20%; Vitamin C 40%; Calcium 6%; Iron 16%
Exchanges: 2 Starch, 3 Very Lean Meat, $^1/_2$ Fat
Carbohydrate Choices: 2

BETTY'S TIPS

⚙ **Success Hint**

To warm tortillas, wrap them in aluminum foil and heat in the oven at 325° for about 15 minutes. Or place them on a paper towel, and microwave on High for about 30 seconds.

Tender, low-fat meats like the turkey tenderloins in this recipe will get dry and tough if overcooked, so follow the cooking times carefully.

⚙ **Serve-With**

Refried beans and a fruit salad with cantaloupe and pineapple chunks are perfect partners for these south-of-the-border sandwiches.

Turkey, Bacon and Avocado Wraps

Muffuletta-Style Steak Hoagies

Muffuletta-Style Steak Hoagies

Prep Time: 20 min Start to Finish: 8 hr 35 min

$1/2$ cup Italian dressing

$1/4$ teaspoon coarsely ground pepper

1 pound beef boneless round steak, 1 inch thick

Olive Salad (below)

4 hoagie buns (about 6 inches long), split

1 medium tomato, thinly sliced

4 slices ($3/4$ ounce each) provolone cheese

1. Mix dressing and pepper in shallow baking dish. Add beef; turn to coat. Cover and refrigerate at least 8 hours but not more than 24 hours.

2. Heat coals or gas grill for direct heat. Make Olive Salad. Remove beef from marinade; discard marinade. Cover and grill beef 4 to 6 inches from medium heat 10 to 12 minutes, turning once or twice, until desired doneness.

3. Cut beef into thin slices. Fill buns with Olive Salad, tomato, warm beef and cheese.

4 sandwiches.

Olive Salad

$1/2$ cup coarsely chopped pitted green olives

$1/2$ cup coarsely chopped pitted ripe olives

$1/2$ cup chopped Grilled Tricolored Bell Peppers (page 102) or purchased roasted bell peppers

$1/4$ cup finely chopped parsley

1 tablespoon Italian dressing

Mix all ingredients in medium bowl.

1 Sandwich: Calories 470 (Calories from Fat 160); Fat 18g (Saturated 6g); Cholesterol 75mg; Sodium 1,280mg; Carbohydrate 42g (Dietary Fiber 4g); Protein 35g
% Daily Value: Vitamin A 44%; Vitamin C 42%; Calcium 26%; Iron 28%
Exchanges: $2^{1}/2$ Starch, 1 Vegetable, 4 Lean Meat, $1/2$ Fat
Carbohydrate Choices: 3

BETTY'S TIPS

✪ **Substitution**
Play around with different flavors of pitted olives for this sandwich. Look for some new varieties in jars as well as in the deli sections of large supermarkets.

✪ **Serve-With**
For a perfect summer picnic lunch, all you need are these hearty sandwiches, a salad or two from the deli, chips and ice-cream novelties.

✪ **Did You Know?**
Back in 1906, the Central Grocery in New Orleans created the Muffuletta, a wonderful specialty sandwich. This famous sandwich is a combination of delicious meats and cheese, but it's the olive salad that makes it unique.

Beef and Pork Barbecue Sandwiches

Prep Time: 25 min Start to Finish: 10 hr 40 min

1¹/₂ pounds beef boneless chuck roast, trimmed of fat

1¹/₂ pounds pork boneless shoulder roast, trimmed of fat

1 large onion, chopped (1 cup)

1 medium green bell pepper, chopped (1 cup)

¹/₂ cup packed brown sugar

¹/₄ cup cider vinegar

1 tablespoon chili powder

1 teaspoon salt

1 teaspoon ground mustard

2 teaspoons Worcestershire sauce

1 can (6 ounces) tomato paste

15 sandwich buns, split

1. Cut beef and pork into 3-inch pieces. Place beef, pork and remaining ingredients except tomato paste and buns in 4- to 5-quart slow cooker.

2. Cover and cook on Low heat setting 8 to 10 hours.

3. Remove beef and pork from cooker, using slotted spoon; place on cutting board. Strain liquid in cooker and return cooked vegetables to cooker. Shred meat, using 2 forks. Return meat to cooker. Stir in tomato paste. Increase heat setting to High. Cover and cook

10 to 15 minutes or until hot. To serve, spoon ¹/₃ cup meat mixture into each bun.

15 sandwiches.

1 Sandwich: Calories 330 (Calories from Fat 115); Fat 13g (Saturated 5g); Cholesterol 55mg; Sodium 500mg; Carbohydrate 30g (Dietary Fiber 2g); Protein 23g
% Daily Value: Vitamin A 10%; Vitamin C 10%; Calcium 6%; Iron 16%
Exchanges: 1 Starch, 1 Other Carbohydrate, 3 Lean Meat, ¹/₂ Fat
Carbohydrate Choices: 2

BETTY'S TIPS

⊛ **Success Hint**
When you strain the liquid in the cooker, set aside some of the liquid. If the meat seems a little dry, stir a little of the liquid back in.

The meat mixture will hold on Low heat setting up to 2 hours. Be sure to stir the mixture occasionally.

⊛ **Serve-With**
Make up a plate of condiments, including rings of red onion, slices of tomato and Cheddar and Swiss cheese, so guests can dress up these sandwiches. Don't forget the ketchup, mustard and pickle relish too!

⊛ **Do-Ahead**
Make this recipe the day before your gathering and put it in the fridge. Reheat it on the stove top just before serving.

Beef and Pork Barbecue Sandwiches

Ham and Cheese Foldover Sandwiches

Prep Time: 20 min Start to Finish: 45 min

2 cups Original Bisquick mix
1/2 cup boiling water
2 teaspoons Dijon mustard
8 ounces deli shaved cooked ham
1 cup shredded Swiss cheese (4 ounces)
1 egg
1 tablespoon water

1. Heat oven to 375°. Spray cookie sheet with cooking spray. Stir Bisquick mix and boiling water with spoon until dough forms. Divide dough into quarters. Place on surface sprinkled with Bisquick mix; roll in Bisquick mix to coat. Press each piece into 6-inch square, 1/4 inch thick.

2. Spread 1/2 teaspoon of the mustard on each dough square to within 1/2 inch of edges. Top with ham and cheese to within 1/2 inch of edges. Fold each square diagonally in half. Press edges with tines of fork to seal. Place on cookie sheet.

3. In small bowl, beat egg and water. Brush over sandwiches. Bake 20 to 25 minutes or until crust is golden brown.

4 sandwiches.
1 Sandwich: Calories 450 (Calories from Fat 190); Fat 21g (Saturated 9g); Cholesterol 110mg; Sodium 1,690mg; Carbohydrate 39g (Dietary Fiber 1g); Protein 26g
% Daily Value: Vitamin A 6%; Vitamin C 0%; Calcium 38%; Iron 16%
Exchanges: 2 1/2 Starch, 2 Lean Meat, 2 Fat
Carbohydrate Choices: 2 1/2

BETTY'S TIPS

⚙ **Serve-With**
Serve with a side of mustard for dipping.

⚙ **Variation**
Try using peppered ham or other seasoned ham in place of the plain ham.

⚙ **Special Touch**
Before baking, brush with beaten egg and sprinkle with caraway, poppy or sesame seed, or use a mixture of all three.

Ham and Cheese Foldover Sandwiches

Jerk Pork Sandwiches

Prep Time: 20 min Start to Finish: 11 hr 20 min

2½- to 3- pound pork boneless shoulder roast
1   medium onion, chopped (½ cup)
3   tablespoons Caribbean jerk seasoning
½   cup chili sauce
½   cup corn relish
2   tablespoons chopped fresh cilantro
1   cup shredded lettuce
8   pita breads

1. Spray 3- to 4-quart slow cooker with cooking spray. Remove netting or strings from pork roast; cut pork into 2-inch pieces. Place pork and onion in cooker. Sprinkle with jerk seasoning; toss to coat. Pour chili sauce over top.

2. Cover and cook on Low heat setting 9 to 11 hours.

3. Place pork on cutting board; use 2 forks to pull pork into shreds. Return pork to cooker. Mix corn relish and cilantro in small bowl. To serve, layer lettuce, pork mixture and corn relish in pita breads.

8 sandwiches.
1 Sandwich: Calories 450 (Calories from Fat 160); Fat 18g (Saturated 6g); Cholesterol 90mg; Sodium 740mg; Carbohydrate 37g (Dietary Fiber 2g); Protein 35g
% Daily Value: Vitamin A 14%; Vitamin C 14%; Calcium 6%; Iron 14%
Exchanges: 2½ Starch, 4 Lean Meat, ½ Fat
Carbohydrate Choices: 2½

BETTY'S TIPS

⚙ **Success Hint**
For accurate cooking times and proper doneness, cut all meats and vegetables into the sizes specified in the recipe.

⚙ **Did You Know?**
Corn relish is a spicy mixture of corn, seasonings and vinegar. Look for it near the other condiments at your supermarket or the deli.

Caribbean jerk seasoning, sometimes called Jamaican jerk seasoning, is a blend of many spices that may include chilies, thyme, garlic, cinnamon and ginger.

Low Fat

Sweet and Saucy Ham Sandwiches

Prep Time: 15 min Start to Finish: 5 hr 15 min

1½   pounds fully cooked smoked ham, chopped
½   cup packed brown sugar
½   cup Dijon mustard
¼   cup chopped green bell pepper
1   tablespoon instant minced onion
1   can (20 ounces) crushed pineapple in juice, undrained
18   sandwich buns, split

1. Mix all ingredients except buns in 3- to 4-quart slow cooker.

2. Cover and cook on Low heat setting 4 to 5 hours.

3. Stir well before serving. To serve, fill each bun with about ¼ cup ham mixture, using slotted spoon. Ham mixture will hold on Low heat setting up to 2 hours; stir occasionally.

18 sandwiches.
1 Sandwich: Calories 235 (Calories from Fat 55); Fat 6g (Saturated 2g); Cholesterol 20mg; Sodium 890mg; Carbohydrate 34g (Dietary Fiber 1g); Protein 11g
% Daily Value: Vitamin A 0%; Vitamin C 4%; Calcium 8%; Iron 12%
Exchanges: 1½ Starch, ½ Fruit, 1 Lean Meat, ½ Fat
Carbohydrate Choices: 2

BETTY'S TIPS

⚙ **Success Hint**
Spray the inside of the slow cooker with cooking spray just before using to keep cleanup to a minimum.

⚙ **Serve-With**
For a super-easy party menu, serve these sandwiches along with an assortment of salads from the deli and a cheesecake from the bakery.

⚙ **Special Touch**
Give these sandwiches a Hawaiian flair by threading one or two chunks of pineapple onto frilly toothpicks and inserting them into the top of each sandwich.

Jerk Pork Sandwiches

Sweet and Saucy Ham Sandwiches

Asian Barbecue Pulled-Pork Sandwiches with Asian Slaw

Prep Time: 15 min Start to Finish: 10 hr 55 min

3 pounds boneless pork shoulder roast, trimmed of fat and cut into 3-inch pieces

$1/2$ teaspoon seasoned salt

1 cup barbecue sauce

$1/2$ cup teriyaki marinade and sauce (from 11-ounce bottle)

4 cups coleslaw mix (from 1-pound bag)

3 medium green onions, sliced (2 tablespoons)

1 tablespoon sugar

$1/4$ cup rice vinegar

3 tablespoons water

$1^1/2$ teaspoons seasoned salt

13 sandwich buns, split

Asian Barbecue Pulled-Pork Sandwiches with Asian Slaw

1. Sprinkle pork with $1/2$ teaspoon seasoned salt. Place in 5- to 6-quart slow cooker.

2. Cover and cook on Low heat setting 8 to 10 hours.

3. Remove pork from cooker, using slotted spoon; place on cutting board. Discard liquid in cooker. Shred pork, using 2 forks. Return to cooker. Mix barbecue sauce and teriyaki marinade in small bowl; pour over pork and mix well. Increase heat setting to High. Cover and cook 30 to 40 minutes or until hot.

4. Mix remaining ingredients except buns in large bowl. To serve, spoon $1/3$ cup pork mixture into each bun and top with $1/4$ cup coleslaw. Pork mixture will hold on Low heat setting up to 2 hours; stir occasionally.

13 sandwiches.
1 Sandwich: Calories 375 (Calories from Fat 135); Fat 15g (Saturated 5g); Cholesterol 65mg; Sodium 1,110mg; Carbohydrate 33g (Dietary Fiber 2g); Protein 27g
% Daily Value: Vitamin A 2%; Vitamin C 8%; Calcium 8%; Iron 14%
Exchanges: 2 Starch, 3 Medium-Fat Meat
Carbohydrate Choices: 2

BETTY'S TIPS

⚙ **Substitution**
Instead of the teriyaki marinade, you can use an additional $1/2$ cup barbecue sauce.

⚙ **Success Hint**
Serving the pork and Asian slaw in small "dollar" buns makes these sandwiches easy to eat at a party—and stretches the recipe too.

⚙ **Serve-With**
Continue the Asian theme with two salads: one of melon chunks drizzled with a citrus dressing, the other a pasta salad tossed with Thai peanut dressing.

Quick

Italian Sausage Burgers

Prep Time: 10 min Start to Finish: 25 min

1	pound lean ground beef
1/2	pound bulk mild or hot Italian sausage
2	tablespoons Progresso Italian Style bread crumbs
6	slices (3/4 ounce each) mozzarella cheese
12	slices Italian bread, 1/2 inch thick
1/2	cup sun-dried tomato mayonnaise
1	cup shredded lettuce
1	medium tomato, thinly sliced

1. Heat coals or gas grill for direct heat. Mix beef, sausage and bread crumbs in large bowl. Shape mixture into 6 patties, about 1/2 inch thick and 3 1/2 inches in diameter.

2. Cover and grill patties 4 to 6 inches from medium heat 12 to 15 minutes, turning once, until meat thermometer inserted in center reads 160°. Top patties with cheese. Cover and grill about 1 minute longer or until cheese is melted. Add bread slices to side of grill for last 2 to 3 minutes of grilling, turning once, until lightly toasted.

3. Spread toasted bread with mayonnaise; top 6 bread slices with lettuce, tomato and patties. Top with remaining bread slices.

6 sandwiches.
1 Sandwich: Calories 515 (Calories from Fat 295); Fat 33g (Saturated 11g); Cholesterol 85mg; Sodium 750mg; Carbohydrate 25g (Dietary Fiber 2g); Protein 30g
% Daily Value: Vitamin A 8%; Vitamin C 4%; Calcium 20%; Iron 18%
Exchanges: 1 1/2 Starch, 3 1/2 High-Fat Meat, 1 Fat
Carbohydrate Choices: 1 1/2

BETTY'S TIPS

⊗ **Substitution**
If you don't have sun-dried tomato mayonnaise, mix up your own by combining 1/3 cup mayonnaise with about 2 tablespoons chopped sun-dried tomatoes. Regular mayonnaise works just fine as well.

⊗ **Success Hint**
To keep food safe and wholesome while grilling, always separate uncooked and cooked foods. Uncooked foods should be kept apart from each other too.

⊗ **Serve-With**
Pair these hearty sandwiches with an Italian-style pasta salad from the deli or a bagged Caesar salad.

Italian Sausage Burgers

Grilled Tricolored Bell Peppers

Prep Time: 10 min Start to Finish: 25 min

- 1 medium green bell pepper, cut lengthwise into quarters and seeded
- 1 medium red bell pepper, cut lengthwise into quarters and seeded
- 1 medium yellow bell pepper, cut lengthwise into quarters and seeded
- 2 tablespoons olive or vegetable oil
- $1/2$ teaspoon seasoned salt
- $1/2$ teaspoon Italian seasoning

1. Heat coals or gas grill for direct heat. Mix bell peppers in large bowl. Drizzle with oil. Sprinkle with seasoned salt and Italian seasoning; toss to coat. Place peppers in grill basket (grill "wok").

2. Cover and grill peppers 4 to 6 inches from medium heat 12 to 15 minutes, shaking basket or stirring peppers frequently, until crisp-tender.

3. Serve peppers as a side dish or cut into smaller pieces to use in salads and sandwiches.

4 servings.
1 Serving: Calories 90 (Calories from Fat 65); Fat 7g (Saturated 1g); Cholesterol 0mg; Sodium 170mg; Carbohydrate 6g (Dietary Fiber 1g); Protein 1g
% Daily Value: Vitamin A 38%; Vitamin C 100%; Calcium 0%; Iron 2%
Exchanges: 1 Vegetable, $1^1/_2$ Fat
Carbohydrate Choices: $1/2$

Veggie Burger and Grilled Pepper Sandwiches

Prep Time: 10 min Start to Finish: 25 min

- 1 package (10 ounces) frozen meatless soy-protein burgers (4 burgers)
- $1/2$ teaspoon salt
- 4 slices ($3/4$ ounce each) mozzarella cheese
- 4 whole-grain sandwich buns, split
- $1/4$ cup roasted-garlic mayonnaise
- 1 cup Grilled Tricolored Bell Peppers (left) or purchased roasted bell peppers
- 1 medium tomato, sliced

1. Heat coals or gas grill for direct heat. Sprinkle burgers with salt.

2. Cover and grill burgers 4 to 6 inches from medium heat 8 to 10 minutes, turning once or twice, until thoroughly heated. Top each burger with cheese. Cover and grill about 1 minute or just until cheese is melted.

3. Spread cut sides of buns with garlic mayonnaise. Thinly slice grilled peppers. Layer tomato, burger and bell peppers in each bun.

4 sandwiches.
1 Sandwich: Calories 440 (Calories from Fat 205); Fat 23g (Saturated 5g); Cholesterol 20mg; Sodium 1,190mg; Carbohydrate 37g (Dietary Fiber 4g); Protein 21g
% Daily Value: Vitamin A 100%; Vitamin C 58%; Calcium 24%; Iron 20%
Exchanges: 2 Starch, 1 Vegetable, 2 Medium-Fat Meat, $2^1/_2$ Fat
Carbohydrate Choices: $2^1/_2$

BETTY'S TIPS

✿ **Substitution**
Make your own hamburger patties or buy frozen patties for this recipe. The frozen ones are super-convenient because you can pop them on the grill without thawing them. Be sure to grill hamburger patties until they're no longer pink in the center.

✿ **Did You Know?**
Garlic mayonnaise is a newer product; look for it with the other mayonnaises. Or make your own by stirring $1/2$ teaspoon garlic powder into $1/4$ cup mayonnaise.

Veggie Burger and Grilled Pepper Sandwiches

Grilled Tricolored Bell Peppers

Chicken and Veggie Pizza

Prep Time: 20 min Start to Finish: 35 min
(Photo on page 89)

       2   cups Original Bisquick mix
    $^1/_3$ cup very hot water
    $^3/_4$ cup spinach dip
       1   cup chopped cooked chicken
       1   medium tomato, seeded and chopped ($^3/_4$ cup)
       1   package (8 ounces) sliced fresh mushrooms
    $1^1/_2$ cups shredded mozzarella cheese (6 ounces)

1. Move oven rack to lowest position. Heat oven to 450°. Spray 12-inch pizza pan with cooking spray.

2. In medium bowl, stir Bisquick mix, hot water and $^1/_4$ cup of the spinach dip with fork until soft dough forms; beat vigorously 20 strokes. Press dough in pizza pan, using fingers dipped in Bisquick mix; pinch edge to form $^1/_2$-inch rim. Bake 7 minutes.

3. Spread remaining $^1/_2$ cup spinach dip over partially baked crust. Sprinkle with chicken, tomato and mushrooms. Sprinkle with cheese.

4. Bake 12 to 15 minutes or until crust is brown and cheese is melted.

8 servings.

1 Serving: Calories 265 (Calories from Fat 115); Fat 13g (Saturated 5g); Cholesterol 30mg; Sodium 690mg; Carbohydrate 23g (Dietary Fiber 1g); Protein 14g
% Daily Value: Vitamin A 16%; Vitamin C 4%; Calcium 22%; Iron 8%
Exchanges: $1^1/_2$ Starch, $1^1/_2$ High-Fat Meat
Carbohydrate Choices: $1^1/_2$

BETTY'S TIPS

❂ **Success Hint**
Keep your pizza from becoming soft and soggy by seeding the tomato. This removes much of the liquid from the tomato, so it won't soak into the pizza crust.

❂ **Serve-With**
If the tomato sauce is your favorite part of pizza, try serving this recipe with a side of tomato pasta sauce to spoon on top.

❂ **Did You Know?**
There's spinach in this pizza! Spinach dip from the refrigerator section or deli adds color and flavor to the pizza crust and provides a creamy "sauce" for this pizza.

Cowboy BBQ Chicken Pizza

Prep Time: 10 min Start to Finish: 35 min

2 cups Original Bisquick mix

¼ cup sour cream

¼ cup very hot water

1 container (18 ounces) Lloyd's® refrigerated fully cooked original barbecue sauce with shredded chicken

¼ cup chopped cooked bacon (about 4 slices from 2.2-ounce package)

1½ cups shredded Colby-Monterey Jack cheese (6 ounces)

1. Heat oven to 400°. In medium bowl, stir Bisquick mix, sour cream and hot water with fork until soft dough forms. Place on surface dusted with Bisquick mix. Shape into a ball; knead 5 times. Roll dough into 14-inch circle; fold circle in half. Place on ungreased large cookie sheet and unfold.

2. Spread chicken mixture over dough to within 2 inches of edge. Fold edge just to chicken mixture. Top with half of bacon. Sprinkle with cheese and remaining bacon.

3. Bake 20 to 25 minutes or until crust is light golden brown and cheese is melted.

8 servings.
1 Serving: Calories 390 (Calories from Fat 170); Fat 19g (Saturated 7g); Cholesterol 70mg; Sodium 1,380mg; Carbohydrate 35g (Dietary Fiber 0g); Protein 20g
% Daily Value: Vitamin A 12%; Vitamin C 4%; Calcium 24%; Iron 18%
Exchanges: 2 Starch, 2 Medium Meat, 2 Fat
Carbohydrate Choices: 2

BETTY'S TIPS

⊗ **Substitution**
A terrific convenience produce and a real time-saver, cooked bacon is available both sliced and chopped. You can also cook, drain and chop 4 slices of bacon to use in this recipe.

⊗ **Serve-With**
Create an Old West meal with baked beans and creamy coleslaw. For dessert, serve fruit cobbler and a cup of hot coffee.

⊗ **Variation**
Barbecued chicken is great on this pizza, but you may also want to try a container of barbecued pork.

Cowboy BBQ Chicken Pizza

Sun-Dried Tomato and Prosciutto Pizza

Prep Time: 5 min Start to Finish: 15 min

1 package (10 ounces) ready-to-serve thin Italian pizza crust (12 inch)

1/4 cup sun-dried tomato spread

3 ounces thinly sliced prosciutto, cut into thin strips

2 tablespoons shredded fresh basil leaves

1 cup finely shredded mozzarella cheese (4 ounces)

1. Heat oven to 450°. Place pizza crust on ungreased cookie sheet. Spread with tomato spread. Top with prosciutto, basil and cheese.

2. Bake about 8 minutes or until cheese is melted. Cut into small squares or wedges.

16 servings.
1 Serving: Calories 95 (Calories from Fat 35); Fat 4g (Saturated 2g); Cholesterol 10mg; Sodium 220mg; Carbohydrate 10g (Dietary Fiber 0g); Protein 5g
% Daily Value: Vitamin A 2%; Vitamin C 0%; Calcium 6%; Iron 4%
Exchanges: 1/2 Starch, 1/2 High-Fat Meat
Carbohydrate Choices: 1/2

BETTY'S TIPS

⚙ **Kitchen Tip**
To easily shred basil, tightly roll up the leaves like a cigar and cut into thin crosswise strips.

You can assemble the pizza up to 2 hours ahead of time. Keep it covered in the refrigerator, and bake just before serving.

Sun-Dried Tomato and Prosciutto Pizza

Sausage and Pineapple Pizza

Prep Time: 20 min Start to Finish: 35 min

1 pound bulk mild Italian sausage
1 medium onion, chopped ($^1/_2$ cup)
1 can (20 ounces) pineapple tidbits
3 cups Original Bisquick mix
$^2/_3$ cup very hot water
2 tablespoons olive or vegetable oil
1 can (15 ounces) pizza sauce
3 cups shredded mozzarella cheese (12 ounces)

1. Move oven rack to lowest position. Heat oven to 450°. Spray two 12-inch pizza pans with cooking spray.

2. In 10-inch skillet, cook sausage and onion over medium heat, stirring occasionally, until sausage is no longer pink; drain. Drain pineapple; press between paper towels to absorb excess moisture.

3. In large bowl, stir Bisquick mix, hot water and oil with fork until soft dough forms; beat vigorously 20 strokes. Divide dough in half. Pat or press half of dough in each pizza pan, using fingers dipped in Bisquick mix; pinch edge to form $^1/_2$-inch rim.

4. Spread half of the pizza sauce on each pizza crust. Top each with half of the sausage and pineapple. Sprinkle each pizza with $1^1/_2$ cups cheese.

5. Bake 12 to 15 minutes or until crust is golden brown and cheese is melted.

2 pizzas (4 servings each).
1 Serving: Calories 550 (Calories from Fat 270); Fat 30g (Saturated 11g); Cholesterol 55mg; Sodium 1,500mg; Carbohydrate 46g (Dietary Fiber 2g); Protein 24g
% Daily Value: Vitamin A 12%; Vitamin C 16%; Calcium 42%; Iron 14%
Exchanges: 2 Starch, 1 Fruit, $2^1/_2$ Medium-Fat Meat, 3 Fat
Carbohydrate Choices: 3

BETTY'S TIPS

⊙ **Success Hint**
If you're baking the pizzas right away, don't worry about pressing the pineapple with paper towels. For freezing and then baking the pizzas, though, this extra step helps absorb the excess liquid from the pineapple, so the crust stays nice and crispy.

⊙ **Serve-With**
For a quick meal, simply take the frozen pizza out of the freezer and pop it in the oven while you toss a quick Caesar salad and cut up some fresh fruit.

⊙ **Variation**
For a spicier version of this pizza pie, use hot sausage rather than mild.

Sausage and Pineapple Pizza

Stuffed-Crust Pepperoni Pizza

Prep Time: 20 min Start to Finish: 35 min

3 cups Original Bisquick mix

$^2/_3$ cup very hot water

2 tablespoons olive or vegetable oil

$^3/_4$ cup diced pepperoni

4 sticks Colby-Monterey Jack cheese (from 10-ounce package), cut lengthwise in half

1 can (8 ounces) pizza sauce

2 cups shredded Italian cheese blend (8 ounces)

1 cup sliced fresh mushrooms

1 small green bell pepper, chopped ($^1/_2$ cup)

1 can (2.25 ounces) sliced ripe olives, drained

1. Move oven rack to lowest position. Heat oven to 450°. Spray 12-inch pizza pan with cooking spray. Stir Bisquick mix, hot water and oil with fork until soft dough forms; beat vigorously 20 strokes. Let stand 8 minutes.

2. Pat or press dough in bottom and 1 inch over side of pizza pan. Lightly press $^1/_4$ cup of the pepperoni along edge of dough. Place string cheese over pepperoni along edge of dough, overlapping if necessary. Fold 1-inch edge of dough over and around cheese and pepperoni; press to seal. Bake 7 minutes.

3. Spread pizza sauce over crust. Sprinkle with 1 cup of the Italian cheese, remaining $^1/_2$ cup pepperoni, mushrooms, bell pepper and olives. Sprinkle with remaining 1 cup Italian cheese. Bake 9 to 12 minutes or until crust is golden brown and cheese is melted.

8 servings.
1 Serving: Calories 430 (Calories from Fat 235); Fat 26g (Saturated 10g); Cholesterol 35mg; Sodium 1,300mg; Carbohydrate 32g (Dietary Fiber 2g); Protein 17g
% Daily Value: Vitamin A 10%; Vitamin C 12%; Calcium 40%; Iron 12%
Exchanges: 2 Starch, 1$^1/_2$ High-Fat Meat, 2$^1/_2$ Fat
Carbohydrate Choices: 2

Stuffed-Crust Pepperoni Pizza

BETTY'S TIPS

⊛ **Substitution**
If you can't find the Italian cheese blend, shredded mozzarella cheese makes a great substitute.

⊛ **Success Hint**
Cheese sticks may come in slightly different sizes and lengths. If you have a little extra cheese, just slightly overlap the pieces when placing them along the edge of the dough.

⊛ **Variation**
Leave off the pepperoni for a vegetable lover's pizza.

Bewitched Double-Crust Cheese Pizza

Prep Time: 15 min Start to Finish: 35 min

3 cups Original Bisquick mix

2/3 cup very hot water

1 can (8 ounces) pizza sauce

2 cups shredded Mexican cheese blend (8 ounces)

1/2 teaspoon spicy pizza seasoning

1. Move oven rack to lowest position. Heat oven to 450°. Spray 12-inch pizza pan with cooking spray.

2. In large bowl, stir Bisquick mix and hot water with fork until soft dough forms; beat vigorously 20 strokes. Divide dough in half. Press half of the dough in pizza pan, using fingers dipped in Bisquick mix; pinch edge to form 1/2-inch rim. Spread pizza sauce over dough. In medium bowl, mix cheese and pizza seasoning; sprinkle over pizza sauce.

3. Place remaining dough on surface dusted with Bisquick mix; roll in Bisquick mix to coat. Shape into a ball; knead 5 times. Roll dough into 14-inch circle. Use cookie cutters in Halloween shapes to cut shapes from dough (leave 1 inch of dough between cutouts and leave 1 inch of edge of dough uncut). Fold dough circle in half; place over pizza and un-fold. Seal edges. Place dough cutouts on top of pizza if desired.

4. Bake 12 to 15 minutes or until crust is golden brown and cheese is melted.

8 servings.
1 Serving: Calories 305 (Calories from Fat 145); Fat 16g (Saturated 7g); Cholesterol 25mg; Sodium 940mg; Carbohydrate 30g (Dietary Fiber 1g); Protein 10g
% Daily Value: Vitamin A 8%; Vitamin C 4%; Calcium 26%; Iron 10%
Exchanges: 2 Starch, 1/2 High-Fat Meat, 2 Fat
Carbohydrate Choices: 2

Bewitched Double-Crust Cheese Pizza

BETTY'S TIPS

☺ **Substitution**
If you prefer, or if you can't find the Mexican cheese blend, make your own. Mix 1/2 cup each shredded mozzarella, shredded provolone, shredded Cheddar and grated Parmesan cheeses.

☺ **Success Hint**
Small Halloween cutouts will allow you to have a few more designs and make it easier to transfer the cutouts to the pizza.

☺ **Serve-With**
For a trick-or-treat dinner kids are sure to eat, serve with cubes of grape and orange gelatin, carrot sticks, orange soda pop and pumpkin cookies for dessert.

Cheeseburger Calzones

Prep Time: 20 min Start to Finish: 40 min

- ¹/₂ pound lean ground beef
- 3 tablespoons ketchup
- 1 teaspoon yellow mustard
- 1 teaspoon instant minced onion
- 2 cups Original Bisquick mix
- ¹/₂ cup boiling water
- 1 cup shredded Cheddar and American cheese blend (4 ounces)
- 12 dill pickle slices
- 1 egg, beaten
- 1 teaspoon sesame seed

1. Heat oven to 375°. In 10-inch skillet, cook beef over medium-high heat 6 to 8 minutes, stirring occasionally, until brown; drain. Stir in ketchup, mustard and onion.

2. Stir Bisquick mix and boiling water with fork until dough forms. Divide dough into quarters. Place dough pieces on surface dusted with Bisquick mix; roll in Bisquick mix to coat. Press each piece into 6-inch round, ¹/₄ inch thick.

3. Spoon ¹/₄ cup beef mixture onto one side of each dough round to within ¹/₂ inch of edges. Top beef on each round with ¹/₄ cup cheese and 3 pickle slices. Fold dough in half, covering filling. Press edges with tines of fork to seal. Place calzones on ungreased cookie sheet. Brush with egg; sprinkle with sesame seed. Bake 15 to 20 minutes or until golden brown.

4 calzones.
1 Calzone: Calories 510 (Calories from Fat 250); Fat 28g (Saturated 12g); Cholesterol 115mg; Sodium 1,490mg; Carbohydrate 41g (Dietary Fiber 1g); Protein 24g
% Daily Value: Vitamin A 12%; Vitamin C 2%; Calcium 26%; Iron 18%
Exchanges: 2 Starch, 1 Other Carbohydrate, 2¹/₂ Medium-Fat Meat, 2¹/₂ Fat
Carbohydrate Choices: 3

Cheeseburger Calzones

BETTY'S TIPS

⊛ **Success Hint**
These calzones are perfect for a meal on the go. Simply wrap a baked calzone in aluminum foil to keep it warm while you're on the run.

⊛ **Serve-With**
You'll want to have some extra ketchup and mustard on hand to serve with these cheeseburger pockets.

Then, to complete the meal, mix up some creamy chocolate milkshakes.

⊛ **Special Touch**
Top the baked calzones with more of your favorite burger toppings. Try lettuce, crumbled bacon, cheese and chopped tomatoes.

Seafood Main Dishes
The Seashore at Its Best

Louisiana-Style Shrimp Casserole (page 126)

Ginger-Lime Tuna Steaks (page 123)

Quick

Basil-Coated Fish

Prep Time: 10 min Start to Finish: 20 min

1   pound fish fillets, about $^1/_2$ inch thick

2   tablespoons olive or vegetable oil

$^1/_2$ cup Reduced Fat Bisquick mix

$^1/_4$ cup Progresso garlic herb bread crumbs

1   tablespoon chopped fresh or 1 teaspoon dried basil leaves

$^1/_4$ teaspoon salt

1   egg

1. Cut fish into 4 serving pieces. In 10-inch skillet, heat oil over medium heat.

2. In small shallow dish, mix Bisquick mix, bread crumbs, basil and salt. In another shallow dish, beat egg. Dip fish into egg, then coat with Bisquick mixture.

3. Reduce heat to medium-low. Cook fish in oil 8 to 10 minutes, turning once, until fish flakes easily with fork and is brown on both sides.

4 servings.
1 Serving: Calories 240 (Calories from Fat 80); Fat 9g (Saturated 2g); Cholesterol 115mg; Sodium 530mg; Carbohydrate 15g (Dietary Fiber 0g); Protein 25g
% Daily Value: Vitamin A 2%; Vitamin C 0%; Calcium 4%; Iron 8%
Exchanges: 1 Starch, 3 Lean Meat
Carbohydrate Choices: 1

BETTY'S TIPS

⊛ **Success Hint**

Fish fillets may vary in thickness quite a bit. If possible, select fillets that are about $^1/_2$ inch thick. If you have thicker fillets, you may need to add a few more minutes to the cooking time.

Choose a mild-flavored fish for this recipe, such as cod, walleye, snapper or perch.

⊛ **Special Touch**

Serve with regular tartar sauce or whip up a kicked-up tartar sauce to serve with this fish. Mix $^1/_2$ cup mayonnaise or salad dressing and 2 tablespoons basil pesto. Then, garnish with lemon wedges and fresh basil.

Basil-Coated Fish

Corn Flake–Crusted Fish Fillets with Dilled Tartar Sauce

Prep Time: 30 min Start to Finish: 30 min

$^1/_2$ cup mayonnaise (do not use salad dressing)

1 tablespoon finely chopped onion

2 tablespoons dill pickle relish

$^1/_2$ cup Gold Medal all-purpose flour

1 teaspoon salt

2 eggs

3 tablespoons water

3 cups Country® Corn Flakes cereal, crushed (about 1$^2/_3$ cups)

4 cod fillets (4 to 6 ounces each)

$^1/_4$ cup vegetable oil

Corn Flake–Crusted Fish Fillets with Dilled Tartar Sauce

1. In small bowl, mix mayonnaise, onion and pickle relish; cover and refrigerate.

2. Meanwhile, in shallow dish, mix flour and salt. In another shallow dish, beat eggs and water with fork. Place crushed cereal in third shallow dish. Dip fish in flour, coating well; shake off excess. Dip floured fish in egg mixture, then in cereal, coating all sides completely. Place coated fish on ungreased cookie sheet.

3. In 12-inch nonstick skillet, heat oil over medium heat until hot. Keeping at least 1 inch between fish fillets and cooking in batches if needed, cook fish in oil 3 to 4 minutes on each side, turning once, until well browned and fish flakes easily with fork. If needed, place cooked fish on paper towels on cookie sheet and keep warm in 225° oven while cooking remaining fish.

4. Serve fish topped with sauce.

4 servings.
1 Serving: Calories 580 (Calories from Fat 335); Fat 37g (Saturated 6g); Cholesterol 180mg; Sodium 1,190mg; Carbohydrate 33g (Dietary Fiber 1g); Protein 28g
% Daily Value: Vitamin A 10%; Vitamin C 4%; Calcium 22%; Iron 42%
Exchanges: 2 Starch, 3$^1/_2$ Medium-Fat Meat, 3$^1/_2$ Fat
Carbohydrate Choices: 2

BETTY'S TIPS

⚙ **Kitchen Tips**

Please your sweet pickle–relish lovers by adding sweet relish to the tartar sauce instead of the dill pickle relish.

Instead of making the tartar sauce from scratch, buy your favorite brand.

Lemon-Garlic Halibut Steaks

Quick & Low Fat

Lemon-Garlic Halibut Steaks

Prep Time: 20 min Start to Finish: 30 min

1/4 cup lemon juice

1 tablespoon olive or vegetable oil

1/4 teaspoon salt

1/4 teaspoon pepper

2 cloves garlic, finely chopped

4 halibut or tuna steaks, about 1 inch thick (about 2 pounds)

1/4 cup chopped parsley

1 tablespoon grated lemon peel

1. Brush grill rack with vegetable oil. Heat coals or gas grill for direct heat. Mix lemon juice, oil, salt, pepper and garlic in shallow glass or plastic dish or resealable plastic food-storage bag. Add fish; turn several times to coat. Cover dish or seal bag and refrigerate 10 minutes.

2. Remove fish from marinade; reserve marinade. Cover and grill fish over medium heat 10 to 15 minutes, turning once and brushing with marinade, until fish flakes easily with a fork. Discard any remaining marinade.

3. Sprinkle fish with parsley and lemon peel.

4 servings.
1 Serving: Calories 175 (Calories from Fat 35); Fat 4g (Saturated 1g); Cholesterol 95mg; Sodium 230mg; Carbohydrate 1g (Dietary Fiber 0g); Protein 34g
% Daily Value: Vitamin A 6%; Vitamin C 4%; Calcium 2%; Iron 4%
Exchanges: 5 Very Lean Meat
Carbohydrate Choices: 0

BETTY'S TIPS

⌘ **Success Hint**
You will need one large lemon for 1 tablespoon grated lemon peel and 1/4 cup of juice. Room-temperature lemons will yield more juice than those that are cold.

⌘ **Serve-With**
Fish on the grill makes a quick and easy weeknight meal. Serve with grilled lemon halves. Cover and grill lemons, cut sides down, 2 to 3 minutes. Heating helps release the juices.

Quick & Low Fat
Halibut-Asparagus Stir-Fry

Prep Time: 25 min Start to Finish: 25 min

- 2 teaspoons olive or vegetable oil
- 1 pound halibut fillets, cut into 1-inch pieces
- 1 medium onion, thinly sliced
- 3 cloves garlic, finely chopped
- 1 teaspoon finely chopped fresh ginger
- 1 box (9 ounces) Green Giant frozen asparagus cuts, thawed, drained
- 1 package (8 ounces) sliced fresh mushrooms (3 cups)
- 1 medium tomato, cut into thin wedges
- 2 tablespoons reduced-sodium soy sauce
- 1 tablespoon lemon juice

1. In 12-inch nonstick skillet, heat oil over medium-high heat. Add halibut, onion, garlic, fresh ginger and asparagus; stir-fry 2 to 4 minutes or until fish almost flakes with fork.

2. Carefully stir in remaining ingredients. Cook 2 to 3 minutes, stirring frequently, until heated through and fish flakes easily with fork. Serve with additional reduced-sodium soy sauce if desired.

4 servings (1¹/₃ cups each).
1 Serving: Calories 170 (Calories from Fat 30); Fat 3g (Saturated 5g); Cholesterol 60mg; Sodium 370mg; Carbohydrate 10g (Dietary Fiber 3g); Protein 26g
% Daily Value: Vitamin A 15%; Vitamin C 20%; Calcium 4%; Iron 10%
Exchanges: 2 Vegetable, 3 Very Lean Meat, ¹/₂ Fat
Carbohydrate Choices: 0

BETTY'S TIPS

⚙ **Kitchen Tip**
When asparagus is in season and plentiful, substitute 1 pound fresh for the frozen. Wash several times in cold water to remove any sand.

Quick & Low Fat
Salmon with Creamy Cucumber Sauce

Prep Time: 25 min Start to Finish: 25 min

- 8 ounces uncooked spinach fettuccine
- 1 cup plain fat-free yogurt
- 1 tablespoon Gold Medal all-purpose flour
- 1 tablespoon chopped fresh or 1 teaspoon dried dillweed
- 1 teaspoon prepared horseradish
- 1 medium unpeeled cucumber, seeded, chopped (1 cup)
- 1 can (6 ounces) skinless boneless pink salmon, drained, flaked

1. Cook and drain fettuccine as directed on package.

2. Meanwhile, in 2-quart saucepan, mix yogurt and flour. Stir in dillweed and horseradish. Heat over low heat, stirring constantly, until hot (do not boil). Stir in cucumber and salmon. Serve over fettuccine.

4 servings.
1 Serving: Calories 290 (Calories from Fat 45); Fat 4.5g (Saturated 1g); Cholesterol 70mg; Sodium 330mg; Carbohydrate 44g (Dietary Fiber 2g); Protein 19g
% Daily Value: Vitamin A 0%; Vitamin C 0%; Calcium 25%; Iron 15%
Exchanges: 2 Starch, 1 Other Carbohydrate, 1¹/₂ Lean Meat
Carbohydrate Choices: 3

BETTY'S TIPS

⚙ **Kitchen Tip**
You can use regular fettuccine instead of the spinach-flavored if you like.

Salmon with Creamy Cucumber Sauce

Halibut-Asparagus Stir-Fry

Grilled Fish Tacos

Prep Time: 20 min Start to Finish: 20 min

1 pound firm white fish fillets, such as sea bass, red snapper or halibut

1 tablespoon olive or vegetable oil

1 teaspoon ground cumin or chili powder

1/2 teaspoon salt

1/4 teaspoon pepper

8 corn tortillas (6 inches in diameter)

1/4 cup sour cream

Toppers (shredded lettuce, chopped avocado, chopped tomatoes, chopped onion and chopped fresh cilantro), if desired

1/2 cup Old El Paso Thick 'n Chunky salsa

1. Brush grill rack with vegetable oil. Heat coals or gas grill for direct heat.

2. Brush fish with oil; sprinkle with cumin, salt and pepper. Cover and grill fish over medium heat 5 to 7 minutes, turning once, until fish flakes easily with a fork.

3. Heat tortillas as directed on package. Spread sour cream on tortillas. Add fish, toppers and salsa.

8 tacos.
1 Taco: Calories 125 (Calories from Fat 35); Fat 4g (Saturated 1g); Cholesterol 30mg; Sodium 300mg; Carbohydrate 13g (Dietary Fiber 2g); Protein 11g
% Daily Value: Vitamin A 4%; Vitamin C 4%; Calcium 6%; Iron 4%
Exchanges: 1 Starch, 1 Lean Meat
Carbohydrate Choices: 1

BETTY'S TIPS

⚙ **Substitution**
Tacos are usually made with corn tortillas, but you could use small flour tortillas instead.

⚙ **Did You Know?**
Fish tacos originated more than 25 years ago in San Felipe, a Mexican town on the Gulf of California. Because fresh fish was so plentiful!, they wrapped it inside tortillas.

Grilled Fish Tacos

Seafood and Vegetables with Rice

Prep Time: 25 min Start to Finish: 25 min

1   package (8 ounces) sliced fresh mushrooms (3 cups)

1   can (14 ounces) fat-free chicken broth

3   roma (plum) tomatoes, cut into quarters, sliced (1$^1/_2$ cups)

$^1/_2$ cup sliced drained roasted bell peppers (from 7-ounce jar)

$^1/_2$ pound uncooked peeled deveined small shrimp, thawed if frozen, tails removed

$^1/_2$ pound cod fillets, cubed

6   ounces bay scallops

$^1/_2$ cup white wine or chicken broth

$^1/_2$ teaspoon salt

$^1/_4$ to $^1/_2$ teaspoon red pepper sauce

2   cups uncooked parboiled (instant) rice

$^1/_4$ cup chopped fresh cilantro

1. In 3-quart saucepan, heat mushrooms and broth to boiling. Stir in remaining ingredients except rice and cilantro. Heat to boiling; reduce heat. Cover and simmer 5 to 7 minutes or until shrimp are pink and firm.

2. Meanwhile, cook rice as directed on package. Stir cilantro into seafood mixture. Serve in bowls over rice.

6 servings.
1 Serving: Calories 240 (Calories from Fat 15); Fat 1.5g (Saturated 0g); Cholesterol 80mg; Sodium 870mg; Carbohydrate 36g (Dietary Fiber 2g); Protein 21g
% Daily Value: Vitamin A 20%; Vitamin C 20%; Calcium 4%; Iron 20%
Exchanges: 2 Starch, 1 Vegetable, 2 Very Lean Meat
Carbohydrate Choices: 2$^1/_2$

BETTY'S TIPS

✪ **Kitchen Tip**
Roasted red bell peppers are nutrient-rich and fat-free. One-half cup contains fewer than 10 calories.

Seafood and Vegetables with Rice

Pesto-Glazed Salmon Fillet

Prep Time: 5 min Start to Finish: 45 min

   2   pounds salmon fillet
$^1/_3$ cup mayonnaise or salad dressing
$^1/_3$ cup basil pesto

1. Heat oven to 375°. Spray 13 x 9-inch baking dish with cooking spray. Place salmon fillet, skin side down, in dish. In small bowl, stir together mayonnaise and pesto; spread over salmon.

2. Bake uncovered 30 to 35 minutes or until salmon flakes easily with fork. Let stand 5 minutes. Place on serving platter. Cut into serving pieces.

8 servings.
1 Serving: Calories 280 (Calories from Fat 180); Fat 20g (Saturated 3g); Cholesterol 70mg; Sodium 190mg; Carbohydrate 1g (Dietary Fiber 0g); Protein 24g
% Daily Value: Vitamin A 4%; Vitamin C 0%; Calcium 4%; Iron 6%
Exchanges: 3$^1/_2$ Lean Meat, 2 Fat
Carbohydrate Choices: 0

BETTY'S TIPS

✿ **Success Hint**
You'll find prepared pesto, a blend of basil, garlic, olive oil and Parmesan cheese, with the fresh pasta in the refrigerated section of your supermarket.

✿ **Serve-With**
Continue the Italian theme of this dish with a homemade or bagged Caesar salad and Gorgonzola Twice-Baked Potatoes with Bacon (page 218).

✿ **Special Touch**
Place the salmon on a serving platter, and garnish with lemon wedges, fresh basil leaves and red currants for a pretty, festive touch.

Quick

Broiled Salmon with Orange-Mustard Glaze

Prep Time: 5 min Start to Finish: 20 min

   1   pound salmon fillets
   2   tablespoons orange marmalade
   2   teaspoons mustard seed
$^1/_4$ teaspoon salt
$^1/_8$ teaspoon red pepper sauce

1. Set oven control to broil. Spray broiler pan rack with cooking spray. Place salmon, skin side down, on rack in broiler pan. Broil with tops 4 inches from heat for 10 to 15 minutes or until fish flakes easily with fork.

2. Meanwhile, in small bowl, mix remaining ingredients. Spread on salmon during last 5 minutes of broiling.

4 servings.
1 Serving: Calories 190 (Calories from Fat 65); Fat 7g (Saturated 2g); Cholesterol 75mg; Sodium 220mg; Carbohydrate 7g (Dietary Fiber 0g); Protein 25g
% Daily Value: Vitamin A 2%; Vitamin C 2%; Calcium 2%; Iron 4%
Exchanges: $^1/_2$ Fruit, 3$^1/_2$ Very Lean Meat, 1 Fat
Carbohydrate Choices: $^1/_2$

BETTY'S TIPS

✿ **Kitchen Tip**
Fatty fish such as salmon provide omega-3 oils to the diet. Omega-3 oils are thought to contribute to heart health.

Pesto-Glazed Salmon Fillet

Broiled Salmon with Orange-Mustard Glaze

Tuna with Three-Herb Pesto

Prep Time: 25 min Start to Finish: 25 min

1 pound fresh tuna steaks
1 teaspoon olive or vegetable oil
$^1/_4$ teaspoon salt
1 cup loosely packed fresh cilantro leaves
$^1/_2$ cup loosely packed flat-leaf parsley leaves
$^1/_4$ cup loosely packed fresh basil leaves
4 medium green onions, sliced ($^1/_4$ cup)
1 clove garlic, cut in half
2 tablespoons lime juice
2 teaspoons olive or vegetable oil
$^1/_4$ teaspoon salt
$^1/_4$ cup 33%-less-sodium chicken broth
1 tablespoon grated Parmesan cheese

1. Set oven control to broil. Brush both sides of tuna steaks with 1 teaspoon oil. Place on rack in broiler pan. Broil with tops 4 inches from heat 8 to 10 minutes, turning once and sprinkling with $^1/_4$ teaspoon salt, until tuna flakes easily with fork.

2. Meanwhile, in food processor bowl with metal blade, place remaining ingredients except for broth and cheese. Cover and process about 10 seconds or until finely chopped. With processor running, slowly pour in broth and continue processing until almost smooth. Stir in cheese. Serve with tuna.

4 servings (with 3 tablespoons pesto each).
1 Serving: Calories 215 (Calories from Fat 90); Fat 10g (Saturated 2g); Cholesterol 45mg; Sodium 410mg; Carbohydrate 3g (Dietary Fiber 1g); Protein 28g
% Daily Value: Vitamin A 26%; Vitamin C 12%; Calcium 6%; Iron 12%
Exchanges: 4 Lean Meat
Carbohydrate Choices: 0

BETTY'S TIPS

✿ **Kitchen Tip**
Although flat-leaf parsley has more flavor than curly parsley, you can substitute the curly variety if that's what's available.

Be careful not to overcook the tuna. You should cook it just until the tuna flakes. Tuna sometimes retains a slightly pink color, even when thoroughly cooked.

Tuna with Three-Herb Pesto

Ginger-Lime Tuna Steaks

Prep Time: 10 min Start to Finish: 1 hr 25 min
(Photo on page 111)

$1^1/_2$ pounds tuna steaks, $^3/_4$ to 1 inch thick

$^1/_4$ cup lime juice

2 tablespoons olive or vegetable oil

2 teaspoons finely chopped fresh ginger

$^1/_2$ teaspoon salt

$^1/_8$ teaspoon ground red pepper (cayenne)

2 cloves garlic, crushed

Lime wedges, if desired

1. If tuna steaks are large, cut into 6 serving pieces. Mix remaining ingredients except lime wedges in shallow glass or plastic dish or resealable plastic food-storage bag. Add tuna; turn to coat. Cover dish or seal bag and refrigerate, turning tuna once, at least 1 hour but no longer than 24 hours.

2. Heat coals or gas grill for direct heat. Remove tuna from marinade; reserve marinade. Cover and grill tuna about 4 inches from medium heat 11 to 15 minutes, brushing 2 or 3 times with marinade and turning once, until tuna flakes easily with fork. Discard any remaining marinade. Serve tuna with lime wedges.

4 servings.
1 Serving: Calories 280 (Calories from Fat 115); Fat 13g (Saturated 3g); Cholesterol 65mg; Sodium 270mg; Carbohydrate 1g (Dietary Fiber 0g); Protein 40g
% Daily Value: Vitamin A 2%; Vitamin C 2%; Calcium 2%; Iron 10%
Exchanges: $5^1/_2$ Lean Meat, 2 Fat
Carbohydrate Choices: 0

BETTY'S TIPS

⚙ **Substitution**
For variety, try this recipe using swordfish or halibut steaks instead of the tuna steaks.

⚙ **Special Touch**
Arrange the cooked tuna steaks on a pretty platter. Garnish with lime peel curls and fresh cilantro.

⚙ **Did You Know?**
Fresh or frozen tuna steaks have light to dark pink flesh. As the tuna cooks, the flesh lightens to a pale cream color.

Tuna Cobbler

Prep Time: 15 min Start to Finish: 40 min

1½ cups Green Giant frozen mixed vegetables (from 1-pound bag)

2 cans (6 ounces each) tuna, drained

1 can (10.75 ounces) condensed cream of chicken soup

½ cup milk

1 jar (2 ounces) sliced pimientos, drained, if desired

2 tablespoons sweet pickle relish

1 teaspoon lemon juice

1 cup Original Bisquick mix

⅓ cup cold water

Ground paprika, if desired

1. Heat oven to 400°. Spray 1½-quart round casserole with cooking spray.

2. In 2-quart saucepan, stir frozen vegetables, tuna, soup, milk, pimientos, relish and lemon juice until well mixed. Heat over medium heat 6 to 8 minutes, stirring occasionally, until vegetables are thawed and mixture is hot and starts to bubble. Pour into casserole.

3. In medium bowl, stir Bisquick mix and cold water with fork until soft dough forms; beat vigorously 30 seconds. Drop dough by 4 spoonfuls onto tuna mixture; sprinkle with paprika.

4. Bake uncovered 20 to 25 minutes until biscuits are golden brown.

4 servings.
1 Serving: Calories 325 (Calories from Fat 90); Fat 10g (Saturated 3g); Cholesterol 35mg; Sodium 1,350mg; Carbohydrate 31g (Dietary Fiber 2g); Protein 28g
% Daily Value: Vitamin A 28%; Vitamin C 10%; Calcium 12%; Iron 16%
Exchanges: 2 Starch, 3 Lean Meat
Carbohydrate Choices: 2

Tuna Cobbler

BETTY'S TIPS

⚙ **Serve-With**
Sliced melon or cantaloupe sprinkled with a little chopped fresh mint is a refreshing side dish for this creamy cobbler.

⚙ **Variation**
Canned salmon is a simple twist in place of tuna.

⚙ **Special Touch**
Cut 6 slices of American cheese diagonally in half to make triangles. Slightly overlap the triangles on top of the baked casserole, and let stand 5 minutes until the cheese melts.

Jerk Shrimp Kabobs

Prep Time: 20 min Start to Finish: 35 min

2 tablespoons olive or vegetable oil

2 teaspoons Caribbean jerk seasoning (dry)

1/4 teaspoon salt

1 1/2 pounds uncooked peeled deveined large shrimp (21 to 30) or extra-large shrimp (16 to 20), thawed if frozen, tails removed

12 chunks (about 1 inch) fresh pineapple

1 red bell pepper, cut into 16 pieces

1/4 cup pineapple preserves

2 tablespoons lime juice

1. Heat coals or gas grill for direct heat. Mix oil, jerk seasoning and salt in large bowl. Add shrimp, pineapple and bell pepper; toss to coat. Thread shrimp, pineapple and bell pepper alternately on each of four 12- to 15-inch metal skewers, leaving 1/4-inch space between each piece. Mix preserves and lime juice; set aside.

2. Cover and grill kabobs 4 to 6 inches from medium heat 4 minutes. Turn kabobs; brush with preserves mixture. Cover and grill 4 to 8 minutes longer or until shrimp are pink and firm.

4 kabobs.
1 Kabob: Calories 260 (Calories from Fat 65); Fat 7g (Saturated 1g); Cholesterol 240mg; Sodium 440mg; Carbohydrate 22g (Dietary Fiber 1g); Protein 27g
% Daily Value: Vitamin A 42%; Vitamin C 56%; Calcium 6%; Iron 24%
Exchanges: 1 Fruit, 1 Vegetable, 3 1/2 Very Lean Meat, 1 Fat
Carbohydrate Choices: 1 1/2

BETTY'S TIPS

⊛ **Success Hint**
If you don't have long skewers, use eight 8- to 10-inch skewers instead.

To devein the shrimp, use the point of a sharp knife to cut a slit along the back curve of the shrimp. Pull out the dark vein, and rinse the shrimp under cold water.

⊛ **Serve-With**
Continue the Caribbean theme by serving the kabobs on a bed of cooked white rice with fresh fruit and black bean salad from the deli.

⊛ **Did You Know?**
Although the ingredients in Caribbean jerk seasoning vary, it's usually a blend of chilies, thyme, sweet spices, garlic and onions. Traditionally, jerk seasoning is used to flavor grilled meats.

Jerk Shrimp Kabobs

Louisiana-Style Shrimp Casserole

Prep Time: 20 min Start to Finish: 50 min
(Photo on page 111)

2 tablespoons butter or margarine

1 clove garlic, finely chopped

2 cups frozen stir-fry bell peppers and onions (from 1-pound bag)

$1/4$ cup finely chopped celery

2 tablespoons Original Bisquick mix

1 can (14.5 ounces) diced tomatoes, undrained

$1/4$ teaspoon salt

$1/4$ teaspoon red pepper sauce

12 ounces cooked peeled deveined medium shrimp, thawed if frozen, tails removed

$3/4$ cup Original Bisquick mix

$1/4$ cup milk

1 egg

1. Heat oven to 400°. In 10-inch skillet, melt butter over medium-high heat. Cook garlic, stir-fry vegetables and celery in butter about 5 minutes, stirring frequently, until vegetables are crisp-tender.

2. Stir 2 tablespoons Bisquick mix into vegetable mixture until blended. Stir in tomatoes, salt, pepper sauce and shrimp. Reduce heat to medium-low. Cook about 7 minutes, stirring occasionally, until bubbling and thickened. Pour shrimp mixture into ungreased 8-inch square baking dish.

3. In small bowl, stir $3/4$ cup Bisquick mix, milk and egg with fork until smooth. Pour over shrimp mixture.

4. Bake uncovered 20 to 30 minutes or until crust is golden brown.

4 servings.
1 Serving: Calories 310 (Calories from Fat 110); Fat 12g (Saturated 5g); Cholesterol 235mg; Sodium 930mg; Carbohydrate 27g (Dietary Fiber 3g); Protein 23g
% Daily Value: Vitamin A 20%; Vitamin C 44%; Calcium 14%; Iron 24%
Exchanges: 1 Starch, 2 Vegetable, 2 Lean Meat, $1^1/2$ Fat
Carbohydrate Choices: 2

BETTY'S TIPS

✿ **Variation**
This southern favorite tastes just as delicious with 2 cups diced cooked chicken in place of the shrimp.

✿ **Do-Ahead**
Make the shrimp filling ahead, spoon into the baking dish, cover and refrigerate. When ready to bake, just stir up the Bisquick topping and bake as directed.

✿ **Special Touch**
Jazz up the look of this seafood sensation by sprinkling the top of the unbaked casserole with a tablespoon of chopped parsley and a teaspoon of Cajun seasoning.

Alfredo Seafood Casserole

Prep Time: 25 min Start to Finish: 1 hr 20 min

4 cups uncooked mafalda (mini-lasagna noodle) pasta (8 ounces)

2 cups broccoli flowerets

1 jar (1 pound) Alfredo pasta sauce

1/2 cup milk

1/8 teaspoon pepper

1/2 pound cooked peeled deveined medium shrimp, thawed if frozen, tails removed

1 container (8 ounces) refrigerated pasteurized crabmeat, drained and cut up

1/4 cup chopped parsley

1/4 cup shredded Parmesan cheese

1 tablespoon butter or margarine, melted

1/4 cup Progresso Italian-style bread crumbs

1. Heat oven to 350°. Spray 11 x 7-inch (2 quart) baking dish with cooking spray. Cook pasta as directed on package, adding broccoli for the last 2 minutes of cooking. Drain pasta and broccoli.

2. In large bowl, mix Alfredo sauce, milk and pepper. Stir in shrimp, crabmeat, parsley and 2 tablespoons cheese. Add pasta and broccoli; toss gently to mix well. Spoon into baking dish. Cover baking dish with aluminum foil.

3. Bake 35 to 40 minutes or until hot in center.

4. Meanwhile, in small bowl, mix remaining 2 tablespoons cheese, butter and bread crumbs. Sprinkle over casserole. Bake 10 to 15 minutes longer or until top is light golden brown.

6 servings.
1 Serving: Calories 555 (Calories from Fat 270); Fat 30g (Saturated 18g); Cholesterol 195mg; Sodium 660mg; Carbohydrate 41g (Dietary Fiber 2g); Protein 30g
% Daily Value: Vitamin A 34%; Vitamin C 26%; Calcium 36%; Iron 22%
Exchanges: 3 Starch, 3 Medium-Fat Meat, 2 Fat
Carbohydrate Choices: 3

BETTY'S TIPS

⊗ **Kitchen Tip**
Serve this elegant casserole with a tossed Caesar salad, crusty sourdough rolls and a lemon meringue pie from the bakery.

You can make this casserole up to 24 hours ahead. Assemble the ingredients except the topping, then cover and refrigerate. Bake and add the topping as directed.

Alfredo Seafood Casserole

Seafood and Spinach Enchiladas

Prep Time: 30 min Start to Finish: 1 hr 10 min

1 cup Old El Paso Thick 'n Chunky salsa

1/4 cup chili sauce

1/2 teaspoon ground cumin

1/4 cup chopped fresh cilantro

2 packages (8 ounces each) refrigerated imitation crabmeat chunks

2 cups Green Giant frozen cut leaf spinach (from 1-pound bag), thawed, squeezed to drain

1 cup shredded Monterey Jack cheese with jalapeño peppers (4 ounces)

8 flour tortillas (8 inch)*

1 cup shredded mild Cheddar cheese (4 ounces)

Additional chopped fresh cilantro, if desired

1. Heat oven to 350°. Spray 13 x 9-inch (3-quart) baking dish with cooking spray. In small bowl, mix salsa, chili sauce, cumin and 1/4 cup cilantro.

2. Break up crabmeat chunks slightly. In medium bowl, mix crabmeat, spinach, Monterey Jack cheese and 1/4 cup of the sauce mixture. Spread about 1/2 cup sauce mixture over bottom of baking dish. Top each tortilla with about 2/3 cup crabmeat mixture. Roll up tortillas; place seam sides down in baking dish. Top with remaining sauce mixture. Sprinkle with Cheddar cheese. Spray sheet of aluminum foil with cooking spray. Cover baking dish with foil, sprayed side down.

3. Bake 35 to 40 minutes or until thoroughly heated. Garnish with additional cilantro.

* If using thick tortillas, use 2 cups salsa. Serve with additional salsa over the top.

8 servings.
1 Serving: Calories 335 (Calories from Fat 115); Fat 13g (Saturated 7g); Cholesterol 45mg; Sodium 1,120mg; Carbohydrate 34g (Dietary Fiber 3g); Protein 21g
% Daily Value: Vitamin A 58%; Vitamin C 6%; Calcium 28%; Iron 14%
Exchanges: 2 Starch, 1 Vegetable, 1 Medium-Fat Meat
Carbohydrate Choices: 2

BETTY'S TIPS

✿ Kitchen Tip

Imitation crabmeat is also called surimi, and it's formed from pollock or cod. If you buy frozen crabmeat, thaw it before using it in this recipe.

For a change of taste, use half crabmeat chunks and half medium-size cooked shrimp.

Seafood and Spinach Enchiladas

Meatless Main Dishes

Delicious Additions to Any Table

Southwestern Potato Patties (page 131)

Curried Lentil and Brown Rice Casserole (page 137)

Summertime Mushroom-Tomato Kabobs

Prep Time: 15 min Start to Finish: 25 min

- 4 fresh portobello mushroom caps (about 3 ounces each)
- 6 red cherry or miniature plum tomatoes
- 6 yellow cherry tomatoes
- 6 medium green onions, cut into 2-inch pieces
- 1/4 cup red wine vinaigrette or Greek vinaigrette dressing

1. Heat coals or gas grill for direct heat. Scrape underside of mushroom caps, using small spoon, to remove dark gills and stems. Cut each cap into 6 pieces.

2. Thread mushroom pieces, red and yellow tomatoes and onion pieces alternately on each of four 14- to 15-inch metal skewers.

3. Cover and grill kabobs 4 to 6 inches from medium heat 8 to 10 minutes, turning and brushing with dressing occasionally, until mushrooms are tender. Place on serving plate. Drizzle with any remaining dressing.

4 kabobs.
1 Kabob: Calories 115 (Calories from Fat 65); Fat 7g (Saturated 1g); Cholesterol 0mg; Sodium 140mg; Carbohydrate 9g (Dietary Fiber 2g); Protein 4g
% Daily Value: Vitamin A 10%; Vitamin C 12%; Calcium 4%; Iron 8%
Exchanges: 2 Vegetable, 1 1/2 Fat
Carbohydrate Choices: 1/2

BETTY'S TIPS

⊕ **Substitution**
If yellow tomatoes aren't available, make the recipe using only red tomatoes.

⊕ **Success Hint**
When threading the veggies on the skewers, leave about a 1/4-inch space between the pieces, so they cook evenly.

⊕ **Did You Know?**
Portobello mushrooms are fully mature crimini mushrooms. They're very large, dark brown and dense with a meaty texture and rich flavor.

Summertime Mushroom-Tomato Kabobs

Quick

Southwestern Potato Patties

Prep Time: 10 min Start to Finish: 25 min
(Photo on page 129)

1 bag (1 pound 4 ounces) refrigerated Southwest-style shredded hash brown potatoes

3 eggs, beaten

1 cup shredded Cheddar cheese (4 ounces)

$^1/_2$ cup Original Bisquick mix

$^1/_2$ teaspoon garlic salt

$^1/_4$ cup vegetable oil

1 can (11 ounces) Green Giant Mexicorn® whole kernel corn with red and green peppers, drained

1 can (15 ounces) black beans, rinsed and drained

$^1/_4$ cup Old El Paso Thick 'n Chunky salsa

Sour cream, if desired

1. In large bowl, mix potatoes, eggs, cheese, Bisquick mix and garlic salt.

2. In 12-inch skillet, heat 2 tablespoons oil over medium heat. For each patty, spoon about $^1/_2$ cup potato mixture into oil in skillet. Flatten with back of spatula.

3. Cook patties about 4 minutes, turning once until golden brown. Remove from skillet and cover to keep warm while cooking remaining patties. Add remaining 2 tablespoons oil as needed to prevent sticking.

4. In 2-quart saucepan, heat corn, beans and salsa over medium heat 2 to 3 minutes, stirring occasionally, until hot. Serve over patties. Top with sour cream.

5 servings.
1 Serving: Calories 590 (Calories from Fat 215); Fat 24g (Saturated 8g); Cholesterol 150mg; Sodium 1,200mg; Carbohydrate 81g (Dietary Fiber 11g); Protein 23g
% Daily Value: Vitamin A 12%; Vitamin C 20%; Calcium 24%; Iron 22%
Exchanges: 5 Starch, 1 Vegetable, 1 Medium-Fat Meat, 2 Fat
Carbohydrate Choices: 5$^1/_2$

BETTY'S TIPS

⊙ **Substitution**
The seasoned potatoes add a little bit of heat to these patties, but for a more intense kick, use a medium or hot salsa.

⊙ **Special Touch**
Garnish these savory patties with fresh cilantro leaves. If you're a cilantro lover, chop 1 tablespoon cilantro and mix in with the potato mixture as well.

⊙ **Did You Know?**
Potato patties, usually served as a side dish, are popular in many cuisines around the world. In this recipe, the potato patties make a great meatless main dish with a slightly spicy taste.

Your guests will be asking for seconds when you serve this Tex-Mex favorite.

Three-Cheese Rigatoni

Prep Time: 15 min Start to Finish: 45 min

3 cups uncooked rigatoni pasta (9 ounces)

2 medium ribs celery, sliced (1 cup)

1 small carrot, shredded ($^1/_2$ cup)

1 container (8 ounces) sour cream-and-chive dip

1 cup shredded Colby cheese (4 ounces)

1 cup shredded brick or Monterey Jack cheese (4 ounces)

$^1/_4$ cup grated Parmesan cheese

$^1/_4$ cup milk

1 tablespoon chopped fresh or 1 teaspoon dried basil leaves

$^1/_4$ cup Progresso Italian-style bread crumbs

1 tablespoon butter or margarine, melted

1. Heat oven to 375°. Cook and drain pasta as directed on package. Return to saucepan.

2. Stir remaining ingredients except bread crumbs and butter into pasta. In ungreased 2-quart casserole, spread pasta mixture. In small bowl, mix bread crumbs and butter; sprinkle around edge of casserole.

3. Bake uncovered 25 to 30 minutes or until hot and bubbly.

6 servings.

1 Serving: Calories 440 (Calories from Fat 200); Fat 22g (Saturated 13g); Cholesterol 60mg; Sodium 820mg; Carbohydrate 40g (Dietary Fiber 3g); Protein 19g
% Daily Value: Vitamin A 50%; Vitamin C 0%; Calcium 40%; Iron 10%
Exchanges: 2$^1/_2$ Starch, 1$^1/_2$ High-Fat Meat, 2 Fat
Carbohydrate Choices: 2$^1/_2$

BETTY'S TIPS

⊗ **Kitchen Tip**
If you'd like to serve a few more, you can add 1 to 1$^1/_2$ cups cooked ham, chicken or beef to this triple-cheesy pasta bake.

Three-Cheese Rigatoni

Black Bean and Corn Enchiladas

Prep Time: 30 min Start to Finish: 1 hr 5 min

1 can (15 ounces) black beans, rinsed, drained

1 can (11 ounces) Green Giant®Mexicorn whole kernel corn, red and green

1 can (4.5 ounces) Old El Paso chopped green chilies, undrained

2 cups shredded Colby-Monterey Jack cheese (8 ounces)

1 can (10 ounces) Old El Paso enchilada sauce

8 flour tortillas (6 to 7 inch)*

Shredded lettuce, chopped tomatoes, chopped avocado, sour cream and salsa, if desired

1. Heat oven to 350°. Spray 13 x 9-inch (3-quart) baking dish with cooking spray. In medium bowl, mix black beans, corn, green chilies, 1 cup cheese and ¼ cup enchilada sauce.

2. Spread ½ cup enchilada sauce over bottom of baking dish. Spoon ½ cup bean mixture down center of each tortilla. Roll up tortillas; place seam sides down in baking dish. Spoon remaining enchilada sauce over enchiladas. Sprinkle with remaining 1 cup cheese. Spray sheet of aluminum foil with cooking spray. Cover baking dish with foil, sprayed side down.

3. Bake 30 to 35 minutes or until thoroughly heated. Serve topped with lettuce, tomatoes, avocado, sour cream and salsa, if using.

4 servings (2 enchiladas each).

* If using thick tortillas, use two 10-ounce cans or one 19-ounce can enchilada sauce. To serve, spoon sauce in baking dish over enchiladas.

1 Serving: Calories 580 (Calories from Fat 205); Fat 23g (Saturated 13g); Cholesterol 55mg; Sodium 1,700mg; Carbohydrate 76g (Dietary Fiber 12g); Protein 30g
% Daily Value: Vitamin A 30%; Vitamin C 26%; Calcium 56%; Iron 34%
Exchanges: 5 Starch, 2 High-Fat Meat
Carbohydrate Choices: 5

BETTY'S TIPS

✪ **Kitchen Tip**

Canned green chilies are milder than jalapeños, so for a spicier dish, use jalapeños.

Enchiladas are a Mexican favorite usually made with corn tortillas. However, the flour tortillas used in this recipe are easier to roll.

Black Bean and Corn Enchiladas

Rice and Bean Bake

Prep Time: 10 min Start to Finish: 1 hr 15 min

1 cup uncooked regular long-grain rice

1¹/₂ cups boiling water

1 tablespoon vegetable or chicken bouillon granules

1¹/₂ teaspoons chopped fresh or ¹/₂ teaspoon dried marjoram leaves

1 medium onion, chopped (¹/₂ cup)

1 can (15 to 16 ounces) kidney beans, undrained

1 package (9 ounces) Green Giant frozen lima beans, thawed, drained

¹/₂ cup shredded Cheddar cheese (2 ounces)

1. Heat oven to 350°. In ungreased 2-quart casserole, mix all ingredients except cheese.

2. Cover and bake 1 hour to 1 hour 5 minutes or until liquid is absorbed; stir. Sprinkle with cheese.

4 servings (1²/₃ cups each).
1 Serving: Calories 405 (Calories from Fat 55); Fat 6g (Saturated 3g); Cholesterol 15mg; Sodium 1,350mg; Carbohydrate 80g (Dietary Fiber 12g); Protein 22g
% Daily Value: Vitamin A 8%; Vitamin C 8%; Calcium 14%; Iron 32%
Exchanges: 5 Starch, 1 Very Lean Meat
Carbohydrate Choices: 5

BETTY'S TIPS

⚙ **Kitchen Tip**
Frozen chopped onions are a convenient product you'll find with the frozen vegetables. Keep them on hand to use in recipes such as this.

Sage and Garlic Vegetable Bake

Prep Time: 30 min Start to Finish: 1 hr 45 min

1 medium butternut squash, peeled, cut into 1-inch pieces (3 cups)

2 medium parsnips, peeled, cut into 1-inch pieces (2 cups)

2 cans (14 ounces each) stewed tomatoes, undrained

2 cups Green Giant frozen cut green beans (from 1-pound bag)

¹/₂ cup coarsely chopped onion

¹/₂ cup uncooked quick-cooking barley

¹/₂ cup water

1 teaspoon dried sage leaves

¹/₂ teaspoon seasoned salt

2 cloves garlic, finely chopped

1. Heat oven to 375°. In ungreased 3-quart casserole, mix all ingredients, breaking up large pieces of tomatoes.

2. Cover and bake 1 hour to 1 hour 15 minutes or until vegetables and barley are tender.

4 servings (2 cups each).
1 Serving: Calories 235 (Calories from Fat 10); Fat 1g (Saturated 0g); Cholesterol 0mg; Sodium 730mg; Carbohydrate 60g (Dietary Fiber 11g); Protein 7g
% Daily Value: Vitamin A 100%; Vitamin C 40%; Calcium 14%; Iron 16%
Exchanges: 1 Starch, 2 Other Carbohydrate, 2 Vegetable
Carbohydrate Choices: 4

BETTY'S TIPS

⚙ **Kitchen Tip**
Try carrots in this recipe instead of the parsnips.

Butternut squash is peanut shaped and has a peel that ranges from cream to yellow. Inside, the squash is bright orange and sweet.

Sage and Garlic Vegetable Bake

Rice and Bean Bake

Chipotle Red Beans and Rice Casserole

Prep Time: 15 min Start to Finish: 1 hr 30 min

1 cup uncooked regular long-grain rice

1 cup Green Giant Niblets frozen whole kernel corn (from 1-pound bag)

1 can (15 ounces) spicy chili beans in sauce, undrained

1 can (14 ounces) vegetable broth

1 can (14.5 ounces) diced tomatoes with green chilies, undrained

1 chipotle chili in adobo sauce (from 7-ounce can), chopped

1 cup chili cheese-flavored corn chips

1 cup shredded Monterey Jack cheese (4 ounces)

1. Heat oven to 350°. Spray 2-quart casserole or 8-inch square baking dish with cooking spray. In baking dish, mix rice, corn, beans, broth, tomatoes and chili. Cover casserole with aluminum foil.

2. Bake 1 hour. Uncover and stir well. Sprinkle with chips and cheese. Bake uncovered 10 to 15 minutes longer or until bubbly and rice is tender.

4 servings (1$^1/_2$ cups each).
1 Serving: Calories 500 (Calories from Fat 125); Fat 14g (Saturated 6g); Cholesterol 25mg; Sodium 1,620mg; Carbohydrate 82g (Dietary Fiber 8g); Protein 19g
% Daily Value: Vitamin A 28%; Vitamin C 24%; Calcium 28%; Iron 30%
Exchanges: 5$^1/_2$ Starch, 1$^1/_2$ Fat
Carbohydrate Choices: 5$^1/_2$

BETTY'S TIPS

⊛ **Kitchen Tip**
Made from ground chilies, adobo sauce is quite spicy. For a little extra zip, add 1 to 2 tablespoons of the sauce to this casserole.

Chipotle Red Beans and Rice Casserole

Low Fat

Curried Lentil and Brown Rice Casserole

Prep Time: 30 min Start to Finish: 1 hr 50 min

1 medium dark-orange sweet potato, peeled, cut into $^1/_2$- to $^3/_4$-inch pieces (2 cups)

$^3/_4$ cup dried lentils (6 ounces), sorted, rinsed

$^1/_2$ cup uncooked natural whole-grain brown rice

$^1/_2$ cup chopped red bell pepper

$^1/_2$ cup raisins

$2^1/_2$ cups water

2 tablespoons soy sauce

2 teaspoons curry powder

2 tablespoons slivered almonds, if desired

1. Heat oven to 375°. In ungreased 2- or $2^1/_2$-quart casserole, mix all ingredients except almonds.

2. Cover and bake 1 hour to 1 hour 15 minutes or until rice and lentils are tender. Uncover and stir mixture. Let stand 5 minutes before serving. Sprinkle with almonds, if using.

4 servings ($1^1/_2$ cups each).
1 Serving: Calories 265 (Calories from Fat 10); Fat 1g (Saturated 0g); Cholesterol 0mg; Sodium 470mg; Carbohydrate 63g (Dietary Fiber 12g); Protein 13g
% Daily Value: Vitamin A 100%; Vitamin C 36%; Calcium 4%; Iron 26%
Exchanges: 3 Starch, 2 Vegetable
Carbohydrate Choices: 4

BETTY'S TIPS

⚙ **Kitchen Tip**
Lentils are often used as a meat substitute. They're a good source of iron and phosphorus and also contain calcium and vitamins A and B.

This Indian-influenced casserole is excellent with a salad of sliced cucumbers in a mint vinaigrette or yogurt dressing.

Curried Lentil and Brown Rice Casserole

Spinach Pizza Pie

Prep Time: 20 min Start to Finish: 1 hr

2   cans (13.8 ounces each) refrigerated pizza crust dough

1   can (8 ounces) pizza sauce (1 cup)

1   jar (4.5 ounces) Green Giant sliced mushrooms, drained

1/4   cup sliced ripe olives

1 1/2   cups shredded mozzarella cheese (6 ounces)

2   packages (9 ounces each) Green Giant frozen chopped spinach, thawed, squeezed to drain

1   teaspoon olive or vegetable oil

1   tablespoon grated Parmesan cheese

1. Heat oven to 400°. Lightly spray 9-inch glass pie plate with cooking spray.

2. Unroll 1 can of pizza crust dough. Place dough in pie plate; press against bottom and side of pie plate to form crust.

3. In small bowl, mix pizza sauce and mushrooms; spoon onto dough in place. Layer with olives, 3/4 cup mozzarella cheese, spinach and remaining 3/4 cup mozzarella cheese.

4. Unroll remaining can of dough. Press dough into 9-inch circle; place over filling. Pinch edges of dough together to seal; roll up edge of dough or flute to form rim. Cut several slits in dough. Brush with oil; sprinkle with Parmesan cheese.

5. Bake 35 to 40 minutes or until deep golden brown. Cut into wedges.

6 servings.

1 Serving: Calories 490 (Calories from Fat 145); Fat 16g (Saturated 5g); Cholesterol 15mg; Sodium 1,150mg; Carbohydrate 72g (Dietary Fiber 6g); Protein 20g
% Daily Value: Vitamin A 100%; Vitamin C 12%; Calcium 34%; Iron 30%
Exchanges: 4 Starch, 2 Vegetable, 1/2 Medium-Fat Meat, 2 Fat
Carbohydrate Choices: 5

BETTY'S TIPS

✿ **Kitchen Tip**
To make sure the spinach is thoroughly drained, place it in a colander. Once it's thawed, use the back of a wooden spoon to press out the moisture.

Spinach Pizza Pie

Easy Meatless Lasagna

Prep Time: 15 min Start to Finish: 1 hr 30 min

1 container (15 ounces) ricotta cheese

³/₄ cup grated Parmesan cheese

2 tablespoons chopped parsley

1 tablespoon chopped fresh or 1¹/₂ teaspoons dried oregano leaves

1 jar (1 pound 10 ounces) plus 1 jar (14 ounces) tomato paste sauce (any variety)

8 uncooked lasagna noodles

4 cups shredded mozzarella cheese (16 ounces)

1. Heat oven to 350°. In medium bowl, mix ricotta cheese, ¹/₂ cup of the Parmesan cheese, parsley and oregano.

2. In bottom of ungreased 13 x 9-inch pan, spread 1 cup pasta sauce; top with 4 noodles. Spread half (about 1 cup) of ricotta cheese mixture over noodles. Spread with half (about 2 cups) of remaining pasta sauce and 2 cups of mozzarella cheese. Repeat layers with remaining noodles, ricotta cheese mixture, pasta sauce and mozzarella cheese. Sprinkle remaining ¹/₄ cup Parmesan cheese over top.

3. Cover and bake 1 hour. Uncover and bake 10 to 15 minutes longer or until noodles are tender, sauce is hot and bubbly and cheese is beginning to turn light golden brown. Let stand 15 minutes before cutting.

12 servings.

1 Serving: Calories 345 (Calories from Fat 135); Fat 15g (Saturated 8g); Cholesterol 35mg; Sodium 880mg; Carbohydrate 33g (Dietary Fiber 2g); Protein 20g
% Daily Value: Vitamin A 22%; Vitamin C 12%; Calcium 48%; Iron 8%
Exchanges: 2 Starch, 2 Medium-Fat Meat, 1 Fat
Carbohydrate Choices: 2

BETTY'S TIPS

⚙ **Kitchen Tip**
You can use uncooked lasagna noodles because the sauce provides enough liquid to soften and cook the noodles during baking.

Easy Meatless Lasagna

Cheesy Noodle Casserole

Tortellini Minestrone Casserole

Tortellini Minestrone Casserole

Prep Time: 15 min Start to Finish: 1 hr 15 min

- 1 package (9 ounces) refrigerated three-cheese tortellini
- 1 1/2 cups Green Giant frozen mixed vegetables (from 1-pound bag)
- 1 can (14 ounces) diced tomatoes with basil, garlic and oregano, undrained
- 1 can (15 ounces) great northern beans, rinsed, drained
- 1 can (8 ounces) tomato sauce
- 1/2 cup water
- 1/4 cup shredded fresh Parmesan cheese

1. Heat oven to 375°. In ungreased 2-quart casserole or 8-inch square baking dish, mix all ingredients except cheese. Cover with aluminum foil.

2. Bake 45 minutes. Uncover and stir well. Sprinkle with cheese. Bake uncovered 10 to 15 minutes longer or until center is hot and cheese is golden brown.

4 servings (about 1 1/2 cups each).
1 Serving: Calories 290 (Calories from Fat 65); Fat 7g (Saturated 3g); Cholesterol 60mg; Sodium 690mg; Carbohydrate 48g (Dietary Fiber 10g); Protein 20g
% Daily Value: Vitamin A 40%; Vitamin C 28%; Calcium 28%; Iron 32%
Exchanges: 3 Starch, 1 1/2 Very Lean Meat
Carbohydrate Choices: 3

BETTY'S TIPS

⊙ **Kitchen Tip**
For a colorful change, try pinto or red kidney beans in this recipe. Cannellini beans are a good substitute for the great northern beans too.

Cheesy Noodle Casserole

Prep Time: 20 min Start to Finish: 50 min

- 4 cups uncooked wide egg noodles (8 ounces)
- 3 cups Green Giant Select frozen broccoli flowerets (from 14-ounce bag)
- 2 jars (5 ounces each) Cheddar pasteurized process cheese spread
- 3/4 cup milk
- 1/8 teaspoon pepper
- 1/2 cup coarsely crushed bite-size square cheese crackers

1. Heat oven to 375°. Spray 2-quart casserole with cooking spray. Cook noodles as directed on package, adding broccoli for last 2 minutes of cooking time. Drain noodles and broccoli in colander.

2. In same saucepan, stir cheese, milk and pepper until smooth. Stir in noodles and broccoli. Spoon into casserole. Sprinkle with crushed crackers.

3. Bake uncovered 25 to 30 minutes or until bubbly and top is golden brown.

4 servings (1 1/2 cups each).
1 Serving: Calories 550 (Calories from Fat 250); Fat 28g (Saturated 16g); Cholesterol 120mg; Sodium 1,160mg; Carbohydrate 51g (Dietary Fiber 5g); Protein 28g
% Daily Value: Vitamin A 56%; Vitamin C 34%; Calcium 48%; Iron 20%
Exchanges: 3 Starch, 1 Vegetable, 2 1/2 Medium-Fat Meat, 2 Fat
Carbohydrate Choices: 3 1/2

BETTY'S TIPS

⊙ **Kitchen Tip**
Instead of the broccoli florets, try a combo of broccoli, cauliflower and carrots.

Four-Cheese Mashed Potato Casserole

Prep Time: 25 min Start to Finish: 1 hr 35 min

5	pounds white potatoes, peeled and cut into 1-inch pieces (about 14 cups)
1	package (3 ounces) cream cheese, softened
1/4	cup crumbled blue cheese
1	cup shredded Cheddar cheese (4 ounces)
1/4	cup shredded Parmesan cheese
1	container (8 ounces) sour cream
1	teaspoon garlic salt
1/4	teaspoon ground paprika
1	teaspoon chopped fresh chives, if desired

1. In 6-quart saucepan or Dutch oven, place potatoes. Add enough water to cover potatoes. Heat to boiling over high heat; reduce heat to medium. Cook uncovered 15 to 18 minutes or until tender; drain. Mash potatoes in saucepan with potato masher or electric mixer on low speed.

2. Meanwhile, in large bowl, beat cream cheese, blue cheese, Cheddar cheese and Parmesan cheese with electric mixer on low speed until smooth. Beat in sour cream and garlic salt.

3. Heat oven to 350°. Stir cheese mixture into mashed potatoes until well blended. If potatoes are too stiff, stir in milk, 1 tablespoon at a time, until desired consistency. Spoon into ungreased 13 x 9-inch (3 quart) baking dish.

4. Bake uncovered 35 to 40 minutes or until hot and top is lightly browned. Sprinkle with paprika and chives.

24 servings (1/2 cup each).
1 Serving: Calories 135 (Calories from Fat 45); Fat 5g (Saturated 3g); Cholesterol 15mg; Sodium 125mg; Carbohydrate 18g (Dietary Fiber 2g); Protein 4g
% Daily Value: Vitamin A 4%; Vitamin C 4%; Calcium 6%; Iron 2%
Exchanges: 1 Starch, 1 Fat
Carbohydrate Choices: 1

BETTY'S TIPS

❂ **Kitchen Tip**
If you aren't a fan of blue cheese, leave it out or substitute 1/4 cup shredded Asiago cheese.

Up to 2 days ahead, you can make this dish up to the point of baking, then cover and refrigerate. Bake as directed.

Four-Cheese Mashed Potato Casserole

Poultry
Main Dishes
Favorites That Are Sure to Please

Parmesan Chicken, Provolone and Ham Bundles (page 147)

Honey-Spice Roast Turkey with Apple-Pecan Stuffing (page 158)

Barbecue Chicken and Bean Casserole

Prep Time: 15 min Start to Finish: 1 hr 45 min

1 pound boneless skinless chicken thighs

1 can (16 ounces) baked beans

1 can (16 to 19 ounces) cannellini beans, rinsed, drained

1/4 cup barbecue sauce

1 1/2 cups Green Giant frozen cut green beans (from 1-pound bag), thawed, drained

1 cup coarsely chopped carrots (about 2 medium)

1 can (1.75 ounces) shoestring potatoes (1 cup)

1. Heat oven to 375°. Spray 2-quart casserole with cooking spray. Cut each chicken thigh into 4 pieces. In casserole, mix chicken and remaining ingredients except shoestring potatoes.

2. Cover and bake 1 hour, stirring once. Uncover casserole, stir well. Bake uncovered 25 to 30 minutes longer, topping with shoestring potatoes for last 10 minutes, until chicken is no longer pink in center.

4 servings (1 3/4 cups each).
1 Serving: Calories 580 (Calories from Fat 135); Fat 15g (Saturated 5g); Cholesterol 80mg; Sodium 790mg; Carbohydrate 69g (Dietary Fiber 15g); Protein 43g
% Daily Value: Vitamin A 100%; Vitamin C 12%; Calcium 22%; Iron 60%
Exchanges: 4 Starch, 2 Vegetable, 4 Lean Meat
Carbohydrate Choices: 4 1/2

BETTY'S TIPS

❂ **Kitchen Tip**
If your family prefers white meat instead of dark, use boneless skinless chicken breasts, cut into 1-inch pieces.

Barbecue Chicken and Bean Casserole

Buffalo-Style Chicken Nuggets

Prep Time: 10 min Start to Finish: 25 min

1¹/₂ cups Corn Chex® cereal
¹/₂ cup Original Bisquick mix
2 teaspoons ground paprika
¹/₄ teaspoon seasoned salt
¹/₄ teaspoon ground red pepper (cayenne)
1 tablespoon vegetable oil
1 teaspoon red pepper sauce
1 pound boneless skinless chicken breasts, cut into 2-inch pieces
¹/₄ cup sour cream
¹/₄ cup ranch dressing

1. Heat oven to 425°. Place cereal in 1-gallon resealable plastic food-storage bag; crush with rolling pin. Add Bisquick mix, paprika, seasoned salt and red pepper to cereal; mix well.

2. In small bowl, mix oil and red pepper sauce. Coat chicken pieces with oil mixture.

3. Shake about 6 chicken pieces at a time in bag of cereal mixture until coated. Shake off any extra mixture. On ungreased cookie sheet, place chicken pieces in single layer.

4. Bake about 10 minutes or until chicken is no longer pink in center.

5. Meanwhile, in small bowl, mix sour cream and dressing. Serve sauce with chicken.

4 servings.
1 Serving: Calories 365 (Calories from Fat 170); Fat 19g (Saturated 4g); Cholesterol 85mg; Sodium 710mg; Carbohydrate 21g (Dietary Fiber 1g); Protein 28g
% Daily Value: Vitamin A 20%; Vitamin C 2%; Calcium 10%; Iron 28%
Exchanges: 1¹/₂ Starch, 3¹/₂ Lean Meat, 1 Fat
Carbohydrate Choices: 1¹/₂

Buffalo-Style Chicken Nuggets

BETTY'S TIPS

⊛ **Substitution**
If you like, turkey breast tenderloins are a good substitute for the chicken.

⊛ **Serve-With**
Add a side of crunchy dippers such as celery and carrot sticks to serve with these spicy nuggets and zippy sauce.

⊛ **Did You Know?**
Paprika gives these chicken nuggets their red color. Paprika, a bright orange-red to deep-red seasoning, is made from sweet red pepper pods and can range in flavor from very mild to quite pungent.

Quick & Low Fat

Easy Mexican Chicken and Beans

Prep Time: 30 min Start to Finish: 30 min

- 1 pound chicken breast strips for stir-fry
- 1 envelope (1.25 ounces) Old El Paso taco seasoning mix
- 1 can (15 to 16 ounces) black or pinto beans, rinsed, drained
- 1 can (11 ounces) Green Giant Mexicorn whole kernel corn, red and green peppers, undrained
- 1/4 cup water
  Tortillas, if desired

1. Heat 10-inch nonstick skillet over medium-high heat. Cook chicken in skillet 8 to 10 minutes, stirring occasionally, until no longer pink in center.

2. Stir in seasoning mix, beans, corn and water. Cook over medium-high heat 8 to 10 minutes, stirring frequently, until sauce is slightly thickened. Serve with tortillas.

4 servings.
1 Serving: Calories 320 (Calories from Fat 40); Fat 4.5g (Saturated 1g); Cholesterol 70mg; Sodium 1,210mg; Carbohydrate 41g (Dietary Fiber 7g); Protein 34g
% Daily Value: Vitamin A 8%; Vitamin C 10%; Calcium 8%; Iron 25%
Exchanges: 2^1/$_2$ Starch, 4 Very Lean Meat
Carbohydrate Choices: 2

BETTY'S TIPS

⚙ **Kitchen Tip**
Filled with many other important nutrients, beans are an excellent source of fiber that's important for good blood glucose management.

Easy Mexican Chicken and Beans

Parmesan Chicken, Provolone and Ham Bundles

Prep Time: 15 min Start to Finish: 50 min
(Photo on page 143)

2 cups Original Bisquick mix
$^1/_2$ teaspoon garlic powder
$^1/_2$ cup boiling water
4 slices ($^3/_4$ ounce each) provolone cheese
4 thin slices (about 1 ounce each) cooked ham
4 large (about $^1/_2$ pound) chicken breast tenders (not breaded)
1 tablespoon butter or margarine, melted
4 teaspoons grated Parmesan cheese
1 cup tomato pasta sauce, heated

1. Heat oven to 375° (if using dark or nonstick pan, heat oven to 350°).

2. Stir Bisquick mix, garlic powder and boiling water with fork until dough forms. Divide dough into quarters. Place pieces on surface dusted with Bisquick mix; roll in Bisquick mix to coat. Press each piece into 7 x 5-inch rectangle, $^1/_4$ inch thick.

3. Center 1 provolone cheese slice and 1 ham slice on each rectangle, folding to fit if needed. Top each with 1 chicken tender. Starting at 7-inch side, roll up each bundle. Press ends and seam to seal. Tuck ends under. On ungreased cookie sheet, place seam side down. Brush with butter; sprinkle with Parmesan cheese.

4. Bake 25 to 33 minutes or until meat thermometer inserted in center of chicken reads 170° and bundles are golden brown. Serve topped with pasta sauce.

4 sandwiches.
1 Sandwich: Calories 530 (Calories from Fat 215); Fat 24g (Saturated 10g); Cholesterol 75mg; Sodium 1,860mg; Carbohydrate 48g (Dietary Fiber 2g); Protein 30g
% Daily Value: Vitamin A 14%; Vitamin C 8%; Calcium 32%; Iron 18%
Exchanges: 2 Starch, 1 Other Carbohydrate, 3 Medium-Fat Meat, 2 Fat
Carbohydrate Choices: 3

BETTY'S TIPS

✪ **Substitution**
Instead of the pasta sauce, dare to try some other sauces. Need ideas? Try Alfredo sauce, ranch dressing or warmed cheese sauce.

✪ **Health Twist**
Skip the pasta sauce, and serve these tasty bundles on a bed of greens drizzled with a low-fat creamy dressing.

✪ **Serve-With**
All you need to make the meal complete is a quick Caesar salad. A bowl of ice cream topped with a little chocolate or caramel sauce is an easy after-dinner treat.

Quick

Taco Chicken

Prep Time: 10 min Start to Finish: 25 min

1½ cups nacho cheese tortilla chips
(1¾ ounces)

½ cup Original Bisquick mix

4 boneless skinless chicken breast halves
(about 1¼ pounds)

1 egg, beaten

2 tablespoons taco sauce

¼ teaspoon salt

3 tablespoons vegetable oil

1. Place tortilla chips in 1-gallon resealable plastic food-storage bag; crush with rolling pin. Add Bisquick mix to chips; mix well.

2. Between sheets of plastic wrap or waxed paper, flatten each chicken breast half to about ¼-inch thickness. In small shallow dish, mix egg, taco sauce and salt. Dip chicken into egg mixture, then shake in bag to coat with Bisquick mixture.

3. In 12-inch nonstick skillet, heat oil over medium heat. Reduce heat to medium-low. Cook chicken in oil 10 to 12 minutes, turning once, until juice is no longer pink when centers of thickest pieces are cut.

4 servings.
1 Serving: Calories 365 (Calories from Fat 180); Fat 20g (Saturated 4g); Cholesterol 125mg; Sodium 540mg; Carbohydrate 16g (Dietary Fiber 1g); Protein 30g
% Daily Value: Vitamin A 2%; Vitamin C 0%; Calcium 4%; Iron 10%
Exchanges: 1 Starch, 4 Lean Meat, 1½ Fat
Carbohydrate Choices: 1

BETTY'S TIPS

⊗ **Substitution**
Looking for a little spicier version of Taco Chicken? Use spicy nacho cheese chips and medium taco sauce for the coating.

⊗ **Success Hint**
Using a nonstick skillet will work best for cooking this coated chicken. If you don't have a nonstick skillet, you may need to add about 1 tablespoon more oil halfway through cooking.

⊗ **Serve-With**
Serve this crispy chicken alongside Spanish rice, warm flour tortillas or corn muffins and sliced avocados.

Taco Chicken

Chicken Breasts with Wild Rice Alfredo

Prep Time: 25 min Start to Finish: 2 hr 15 min

1¹/₂ cups uncooked wild rice, rinsed and drained

1 can (14 ounces) roasted garlic-seasoned chicken broth

1 cup water

1 teaspoon dried thyme leaves

2 tablespoons butter or margarine

6 boneless skinless chicken breast halves (about 2 pounds)

1 package (8 ounces) sliced fresh mushrooms (3 cups)

1 jar (7 ounces) roasted bell peppers, drained and chopped

1 jar (1 pound) Alfredo pasta sauce (2 cups)

1. In 2-quart saucepan, heat wild rice, broth and water to boiling over high heat. Reduce heat to low. Cover and simmer 45 to 60 minutes or until rice kernels are open and almost tender; drain if necessary. Stir in thyme. Spread rice in ungreased 13 x 9-inch baking dish.

2. Heat oven to 350°. In 12-inch skillet, heat butter over medium-high heat. Cook chicken in butter 8 to 10 minutes, turning once, until brown. Place on cooked rice. Add mushrooms to skillet. Cook 3 to 5 minutes, stirring occasionally, until lightly browned. Stir in bell peppers and Alfredo sauce; pour over chicken.

3. Bake uncovered 45 to 55 minutes or until mixture is bubbly and juice of chicken is no longer pink when centers of thickest pieces are cut.

6 servings.

1 Serving: Calories 720 (Calories from Fat 370); Fat 41g (Saturated 23g); Cholesterol 180mg; Sodium 820mg; Carbohydrate 44g (Dietary Fiber 4g); Protein 44g
% Daily Value: Vitamin A 62%; Vitamin C 42%; Calcium 28%; Iron 14%
Exchanges: 2¹/₂ Starch, 1 Vegetable, 5 Lean Meat, 5 Fat
Carbohydrate Choices: 3

BETTY'S TIPS

❂ **Substitution**
If you can't find chicken broth with garlic, make your own. Just finely chop 2 cloves of garlic and stir into regular chicken broth.

Two cups refrigerated Alfredo sauce can be used instead of the jarred sauce.

❂ **Success Hint**
For the best flavor and texture, make sure the wild rice has cooked long enough to "pop" open to show its white insides. You may need to add more water during cooking.

Chicken Breasts with Wild Rice Alfredo

Oven-Fried Barbecue Chicken

Prep Time: 15 min Start to Finish: 1 hr 5 min

1 cup buttermilk
1 cup Gold Medal all-purpose flour
1 teaspoon salt
1 teaspoon pepper
3 to 3¹/₂ pounds cut-up broiler-fryer chicken
Cooking spray
¹/₂ cup barbecue sauce
2 tablespoons honey

1. Heat oven to 400°. Pour buttermilk into large shallow dish. In large plastic food-storage bag, mix flour, salt and pepper. Dip each chicken piece in buttermilk, then place in bag with flour. Hold bag closed and shake until chicken is coated. Place skin side down in ungreased 15 x 10 x 1-inch pan. Spray chicken generously with cooking spray. Turn chicken; spray other sides generously with cooking spray.

2. Bake uncovered 45 to 50 minutes or until chicken is crisp and juice is no longer pink when centers of thickest pieces are cut.

3. Meanwhile, in small bowl, mix barbecue sauce and honey. Just before serving, brush chicken with sauce mixture.

6 servings.
1 Serving: Calories 370 (Calories from Fat 125); Fat 14g (Saturated 4g); Cholesterol 90mg; Sodium 720mg; Carbohydrate 31g (Dietary Fiber 1g); Protein 30g
% Daily Value: Vitamin A 2%; Vitamin C 0%; Calcium 6%; Iron 14%
Exchanges: 2 Starch, 3¹/₂ Lean Meat, ¹/₂ Fat
Carbohydrate Choices: 2

BETTY'S TIPS

✿ Kitchen Tip
Round out this barbecue chicken dinner with coleslaw from the deli and corn muffins from the bakery.

Give this chicken an Asian twist by using bottled teriyaki baste and glaze instead of the honey and barbecue sauce.

Oven-Fried Barbecue Chicken

Quick

Feta-Topped Chicken

Prep Time: 10 min Start to Finish: 25 min

4 boneless skinless chicken breast halves
   (1¹/₄ pounds)

2 tablespoons balsamic vinaigrette dressing

1 teaspoon Italian seasoning

¹/₄ teaspoon seasoned pepper

1 large roma (plum) tomato, cut into 8 slices

¹/₄ cup crumbled feta cheese (1 ounce)

1. Set oven control to broil. Brush both sides of chicken breasts with dressing. Sprinkle both sides with Italian seasoning and seasoned pepper. Place on rack in broiler pan.

2. Broil with tops 4 inches from heat about 10 minutes, turning once, until chicken is no longer pink when centers of thickest pieces are cut. Top with tomato and cheese. Broil 2 to 3 minutes longer or until cheese is lightly browned.

4 servings.
1 Serving: Calories 200 (Calories from Fat 80); Fat 9g (Saturated 2g); Cholesterol 80mg; Sodium 210mg; Carbohydrate 2g (Dietary Fiber 0g); Protein 28g
% Daily Value: Vitamin A 2%; Vitamin C 2%; Calcium 6%; Iron 6%
Exchanges: 4 Very Lean Meat, 1¹/₂ Fat
Carbohydrate Choices: 0

BETTY'S TIPS

❂ **Kitchen Tip**
You can use ¹/₂ teaspoon each of dried basil and oregano leaves in place of the Italian seasoning.

Feta-Topped Chicken

Three-Herb Chicken

Prep Time: 10 min Start to Finish: 1 hr 30 min

Herb Marinade (right)
4 chicken thighs (about 1 pound)
4 chicken drumsticks (about 1 pound)

1. Make Herb Marinade. Add chicken to marinade; turn to coat. Cover dish and refrigerate, turning chicken occasionally, at least 30 minutes but no longer than 24 hours.

2. Heat coals or gas grill for direct heat. Remove chicken from marinade; reserve marinade. Cover and grill chicken, skin side down, 5 to 6 inches from medium heat 8 to 10 minutes. Turn chicken; brush with marinade. Cover and grill 25 to 35 minutes longer, turning occasionally and brushing with marinade, until juice of chicken is no longer pink when centers of thickest pieces are cut. Discard any remaining marinade.

4 servings.

Herb Marinade

$1/2$ cup vegetable oil
$1/2$ cup lime juice
2 tablespoons chopped fresh or 2 teaspoons dried basil leaves
2 tablespoons chopped fresh or 2 teaspoons dried oregano leaves
2 tablespoons chopped fresh or 2 teaspoons dried thyme leaves
1 teaspoon onion powder
$1/4$ teaspoon lemon pepper

Mix all ingredients in shallow glass or plastic dish.

1 Serving: Calories 425 (Calories from Fat 295); Fat 33g (Saturated 7g); Cholesterol 100mg; Sodium 95mg; Carbohydrate 1g (Dietary Fiber 0g); Protein 31g
% Daily Value: Vitamin A 4%; Vitamin C 4%; Calcium 2%; Iron 12%
Exchanges: 4 Medium-Fat Meat, 3 Fat
Carbohydrate Choices: 0

BETTY'S TIPS

✿ **Substitution**
You could substitute 4 bone-in chicken breasts for the thighs and drumsticks.

✿ **Time-Saver**
Microwave the chicken to partially cook it before grilling. Not only does this save time, but it can also help prevent overcooked chicken.

✿ **Special Touch**
Garnish individual servings or a platter of this delicious chicken with lime slices or sprigs of fresh basil, oregano or thyme.

Three-Herb Chicken

Rosemary Roast Chicken

Prep Time: 20 min Start to Finish: 2 hr 15 min

3 to 3¹/₂	pounds whole broiler-fryer chicken
1¹/₂	pounds buttercup or acorn squash, peeled and cut into ¹/₂-inch rings or slices, then cut crosswise in half
2	medium onions, cut into 1-inch wedges (2 cups)
¹/₂	cup butter or margarine, melted
¹/₄	cup lemon juice
2	tablespoons honey
2	teaspoons dried rosemary leaves, crumbled
1	clove garlic, finely chopped

1. Heat oven to 375°. Fold wings of chicken under back. Tie or skewer drumsticks together. Place chicken, breast side up, on rack in shallow roasting pan. Arrange squash and onions around chicken.

2. In small bowl, mix remaining ingredients; brush on chicken and vegetables just until evenly coated. Reserve remaining butter mixture. Insert meat thermometer in chicken so tip is in thickest part of inside thigh muscle and does not touch bone.

3. Roast uncovered 1 hour. Brush remaining butter mixture on chicken and vegetables. Cover loosely with aluminum foil to prevent overbrowning. Bake 45 to 55 minutes longer or until thermometer reads 180° and juice of chicken is no longer pink when center of thigh is cut and squash is tender.

6 servings.
1 Serving: Calories 440 (Calories from Fat 260); Fat 29g (Saturated 13g); Cholesterol 125mg; Sodium 190mg; Carbohydrate 17g (Dietary Fiber 3g); Protein 28g
% Daily Value: Vitamin A 66%; Vitamin C 10%; Calcium 4%; Iron 8%
Exchanges: 1 Starch, 3¹/₂ Medium-Fat Meat, 2 Fat
Carbohydrate Choices: 1

BETTY'S TIPS

✿ **Kitchen Tip**
Cube any leftover chicken and add to Super Stuffing, page 222, for a quick one-dish meal.

Add steamed broccoli spears or green beans to make your meal complete.

Rosemary Roast Chicken

Tomato-Basil Chicken Casserole

Seasoned Oven-Roasted Chicken

Tomato-Basil Chicken Casserole

Prep Time: 25 min Start to Finish: 1 hr 15 min

2 cups uncooked gemelli pasta (8 ounces)

2 cups diced Seasoned Oven-Roasted Chicken (right) or purchased diced cooked chicken

1 jar (26 ounces) tomato paste sauce (any hearty or thick variety)

1 medium zucchini, cut lengthwise in half, then cut into slices ($1\frac{1}{2}$ cups)

1 can (3.8 ounces) sliced ripe olives, drained

1 teaspoon dried basil leaves

$\frac{1}{4}$ cup shredded fresh Parmesan cheese

1. Heat oven to 375°. Spray 2-quart casserole with cooking spray. Cook and drain pasta as directed on package.

2. In casserole, mix pasta and remaining ingredients except cheese.

3. Cover and bake 30 minutes. Sprinkle with cheese. Bake uncovered 15 to 20 minutes longer or until bubbly and thoroughly heated.

6 servings ($1\frac{1}{3}$ cups each).
1 Serving: Calories 400 (Calories from Fat 90); Fat 10g (Saturated 2g); Cholesterol 40mg; Sodium 990mg; Carbohydrate 55g (Dietary Fiber 4g); Protein 23g
% Daily Value: Vitamin A 22%; Vitamin C 18%; Calcium 12%; Iron 20%
Exchanges: 3 Starch, 2 Vegetable, $1\frac{1}{2}$ Lean Meat, $\frac{1}{2}$ Fat
Carbohydrate Choices: $3\frac{1}{2}$

BETTY'S TIPS

✿ **Kitchen Tip**
Gemelli is a pasta that looks like two strands of spaghetti twisted together. Rotini or penne pasta would work well in this recipe too.

Low Fat
Seasoned Oven-Roasted Chicken

Prep Time: 10 min Start to Finish: 1 hr

8 boneless skinless chicken breast halves (about 2 pounds)

1 tablespoon olive or vegetable oil

$1\frac{1}{2}$ teaspoons parsley flakes

1 teaspoon seasoned salt

1 teaspoon garlic pepper blend

1 teaspoon dried basil leaves

1. Heat oven to 400°. Spray 13 x 9-inch (3-quart) baking dish with cooking spray. Brush both sides of chicken with oil. Sprinkle both sides with parsley, seasoned salt, garlic pepper and basil. Place in baking dish.

2. Bake uncovered 25 to 35 minutes or until juice of chicken is no longer pink when centers of thickest pieces are cut.

3. Cool chicken 10 to 15 minutes. Cut into desired size pieces for recipes calling for cooked chicken. Wrap tightly and refrigerate up to 2 days or freeze up to 1 month.

About 4 cups cut-up chicken.
$\frac{1}{2}$ Cup: Calories 165 (Calories from Fat 55); Fat 6g (Saturated 1g); Cholesterol 75mg; Sodium 240mg; Carbohydrate 0g (Dietary Fiber 0g); Protein 27g
% Daily Value: Vitamin A 0%; Vitamin C 0%; Calcium 2%; Iron 6%
Exchanges: 4 Very Lean Meat, $\frac{1}{2}$ Fat
Carbohydrate Choices: 0

Chicken and Dumplings

Prep Time: 10 min Start to Finish: 30 min

1¹/₂ cups milk
1 cup frozen peas and carrots (from 1-pound bag)
1 cup cut-up cooked chicken
1 can (10.75 ounces) condensed cream of chicken or cream of mushroom soup
1 cup Original Bisquick mix
¹/₃ cup milk

1. In 3-quart saucepan, heat 1¹/₂ cups milk, peas and carrots, chicken and soup to boiling, stirring occasionally.

2. In small bowl, stir Bisquick and ¹/₃ cup milk with fork until soft dough forms. Drop dough by 8 spoonfuls onto boiling chicken mixture. Reduce heat to medium.

3. Cook uncovered 10 minutes. Cover and cook 10 minutes longer.

4 servings.
1 Serving: Calories 340 (Calories from Fat 125); Fat 14g (Saturated 4g); Cholesterol 45mg; Sodium 1,080mg; Carbohydrate 34g (Dietary Fiber 2g); Protein 19g
% Daily Value: Vitamin A 84%; Vitamin C 2%; Calcium 20%; Iron 12%
Exchanges: 2 Starch, 1 Vegetable, 1¹/₂ Medium-Fat Meat, 1 Fat
Carbohydrate Choices: 2

Chicken and Dumplings

Chicken and Broccoli Casserole with Cheesy Biscuit Topping

Prep Time: 20 min Start to Finish: 1 hr 5 min

- 1 can (10¾ ounces) condensed cream of chicken soup
- ½ cup milk
- 2 cups diced Seasoned Oven-Roasted Chicken (page 155) or purchased diced cooked chicken
- 1 bag (1 pound) Green Giant frozen cut broccoli, thawed, drained
- 1 jar (2 ounce) chopped pimientos, drained
- 1 pouch (7.75 ounces) Bisquick Complete cheese-garlic biscuit mix
- ½ cup water
- 1 tablespoon chopped fresh chives, if desired

1. Heat oven to 425°. Spray 2-quart casserole or 8-inch square baking dish with cooking spray. In baking dish, mix soup and milk until well blended. Stir in chicken, broccoli and pimientos. Cover casserole with aluminum foil.

2. Cover cookie sheet with foil; place on lower oven rack to catch drips from casserole. Place casserole in center of oven over cookie sheet. Bake about 25 minutes or until bubbly.

3. About 5 minutes before removing casserole from oven, make biscuit mix as directed on package, using water. Drop dough by 8 large spoonfuls onto chicken mixture around the edges. Sprinkle with chives.

4. Bake uncovered 12 to 17 minutes or until bubbly and biscuits are golden brown.

4 servings.
1 Serving: Calories 520 (Calories from Fat 170); Fat 19g (Saturated 5g); Cholesterol 80mg; Sodium 1,650mg; Carbohydrate 50g (Dietary Fiber 4g); Protein 37g
% Daily Value: Vitamin A 50%; Vitamin C 44%; Calcium 20%; Iron 22%
Exchanges: 3 Starch, 1 Vegetable, 3½ Lean Meat, 1½ Fat
Carbohydrate Choices: 3

BETTY'S TIPS

✿ Kitchen Tip
Pair this easy supper with a bagged salad tossed with a tangy dressing such as raspberry vinaigrette, or serve with a fresh fruit salad.

Chicken and Broccoli Casserole with Cheesy Biscuit Topping

Honey-Spice Roast Turkey with Apple-Pecan Stuffing

Prep Time: 20 min Start to Finish: 4 hr 50 min
(Photo on page 143)

Turkey

12- to 15- pound turkey, thawed if frozen

$1/4$ cup honey

2 tablespoons butter or margarine, melted

2 teaspoons chili powder

$1/2$ teaspoon ground allspice

$1/2$ teaspoon ground cumin

Apple-Pecan Stuffing

$1/4$ cup butter or margarine

$1/2$ cup pecan pieces

1 medium apple, chopped (1 cup)

4 cups herb-seasoned stuffing mix (from 14- to 16-ounce package)

2 cups apple juice

1. Heat oven to 325°. Starting at back opening of turkey, gently separate skin from turkey breast, using fingers. In small bowl, stir together honey, 2 tablespoons melted butter, chili powder, allspice and cumin; brush half of mixture over turkey breast under skin (reserve remaining honey mixture).

2. In 4-quart Dutch oven, melt $1/4$ cup butter over medium-high heat. Cook pecans in butter 1 to 2 minutes, stirring occasionally, until lightly toasted. Lightly stir in apple, stuffing mix and apple juice until moistened.

3. Stuff turkey just before baking. Fill wishbone area with stuffing first. Fasten neck skin to back with skewer. Fold wings across back with tips touching. Fill body cavity lightly with remaining stuffing. (Do not pack—stuffing will expand while cooking.) Tuck drumsticks under band of skin at tail, or tie together with heavy string, then tie to tail. Place turkey breast side up on rack in shallow roasting pan. Insert meat thermometer so tip is in thickest part of inside thigh muscle and does not touch bone. Do not add water.

4. Cover with aluminum foil and bake 3 to 4 hours, uncovering and brushing with remaining honey mixture for last 30 minutes of baking, until thermometer reads 180° and juice is no longer pink when center of thigh is cut. Drumsticks should move easily when lifted or twisted.

5. Place turkey on warm platter; cover with foil to keep warm. Let stand at least 15 minutes for easiest carving. Cover and refrigerate any remaining turkey and stuffing separately.

12 to 15 servings.

1 Serving: Calories 725 (Calories from Fat 295); Fat 33g (Saturated 11g); Cholesterol 225mg; Sodium 570mg; Carbohydrate 30g (Dietary Fiber 2g); Protein 77g
% Daily Value: Vitamin A 10%; Vitamin C 0%; Calcium 8%; Iron 26%
Exchanges: 2 Starch, 10 Lean Meat
Carbohydrate Choices: 2

BETTY'S TIPS

⊕ **Success Hint**
Let one of the new meat thermometers help you know when the turkey is done. Place the probe in the turkey and the digital readout on the counter. No more opening the oven to check the temp!

⊕ **Variation**
Love extra stuffing? Double the recipe, and use half for the bird. Place the other half in a greased 2-quart casserole. Cover and bake at 325° for 30 minutes; uncover and bake 10 to 15 minutes longer or until the top is lightly toasted.

⊕ **Special Touch**
Spoon the stuffing into a serving bowl, and sprinkle with chopped parsley for a spritz of color.

Chipotle Turkey Breast

Prep Time: 10 min Start to Finish: 2 hr 15 min

8 to 10	cloves garlic
2 to 2½	pounds bone-in skin-on turkey breast half
⅓	cup real maple syrup
2	tablespoons vegetable oil
1 or 2	chipotle chilies in adobo sauce (from 7-ounce can)
1	tablespoon soy sauce
1 or 2	cloves garlic, peeled

1. Heat oven to 325°. Tuck 8 to 10 cloves of garlic under skin of turkey. In shallow roasting pan, place turkey on rack.

2. In mini food processor or blender, add remaining ingredients. Cover and process until smooth. Brush over turkey. Insert ovenproof meat thermometer so tip is in thickest part of turkey and does not touch bone.

3. Bake uncovered 1 hour 30 minutes to 2 hours, turning occasionally and brushing with chipotle mixture, until meat thermometer reads 170° and juice is no longer pink when center is cut. Let stand 5 minutes before serving. Discard any remaining chipotle mixture.

6 servings.
1 Serving: Calories 285 (Calories from Fat 110); Fat 12g (Saturated 3g); Cholesterol 80mg; Sodium 280mg; Carbohydrate 15g (Dietary Fiber 0g); Protein 29g
% Daily Value: Vitamin A 2%; Vitamin C 0%; Calcium 2%; Iron 6%
Exchanges: 1 Other Carbohydrate, 4 Lean Meat
Carbohydrate Choices: 1

Chipotle Turkey Breast

BETTY'S TIPS

✪ **Substitution**
Maple-flavored syrup or honey can be used for the real maple syrup in the marinade.

✪ **Success Hint**
Look for chipotle chilies in adobo sauce in the ethnic-foods section of your supermarket. For maximum flavor, include some of the sauce with the chilies.

✪ **Did You Know?**
Letting meat stand before cutting allows it to finish cooking and seal in the juices, so they aren't lost when the meat is sliced.

Garlic-Spiked Turkey Breast with Fresh Basil Mayonnaise

Prep Time: 30 min Start to Finish: 9 hr 30 min

6¹/₂- pound bone-in turkey breast, thawed if frozen

6 cloves garlic, thinly sliced

¹/₄ cup grated lemon peel (from 3 medium or 2 large lemons)

2 tablespoons chopped parsley

1¹/₂ teaspoons lemon pepper seasoning salt

1 tablespoon olive or vegetable oil

1 cup loosely packed fresh basil leaves

3 tablespoons olive or vegetable oil

1 cup mayonnaise or salad dressing

1. Remove gravy packet or extra parts from turkey breast. Remove skin from turkey. Make cuts, ¹/₄ to ¹/₂ inch deep and ¹/₄ to ¹/₂ inch wide, in top of turkey, using small paring knife. Insert garlic slices into cuts.

2. Mix lemon peel, parsley and lemon pepper seasoning salt; rub onto turkey. Heat 1 tablespoon oil in 12-inch skillet over medium-high heat. Cook turkey in oil until brown on all sides.

3. Place turkey and any drippings in 5- to 6-quart slow cooker. Cover and cook on Low heat setting 8 to 9 hours.

4. Place basil and 3 tablespoons oil in food processor. Cover and process until basil is chopped. Add mayonnaise. Cover and process until smooth. Serve sliced turkey with mayonnaise.

12 servings.

1 Serving: Calories 485 (Calories from Fat 290); Fat 32g (Saturated 6g); Cholesterol 140mg; Sodium 380mg; Carbohydrate 2g (Dietary Fiber 0g); Protein 47g
% Daily Value: Vitamin A 8%; Vitamin C 2%; Calcium 4%; Iron 10%
Exchanges: 6¹/₂ Medium-Fat Meat
Carbohydrate Choices: 0

BETTY'S TIPS

⚙ **Success Hint**

Use a small paring knife with a sharp point to make the cuts in the turkey breast.

An electric knife makes slicing the turkey a snap.

Look for packages or bunches of fresh basil in the produce section of the grocery store. It should be a rich green color without any sign of mold and have a fragrant aroma.

Garlic-Spiked Turkey Breast with Fresh Basil Mayonnaise

Honey-Dijon Brined Turkey Breast

Prep Time: 15 min Start to Finish: 14 hr 15 min

11	cups cold water
1	cup honey
1/2	cup Dijon mustard
1/3	cup salt
5- to 6-	pound bone-in whole turkey breast, thawed if frozen
3	tablespoons olive or vegetable oil
1	teaspoon dried marjoram leaves
1	teaspoon ground mustard
1	teaspoon garlic pepper

1. Stir water, honey, mustard and salt in 6-quart container until salt and honey are dissolved. Add turkey to brine mixture. Cover and refrigerate at least 12 hours but no longer than 24 hours.

2. If using charcoal grill, place drip pan directly under grilling area, and arrange coals around edge of firebox. Heat coals or gas grill for indirect heat. Remove turkey from brine mixture; rinse thoroughly under cool running water and pat dry. Discard brine. Mix remaining ingredients; brush over turkey.

3. Cover and grill turkey over drip pan or over unheated side of gas grill and 4 to 6 inches from medium heat 1 hour 45 minutes to 2 hours, rotating turkey 1/2 turn after 1 hour, until juice of turkey is no longer pink when center is cut and thermometer reads 170°.

8 servings.
1 Serving: Calories 400 (Calories from Fat 160); Fat 18g (Saturated 5g); Cholesterol 145mg; Sodium 460mg; Carbohydrate 5g (Dietary Fiber 0g); Protein 54g
% Daily Value: Vitamin A 2%; Vitamin C 0%; Calcium 2%; Iron 10%
Exchanges: 7 1/2 Lean Meat
Carbohydrate Choices: 0

BETTY'S TIPS

⊛ **Success Hint**
Because the brine mixture adds salt and flavor to the turkey, buy a turkey that hasn't been injected with a saline solution. Although a turkey that has been injected will work fine in this recipe, it will turn out a little saltier.

Allow the turkey breast to stand for 5 to 10 minutes before slicing. This "standing" time locks juices into the meat so that it will be moist and tender.

⊛ **Serve-With**
For a summery meal, serve the turkey with herbed new potatoes, mixed spring greens tossed with balsamic vinaigrette dressing and sourdough bread. Strawberry shortcake for dessert is the crowning touch.

Honey-Dijon Brined Turkey Breast

Turkey and Stuffing Bake

Prep Time: 20 min Start to Finish: 1 hr

- 3 cups chopped cooked turkey
- 1 bag (14 ounces) Green Giant Select frozen broccoli flowerets, thawed and drained
- 1 can (10.75 ounces) cream of chicken soup
- 1/2 cup sour cream
- 1 1/2 cups shredded Swiss cheese (6 ounces)
- 1 package (6 ounces) stuffing mix for turkey
- 3/4 cup hot water

1. Heat oven to 350°. Spread turkey in ungreased 13 x 9-inch baking dish. Top with broccoli.

2. In medium bowl, stir together soup, sour cream and cheese; spread over broccoli. In large bowl, stir together stuffing mix and hot water; sprinkle over casserole.

3. Bake uncovered 35 to 40 minutes or until hot and bubbly.

8 servings.
1 Serving: Calories 340 (Calories from Fat 145); Fat 16g (Saturated 7g); Cholesterol 75mg; Sodium 730mg; Carbohydrate 23g (Dietary Fiber 2g); Protein 26g
% Daily Value: Vitamin A 24%; Vitamin C 14%; Calcium 26%; Iron 10%
Exchanges: 1 Starch, 1 Vegetable, 3 Lean Meat, 1/2 Fat
Carbohydrate Choices: 1 1/2

BETTY'S TIPS

✿ **Success Hint**
This recipe makes perfect use of that leftover cooked turkey!

✿ **Serve-With**
For festive color and refreshing crunch, serve this casserole with Orange, Kiwifruit and Poppy Seed Salad (page 86).

✿ **Variation**
For Chicken and Stuffing Bake, use leftover cooked chicken and chicken stuffing mix.

Turkey and Green Chili Stuffing Casserole

Prep Time: 25 min Start to Finish: 1 hr 40 min

- 2 tablespoons butter or margarine
- 1 medium onion, chopped (1/2 cup)
- 1 small red bell pepper, chopped (1/2 cup)
- 4 cups seasoned corn bread stuffing mix
- 1 cup Green Giant Niblets frozen whole kernel corn (from 1-pound bag)
- 1 can (4.5 ounces) Old El Paso chopped green chilies, undrained
- 1 1/2 cups water
- 2 turkey breast tenderloins (about 3/4 pound each)
- 1/2 teaspoon chili powder
- 1/2 teaspoon peppered seasoned salt

1. Heat oven to 350°. Spray 11 x 7-inch (2-quart) baking dish with cooking spray. In 12-inch nonstick skillet, melt butter over medium-high heat. Cook onion and bell pepper in butter 2 to 3 minutes, stirring frequently, until tender. Stir in stuffing mix, corn, chilies and water. Spread stuffing mixture in baking dish.

2. Sprinkle both sides of turkey tenderloins with chili powder and peppered seasoned salt. Place on stuffing, pressing into stuffing mixture slightly. Spray sheet of aluminum foil with cooking spray. Cover baking dish with foil, sprayed side down.

3. Bake 1 hour. Uncover and bake 10 to 15 minutes longer or until juice of turkey is no longer pink when centers of thickest pieces are cut.

6 servings.
1 Serving: Calories 365 (Calories from Fat 65); Fat 7g (Saturated 3g); Cholesterol 85mg; Sodium 990mg; Carbohydrate 43g (Dietary Fiber 3g); Protein 33g
% Daily Value: Vitamin A 22%; Vitamin C 26%; Calcium 6%; Iron 20%
Exchanges: 3 Starch, 3 1/2 Very Lean Meat
Carbohydrate Choices: 3

BETTY'S TIPS

✿ **Kitchen Tip**
Look for the corn bread stuffing mix in bags near the other packages of stuffing at the grocery store.

Cut down on prep time by using frozen chopped onions and bell peppers. Look for them in the vegetable section of the freezer case.

Turkey and Green Chili Stuffing Casserole

Turkey and Stuffing Bake

Turkey-Butternut Squash Ragout

Prep Time: 15 min Start to Finish: 8 hr 15 min

2 turkey thighs (about 1¹/₂ pounds), skin removed

1 small butternut squash (about 2 pounds), peeled, seeded and cut into 1¹/₂-inch pieces (3 cups)

1 medium onion, cut in half and sliced

1 can (16 ounces) baked beans, undrained

1 can (14.5 ounces) diced tomatoes with Italian seasonings, undrained

2 tablespoons chopped parsley

1. Spray 3- to 4-quart slow cooker with cooking spray. Mix all ingredients except parsley in cooker.

2. Cover and cook on Low heat setting 7 to 8 hours.

3. Place turkey on cutting board. Remove meat from bones; discard bones. Return turkey to cooker. Just before serving, sprinkle with parsley.

4 servings.
1 Serving: Calories 355 (Calories from Fat 55); Fat 6g (Saturated 2g); Cholesterol 115mg; Sodium 740mg; Carbohydrate 49g (Dietary Fiber 10g); Protein 35g
% Daily Value: Vitamin A 100%; Vitamin C 42%; Calcium 20%; Iron 44%
Exchanges: 3 Starch, 1 Vegetable, 3 Very Lean Meat
Carbohydrate Choices: 3

BETTY'S TIPS

❂ **Success Hint**
Cut winter squash, such as the butternut in this recipe, with a sharp knife, then remove the seeds with a spoon. Peel away the tough skin with a vegetable peeler or paring knife.

❂ **Health Twist**
Butternut squash, rich in color, is an excellent source of vitamin A.

❂ **Serve-With**
A tossed green salad with a splash of balsamic vinaigrette and crusty French rolls complete this slow-cooked meal. Low-fat frozen yogurt adds a cool, tangy ending.

Turkey-Butternut Squash Ragout

Pork
Main Dishes

Savory Selections to Enjoy

Oven-Fried Pork Cutlets with Apple Slaw (page 172)

Slow-Cooked Pork Burrito Bowls (page 177)

Greek Pork Kabobs

Prep Time: 15 min Start to Finish: 30 min

¹/₂ cup Greek vinaigrette dressing

1 tablespoon chopped parsley

1 pound pork boneless loin, cut into 1-inch cubes

1 red onion, cut into 8 wedges

1 large red or green bell pepper, cut into 8 pieces

1. Heat coals or gas grill for direct heat. Mix dressing and parsley in large bowl; stir in pork, onion and bell pepper. Thread pork, onion and pepper alternately on each of four 15-inch metal skewers, leaving ¹/₄-inch space between each piece. Reserve remaining dressing in bowl.

2. Cover and grill kabobs 4 to 6 inches from medium heat 10 to 15 minutes, turning kabobs 2 or 3 times and brushing with dressing during last 5 minutes of grilling, until pork is no longer pink in center. Discard any remaining dressing.

4 servings.
1 Serving: Calories 295 (Calories from Fat 155); Fat 17g (Saturated 4g); Cholesterol 75mg; Sodium 280mg; Carbohydrate 9g (Dietary Fiber 1g); Protein 26g
% Daily Value: Vitamin A 2%; Vitamin C 0%; Calcium 2%; Iron 6%
Exchanges: 1 Vegetable, 3¹/₂ Lean Meat, 1¹/₂ Fat
Carbohydrate Choices: ¹/₂

BETTY'S TIPS

✪ **Substitution**
Eight marinated sweet cherry peppers can be substituted for the bell pepper. Look for them in the deli next to the olives.

✪ **Success Hint**
Skewers with flat sides (rather than round) hold ingredients more securely and keep pieces in place when you turn the kabobs.

✪ **Serve-With**
For a Greek flair, serve these kabobs with cooked new potatoes tossed with butter and chopped parsley, and sliced cucumbers drizzled with an herb vinaigrette and sprinkled with crumbled feta cheese.

Greek Pork Kabobs

Caribbean Pork Ribs

Prep Time: 10 min Start to Finish: 7 hr 35 min

3 pounds pork loin back ribs
³/₄ cup ketchup
³/₄ cup pineapple preserves
¹/₂ cup teriyaki marinade and sauce
2 tablespoons packed brown sugar
2 cloves garlic, finely chopped
2 tablespoons cornstarch
1 can (20 ounces) pineapple chunks in juice, drained and ¹/₄ cup juice reserved
1 bag (1 pound) frozen stir-fry bell peppers and onions

1. Spray inside of 4- to 5-quart slow cooker with cooking spray. Cut ribs into 2- or 3-rib portions; place in slow cooker. Stir together ketchup, preserves, teriyaki marinade, brown sugar and garlic in small bowl; pour over ribs.

2. Cover and cook on Low heat setting 6 to 7 hours. Skim fat if necessary. Remove ribs from cooker and cover to keep warm.

3. Mix cornstarch and reserved ¹/₄ cup pineapple juice in small bowl; stir into liquid in cooker. Increase heat setting to High. Cover and cook about 25 minutes or until thickened.

4. Mix pineapple chunks and stir-fry vegetables in large microwavable bowl. Microwave uncovered on High 5 to 7 minutes or until heated through; drain. Stir vegetable mixture into sauce in cooker. Serve vegetable mixture over ribs.

8 servings.
1 Serving: Calories 535 (Calories from Fat 225); Fat 25g (Saturated 9g); Cholesterol 100mg; Sodium 1,050mg; Carbohydrate 52g (Dietary Fiber 2g); Protein 26g
% Daily Value: Vitamin A 8%; Vitamin C 34%; Calcium 8%; Iron 14%
Exchanges: 1 Starch, 2 Fruit, 1 Vegetable, 3 Medium-Fat Meat, 1 Fat
Carbohydrate Choices: 3¹/₂

BETTY'S TIPS

☉ **Success Hint**
A clever trick for skimming fat from the cooked meat is to place a slice of bread on top of the mixture for a few minutes to absorb the fat. Or you can use a spoon.

☉ **Variation**
For a terrific riblet appetizer, ask your meat cutter at your supermarket to cut across the ribs horizontally.

Caribbean Pork Ribs

Hoisin-Glazed Pork Chops

Prep Time: 10 min Start to Finish: 25 min

1/2 cup barbecue sauce

1/4 cup hoisin sauce

2 tablespoons dry sherry, if desired

1 tablespoon honey

4 pork boneless loin chops, about 1/2 inch thick (about 1 pound)

1/2 teaspoon garlic pepper

1/4 teaspoon salt

1/4 teaspoon ground ginger

1. Heat coals or gas grills for direct heat. Mix barbecue sauce, hoisin sauce, sherry, if using, and honey in 1-quart saucepan. Cook over medium heat about 5 minutes, stirring occasionally, until flavors are blended.

2. Sprinkle pork with garlic pepper, salt and ginger. Cover and grill pork 4 to 6 inches from medium heat 10 to 12 minutes, turning frequently and brushing with hoisin glaze during last 5 minutes of grilling, until pork is no longer pink in center.

3. Heat remaining glaze to boiling; boil and stir 1 minute. Serve pork with remaining glaze.

4 servings.
1 Serving: Calories 265 (Calories from Fat 80); Fat 9g (Saturated 3g); Cholesterol 65mg; Sodium 760mg; Carbohydrate 22g (Dietary Fiber 1g); Protein 24g
% Daily Value: Vitamin A 6%; Vitamin C 2%; Calcium 2%; Iron 8%
Exchanges: 1 Starch, 1/2 Other Carbohydrate, 3 Lean Meat
Carbohydrate Choices: 1 1/2

BETTY'S TIPS

⊛ **Success Hint**
Turn the pork chops frequently with tongs instead of a fork, so you don't pierce the meat during cooking and release the juices.

⊛ **Serve-With**
These Asian-inspired pork chops go great with your favorite fried rice mix, sliced fresh tomatoes and egg rolls from the deli or frozen-foods section of your supermarket.

⊛ **Did You Know?**
Hoisin is a thick, reddish brown sauce with a spicy-sweet flavor that's often used in Chinese cooking. It's a blend of soybeans, garlic, chilies and spices. Look for it in the ethnic-foods section of the grocery store.

Hoisin-Glazed Pork Chops

Quick

Cajun Smothered Pork Chops

Prep Time: 15 min Start to Finish: 15 min

4 bone-in pork loin chops, $^1/_2$ inch thick (about 1 pound), trimmed of fat

2 teaspoons salt-free extra-spicy seasoning blend

2 teaspoons vegetable oil

$^1/_2$ medium onion, sliced

1 can (14.5 ounces) zesty diced tomatoes with jalapeño peppers, undrained

1. Sprinkle both sides of pork chops with seasoning blend. In 12-inch nonstick skillet, heat oil over medium-high heat. Add onion; cook about 2 minutes, stirring occasionally, until slightly tender. Push onion to one side of skillet.

2. Add pork to other side of skillet. Cook about 3 minutes, turning once, until browned. Add tomatoes. Heat to boiling; reduce heat. Cover and cook 4 to 8 minutes or until pork is no longer pink in center.

4 servings (with $^1/_4$ cup sauce each).
1 Serving: Calories 220 (Calories from Fat 100); Fat 11g (Saturated 3g); Cholesterol 65mg; Sodium 410mg; Carbohydrate 6g (Dietary Fiber 2g); Protein 24g
% Daily Value: Vitamin A 8%; Vitamin C 12%; Calcium 4%; Iron 8%
Exchanges: 1 Vegetable, 3 Lean Meat, $^1/_2$ Fat
Carbohydrate Choices: $^1/_2$

BETTY'S TIPS

⊛ **Kitchen Tip**
For a less spicy dish, use plain diced tomatoes instead of the diced tomatoes with jalapeño peppers.

Cajun Smothered Pork Chops

Balsamic Pork with Mixed Herbs

Balsamic Pork with Mixed Herbs

Prep Time: 30 min Start to Finish: 1 hr 30 min

2	pork tenderloins (about $3/4$ pound each)
8	large sprigs rosemary
8	large sprigs thyme
$1/2$	cup balsamic vinegar
3	tablespoons olive or vegetable oil

1. Cut each pork tenderloin crosswise into 6 pieces. Press each piece, cut side down, to form a round, 1 to $1^1/4$ inches thick.

2. Place rosemary and thyme sprigs in shallow glass or plastic dish or resealable plastic food-storage bag. Stir in vinegar and oil. Add pork; turn to coat. Cover dish or seal bag and refrigerate, turning pork 2 or 3 times, at least 1 hour but no longer than 24 hours.

3. Heat coals or gas grill for direct heat. Remove pork from marinade; reserve marinade.

4. Cover and grill pork over medium heat 7 minutes, turning and brushing frequently with marinade. Discard any remaining marinade. Cover and grill pork 6 to 8 minutes longer, turning frequently, until pork has slight blush of pink in center and meat thermometer inserted in center reads 160°.

6 servings.
1 Serving: Calories 190 (Calories from Fat 80); Fat 9g (Saturated 2g); Cholesterol 70mg; Sodium 50mg; Carbohydrate 1g (Dietary Fiber 0g); Protein 26g
% Daily Value: Vitamin A 0%; Vitamin C 0%; Calcium 0%; Iron 8%
Exchanges: $3^1/2$ Lean Meat
Carbohydrate Choices: 0

BETTY'S TIPS

⚙ **Success Hint**
Be sure to use pork tenderloins—not pork loins—in this recipe. Pork loins are much larger and less tender.

⚙ **Special Touch**
If you're using a charcoal grill, remove the herbs from the marinade and place them directly on the hot coals for added herb flavor and aroma.

Oven-Fried Pork Cutlets with Apple Slaw

Prep Time: 10 min Start to Finish: 30 min
(Photo on page 165)

Pork Cutlets

4	pork boneless loin chops, $^1/_2$ inch thick
8	saltine crackers, finely crushed ($^1/_3$ cup)
$^1/_2$	cup Original Bisquick mix
$^1/_2$	teaspoon ground paprika
$^1/_4$	teaspoon pepper
1	egg
1	tablespoon water

Apple Slaw

4	cups coleslaw mix
1	small tart red apple, coarsely chopped (1 cup)
$^1/_4$	cup chopped onion
$^1/_3$	cup coleslaw dressing
$^1/_8$	teaspoon celery seed

1. Heat oven to 425°. Generously spray 15 x 10 x 1-inch pan with cooking spray. Between sheets of plastic wrap or waxed paper, flatten each pork chop to about $^1/_4$-inch thickness.

2. In shallow dish, mix crackers, Bisquick mix, paprika and pepper. In another shallow dish, beat egg and water. Dip pork chops into egg, then coat with Bisquick mixture. Repeat dipping coated pork in egg and in Bisquick mixture. Place in pan. Generously spray tops of pork with cooking spray.

3. Bake about 20 minutes or until golden brown and no longer pink in center. Toss all apple slaw ingredients.

4 servings.
1 Serving: Calories 395 (Calories from Fat 180); Fat 20g (Saturated 5g); Cholesterol 130mg; 63; Carbohydrate 27g (Dietary Fiber 3g); Protein 27g
% Daily Value: Vitamin A 2%; Vitamin C 0%; Calcium 2%; Iron 6%
Exchanges: $1^1/_2$ Starch, 1 Vegetable, 3 Lean Meat, 2 Fat
Carbohydrate Choices: 2

BETTY'S TIPS

❂ **Time-Saver**
Get a jump start on this recipe by making the cracker crumb mixture a day ahead. Keep it in a resealable plastic bag so it stays crisp and crunchy.

❂ **Variation**
Instead of the pork cutlets, you can use boneless skinless chicken breast halves. Flatten the chicken as directed in step 1 for the pork chops, and continue as directed.

❂ **Special Touch**
Add some thin apple wedges around the edge of the platter for a pretty finish to this fabulous dish.

Grilled Pork Tenderloin with Firecracker Marinade

Prep Time: 45 min Start to Finish: 2 hr 45 min

Firecracker Marinade (below)

3 pork tenderloins (about $3/4$ pound each)

3 large red or yellow bell peppers, roasted and cut into strips

2 tablespoons olive or vegetable oil

1 tablespoon balsamic vinegar

   Salt, to taste

2 cloves garlic, finely chopped

1. Make Firecracker Marinade in shallow glass or plastic dish or resealable plastic food-storage bag. Add pork; turn to coat. Cover dish or seal bag and refrigerate, turning pork occasionally, at least 2 hours but no longer than 12 hours.

2. Mix bell peppers, oil, vinegar, salt and garlic in medium bowl. Set aside.

3. Heat coals or gas grill for direct heat. Remove pork from marinade; reserve marinade. Cover and grill pork over medium heat 20 to 25 minutes, brushing occasionally with marinade and turning once, until pork has slight blush of pink in center and meat thermometer inserted in center reads 160°. Discard any remaining marinade.

4. Cut pork into slices; arrange on serving platter with bell pepper mixture.

8 servings.

Firecracker Marinade

  $1/2$ cup barbecue sauce

  2 tablespoons packed brown sugar

  2 tablespoons olive or vegetable oil

  2 tablespoons white wine vinegar

  2 tablespoons soy sauce

1 to 2 teaspoons red pepper sauce

  2 cloves garlic, finely chopped

Mix all ingredients.

Grilled Pork Tenderloin with Firecracker Marinade

1 Serving: Calories 260 (Calories from Fat 100); Fat 11g (Saturated 3g); Cholesterol 80mg; Sodium 420mg; Carbohydrate 10g (Dietary Fiber 1g); Protein 30g
% Daily Value: Vitamin A 15%; Vitamin C 70%; Calcium 2%; Iron 10%
Exchanges: 2 Vegetable, 4 Very Lean Meat, $1 1/2$ Fat
Carbohydrate Choices: $1/2$

BETTY'S TIPS

⊙ **Success Hint**
To roast the bell peppers, broil them with tops 5 inches from heat about 10 minutes, turning occasionally, until skin is blistered and evenly browned but not burned. Place in plastic or paper bag, and close tightly. Let stand 10 minutes, then peel, seed and cut into strips.

⊙ **Do-Ahead**
Make the bell pepper mixture and the marinade up to 2 days ahead of time. Cover and refrigerate.

Quick

Peppered Pork Medallions in Tangy Mushroom Sauce

Prep Time: 30 min Start to Finish: 30 min

1 pound pork tenderloin
1 teaspoon mixed-pepper seasoning
1/4 teaspoon salt
2 teaspoons vegetable oil
1 cup 33%-less-sodium chicken broth
2 tablespoons Gold Medal all-purpose flour
2 tablespoons balsamic vinegar
2 teaspoons dried rosemary leaves, crumbled
1 package (8 ounces) fresh whole mushrooms

1. Cut pork into four 4-ounce pieces. Between sheets of plastic wrap or waxed paper, flatten pork pieces with meat mallet to 4 x 3 1/2 inches in diameter, less than 1/2 inch thick.

2. Sprinkle both sides of pork medallions with mixed-pepper seasoning and salt; press in seasonings. In 12-inch nonstick skillet, heat oil over medium-high heat. Add pork; cook about 5 minutes, turning once, until browned.

3. Meanwhile, in small bowl, mix broth and flour until smooth. Add broth mixture and remaining ingredients to skillet. Heat to boiling; reduce heat. Cover and cook 8 to 10 minutes, stirring occasionally, until pork is no longer pink in center and mushrooms are tender.

4 servings.
1 Serving: Calories 205 (Calories from Fat 65); Fat 7g (Saturated 2g); Cholesterol 70mg; Sodium 320mg; Carbohydrate 6g (Dietary Fiber 1g); Protein 29g
% Daily Value: Vitamin A 0%; Vitamin C 0%; Calcium 0%; Iron 12%
Exchanges: 1 Vegetable, 4 Very Lean Meat, 1 Fat
Carbohydrate Choices: 1/2

BETTY'S TIPS

⊛ **Kitchen Tip**

If your family doesn't care for the flavor of rosemary, you could try thyme, parsley or oregano instead.

Small crimini mushrooms can be used in place of the regular white mushrooms. They have a slightly more earthly flavor and meatier texture.

Peppered Pork Medallions in Tangy Mushroom Sauce

Roast Pork with Apples and Sweet Potatoes

Prep Time: 15 min Start to Finish: 1 hr 15 min

1/4 cup packed brown sugar

6 tablespoons butter or margarine, melted

1 tablespoon cider vinegar

1 teaspoon salt

1/2 teaspoon garlic powder

1/2 teaspoon pepper

2 medium red cooking apples, sliced (about 2 cups)

2 medium dark-orange sweet potatoes, peeled and thinly sliced (about 2 1/2 cups)

1 medium onion, chopped (1/2 cup)

2 pork tenderloins (1 pound each)

1. Heat oven to 425°. In medium bowl, mix brown sugar, butter, vinegar, salt, garlic powder and pepper. Reserve 2 tablespoons of the butter mixture. Add apples, sweet potatoes and onion to remaining butter mixture; toss to coat. Arrange apple mixture in roasting pan or 13 x 9-inch (3-quart) baking dish. Cover tightly with aluminum foil and bake 20 minutes.

2. Meanwhile, brush pork with reserved butter mixture. Heat 10-inch nonstick skillet over medium-high heat until hot. Cook pork in skillet about 3 minutes, turning to brown all sides evenly.

3. Place pork on apple mixture. Bake uncovered 30 to 40 minutes or until pork has slight blush of pink in center and meat thermometer inserted in center reads 160°.

6 servings.

1 Serving: Calories 410 (Calories from Fat 160); Fat 18g (Saturated 9g); Cholesterol 125mg; Sodium 550mg; Carbohydrate 27g (Dietary Fiber 3g); Protein 35g
% Daily Value: Vitamin A 50%; Vitamin C 10%; Calcium 4%; Iron 12%
Exchanges: 1 Starch, 1 Fruit, 4 1/2 Lean Meat, 1/2 Fat
Carbohydrate Choices: 2

BETTY'S TIPS

✿ Kitchen Tip

Be sure to use pork tenderloins—not pork loins—in this recipe. Pork loins are much larger and less tender.

All this meal needs to be complete is coleslaw from the deli or a tossed salad with blue cheese dressing.

Roast Pork with Apples and Sweet Potatoes

Pork Loin with Apricot Rosemary Glaze

Prep Time: 10 min Start to Finish: 1 hr 50 min

   3   pounds pork loin roast
   1   teaspoon salt
$^1/_4$ teaspoon pepper
   1   cup apricot preserves
$^1/_4$ cup dry sherry, cooking sherry or apple juice
   2   teaspoons dried rosemary leaves, crumbled
   2   cloves garlic, finely chopped

1. Heat oven to 350°. Trim fat from pork. Place pork in 13 x 9-inch baking dish. Sprinkle with salt and pepper.

2. In 10-inch skillet, heat preserves, sherry, rosemary and garlic over medium heat, stirring frequently, until thickened. If necessary, mash apricot pieces with fork into small pieces. Spoon $^1/_4$ cup apricot mixture onto pork (reserve remaining apricot mixture). Insert meat thermometer so tip is in center of thickest part of pork.

3. Bake uncovered 1 hour 15 minutes to 1 hour 30 minutes or until thermometer reads 155°. Cover pork with aluminum foil; let stand 15 to 20 minutes or until thermometer reads 160°. (Temperature will continue to rise about 5°, and pork will be easier to carve.) Cut pork into slices. Heat remaining apricot mixture, serve with pork.

10 servings.
1 Serving: Calories 305 (Calories from Fat 100); Fat 11g (Saturated 4g); Cholesterol 85mg; Sodium 300mg; Carbohydrate 22g (Dietary Fiber 0g); Protein 30g
% Daily Value: Vitamin A 0%; Vitamin C 2%; Calcium 0%; Iron 6%
Exchanges: 1 Fruit, $^1/_2$ Other Carbohydrate, 4 Lean Meat
Carbohydrate Choices: $1^1/_2$

Pork Loin with Apricot Rosemary Glaze

BETTY'S TIPS

⊗ **Substitution**
   If you have fresh rosemary, chop about 1 tablespoon of the leaves for the sauce. Arrange some of the rosemary sprigs, along with fresh or dried apricots, around the roast when serving.

⊗ **Success Hint**
   When checking the doneness of the roast, remove it from the oven when the thermometer reads 5° less than the desired temperature. The roast will continue to cook as it stands, covered, before being sliced.

⊗ **Serve-With**
   Seasoned rice pilaf, buttered carrots and lettuce wedges with blue cheese dressing complement the rich flavors of this roast.

Slow-Cooked Pork Burrito Bowls

Prep Time: 15 min Start to Finish: 8 hr 15 min

2 pounds pork boneless shoulder roast

1 can (15 to 16 ounces) pinto beans, rinsed and drained

1 envelope (1.25 ounces) Old El Paso taco seasoning mix

1 can (4.5 ounces) Old El Paso diced green chilies, undrained

2 packages (7.6 ounces each) Old El Paso Spanish rice mix

5 cups water

2 tablespoons butter or margarine

2$^1/_4$ cups shredded Mexican blend cheese (9 ounces)

2$^1/_4$ cups shredded lettuce

$^3/_4$ cup Old El Paso Thick 'n Chunky salsa

1. If pork roast comes in netting or is tied, remove netting or strings. In 3- to 4-quart slow cooker, place pork. Pour beans around pork. Sprinkle dry taco seasoning mix over pork. Pour green chilies over beans.

2. Cover and cook on Low heat setting 8 to 10 hours.

3. About 45 minutes before serving, in 3-quart saucepan, make rice mixes as directed on package, using water and butter.

4. Remove pork from cooker; place on cutting board. Use 2 forks to pull pork into shreds. Return pork to cooker; gently stir to mix with beans.

5. To serve, spoon about 1 cup rice into each serving bowl, top with $^1/_2$ cup pork mixture, $^1/_4$ cup cheese, $^1/_4$ cup lettuce and about 1 teaspoon salsa.

9 servings.
1 Serving: Calories 485 (Calories from Fat 225); Fat 25g (Saturated 12g); Cholesterol 100mg; Sodium 810mg; Carbohydrate 30g (Dietary Fiber 5g); Protein 35g
% Daily Value: Vitamin A 20%; Vitamin C 8%; Calcium 20%; Iron 18%
Exchanges: 2 Starch, 4 Medium-Fat Meat, $^1/_2$ Fat
Carbohydrate Choices: 2

BETTY'S TIPS

✿ **Kitchen Tip**
If you can't find Old El Paso Spanish rice mix, use any Spanish rice mix and just follow the package directions.

You'll find that pork boneless shoulder roasts also may be called shoulder blade roast, Boston roast or Boston butt.

Swiss Pork Chop and Potato Casserole

Prep Time: 20 min Start to Finish: 1 hr 25 min

1 envelope (1.8 ounces) white sauce mix

2 cups milk

1 cup shredded Swiss cheese (4 ounces)

1/2 teaspoon dried rosemary leaves, crumbled

3 medium Yukon gold potatoes, peeled, sliced (4 cups)

1 medium dark-orange sweet potato, peeled, sliced (1 1/2 cups)

1 medium onion, thinly sliced

4 bone-in pork loin chops, 1/2 inch thick

1/2 teaspoon peppered seasoned salt

1. Heat oven to 350°. Spray 11 x 7-inch (2-quart) baking dish with cooking spray. In 1 1/2-quart saucepan, mix sauce mix and milk. Heat to boiling over medium heat, stirring constantly with wire whisk. Stir in cheese and rosemary until cheese is melted.

2. In baking dish, layer half of Yukon gold potatoes, all of sweet potatoes and half of onion. Spread about half of sauce over top. Layer with remaining potatoes and onion; cover with remaining sauce.

3. Cover and bake 30 minutes. Meanwhile, heat 12-inch nonstick skillet over medium-high heat. Sprinkle both sides of pork chops with peppered seasoned salt. Cook pork in skillet 4 to 5 minutes, turning once, until brown.

4. Place pork on potatoes. Bake uncovered 30 to 35 minutes longer or until pork is no longer pink when cut near bone and potatoes are tender.

4 servings.

1 Serving: Calories 515 (Calories from Fat 160); Fat 18g (Saturated 9g); Cholesterol 100mg; Sodium 1,290mg; Carbohydrate 48g (Dietary Fiber 4g); Protein 40g
% Daily Value: Vitamin A 96%; Vitamin C 16%; Calcium 50%; Iron 8%
Exchanges: 3 Starch, 4 1/2 Lean Meat, 1/2 Fat
Carbohydrate Choices: 3

BETTY'S TIPS

❂ **Kitchen Tip**

If you don't have seasoned salt on hand, sprinkle the chops with salt and pepper. Boneless chops work well in this recipe too.

Yukon gold potatoes are moist and buttery with a golden flesh. If they're not available, use red-skinned potatoes instead.

Swiss Pork Chop and Potato Casserole

Onion-Topped Sausage and Potato Dinner

Prep Time: 15 min Start to Finish: 1 hr 25 min

1 can (10$^3/_4$ ounces) condensed cream of potato or cream of celery soup

$^1/_2$ cup chive-and-onion sour cream

1$^1/_4$ cups shredded Cheddar cheese (5 ounces)

1 bag (1 pound 4 ounces) refrigerated cooked new potato wedges

1 cup Green Giant frozen cut green beans (from 1-pound bag), thawed, drained

8 ounces fully cooked smoked Polish sausage, sliced

1 cup French-fried onions (from 2.8-ounce can)

1. Heat oven to 350°. Spray 11 x 7-inch baking dish or 2-quart casserole with cooking spray.

2. In large bowl, mix soup, sour cream and 1 cup cheese. Stir in potatoes, green beans and sausage. Spoon into baking dish. Cover baking dish with aluminum foil or cover casserole with lid.

3. Bake 45 to 55 minutes or until bubbly around edges and potatoes are tender. Sprinkle with onions and remaining $^1/_4$ cup cheese. Bake uncovered 10 to 15 minutes longer or until onions are golden brown.

5 servings.
1 Serving: Calories 495 (Calories from Fat 295); Fat 33g (Saturated 15g); Cholesterol 75mg; Sodium 1,150mg; Carbohydrate 33g (Dietary Fiber 4g); Protein 16g
% Daily Value: Vitamin A 12%; Vitamin C 12%; Calcium 22%; Iron 14%
Exchanges: 2 Starch, 1$^1/_2$ High-Fat Meat, 4 Fat
Carbohydrate Choices: 2

BETTY'S TIPS

⚙ **Kitchen Tip**
If you have only regular sour cream on hand, season the sauce mixture with 1 teaspoon freeze-dried chives and $^1/_4$ teaspoon onion powder.

Onion-Topped Sausage and Potato Dinner

Sweet and Spicy Glazed Ham

Ham and Corn Bread Casserole

Ham and Corn Bread Casserole

Prep Time: 15 min Start to Finish: 1 hr 15 min

2 cups Original Bisquick mix
1 cup finely chopped fully cooked ham
1 cup shredded Cheddar cheese (4 ounces)
$1/4$ cup butter or margarine, melted
8 medium green onions, sliced ($1/2$ cup)
3 eggs, slightly beaten
1 can (14.75 ounces) Green Giant cream-style corn
1 can (11 ounces) Green Giant Mexicorn whole kernel corn, red and green peppers, drained

1. Heat oven to 350°. Spray 11 x 7-inch (2-quart) baking dish with cooking spray.

2. In large bowl, mix all ingredients. Pour into baking dish.

3. Bake uncovered 45 to 55 minutes or until golden brown and set. Let stand 5 minutes before cutting. Cut into squares.

6 to 8 servings.
1 Serving: Calories 500 (Calories from Fat 240); Fat 27g (Saturated 11g); Cholesterol 160mg; Sodium 1,300mg; Carbohydrate 49g (Dietary Fiber 3g); Protein 19g
% Daily Value: Vitamin A 15%; Vitamin C 10%; Calcium 20%; Iron 15%
Exchanges: 3 Starch, $1^1/2$ High-Fat Meat, $2^1/2$ Fat
Carbohydrate Choices: 3

BETTY'S TIPS

⚙ **Kitchen Tip**
Make broccoli slaw to serve with this casserole. Toss purchased broccoli slaw with 2 or 3 thinly sliced green onions and bottled coleslaw dressing.

Low Fat
Sweet and Spicy Glazed Ham

Prep Time: 10 min Start to Finish: 2 hr 25 min

6 to 8 pounds fully cooked smoked bone-in ham
$1/2$ cup packed brown sugar
$1/3$ cup maple-flavored syrup
$1/2$ teaspoon ground mustard
$1/8$ teaspoon ground cinnamon
$1/8$ teaspoon ground ginger
$1/8$ teaspoon ground cloves
Dash of ground nutmeg

1. Heat oven to 325°. Line shallow roasting pan with aluminum foil. Place ham, cut side down, on rack in pan. Insert ovenproof meat thermometer so tip is in thickest part of ham and does not touch bone.

2. Bake uncovered about 1 hour 30 minutes or until thermometer reads 135° to 140°. Meanwhile, in small bowl, mix remaining ingredients. Brush over ham during last 30 minutes of baking.

3. Cover ham loosely with foil and let stand 10 to 15 minutes for easier carving.

20 servings.
1 Serving: Calories 130 (Calories from Fat 35); Fat 4g (Saturated 1g); Cholesterol 35mg; Sodium 800mg; Carbohydrate 10g (Dietary Fiber 0g); Protein 14g
% Daily Value: Vitamin A 0%; Vitamin C 0%; Calcium 0%; Iron 6%
Exchanges: $1/2$ Other Carbohydrate, 2 Very-Lean Meat, $1/2$ Fat
Carbohydrate Choices: $1/2$

BETTY'S TIPS

⚙ **Substitution**
You can use a 4-pound boneless ham instead of the bone-in ham. Remember to reduce the baking time to 1 hour 15 minutes.

⚙ **Special Touch**
Set out a bowl of chutney, honey mustard or pineapple sauce to spoon over the ham.

Quick

Ham Steak with Mustard Glaze

Prep Time: 10 min Start to Finish: 20 min

1 pound ham steak, $^1/_2$ inch thick
1 tablespoon Dijon mustard
1 tablespoon honey
1 tablespoon apricot preserves

1. Heat coals or gas grill for direct heat. Cut outer edge of fat on ham diagonally at 1-inch intervals to prevent curling (do not cut into ham). Mix mustard, honey and preserves.

2. Grill ham uncovered 4 to 6 inches from medium-high heat 4 minutes. Turn ham; brush with mustard mixture. Grill 4 minutes longer. Turn ham; brush with remaining mustard mixture. Grill about 2 minutes longer or until heated through.

4 servings.
1 Serving: Calories 200 (Calories from Fat 80); Fat 9g (Saturated 3g); Cholesterol 55mg; Sodium 1,540mg; Carbohydrate 8g (Dietary Fiber 0g); Protein 22g
% Daily Value: Vitamin A 0%; Vitamin C 0%; Calcium 0%; Iron 8%
Exchanges: $^1/_2$ Fruit, 3 Lean Meat
Carbohydrate Choices: $^1/_2$

BETTY'S TIPS

⚙ **Substitution**
Try using 4 smoked pork chops instead of the ham steak in this recipe.

⚙ **Serve-With**
Creamy coleslaw from the deli and roasted sweet potatoes are tasty accompaniments to this easy entrée. Wrap the sweet potatoes in foil, and start grilling them before you add the ham steak. They'll cook in 30 to 40 minutes over medium heat.

⚙ **Did You Know?**
Ham steak, sometimes labeled "ham slice," is a center-cut piece of ham that's usually fairly lean. Look for it with the other ham in the meat department.

Ham Steak with Mustard Glaze

Beef
Main Dishes

Hearty Choices for Delicious Dinners

Italian Steak and Vegetables (page 190)

Ground Beef Shepherd's Pie with Cheesy Garlic Mashed Potatoes (page 204)

Gorgonzola- and Mushroom-Stuffed Beef Tenderloin with Merlot Sauce

Prep Time: 20 min Start to Finish: 1 hr 20 min

1 beef tenderloin (about 2$^1/_2$ pounds)
1 tablespoon butter or margarine
1 cup sliced fresh mushrooms (3 ounces)
1 cup soft bread crumbs (about 1$^1/_2$ slices bread)
$^1/_2$ cup crumbled Gorgonzola or Roquefort cheese
$^1/_4$ cup chopped parsley
1 tablespoon olive or vegetable oil
$^1/_4$ teaspoon coarse kosher salt, coarse sea salt or regular salt

Merlot Sauce

$^1/_2$ cup currant jelly
$^1/_2$ cup Merlot, Zinfandel or nonalcoholic red wine
$^1/_4$ cup beef broth
1 tablespoon butter or margarine

1. Heat oven to 425°. To cut beef so that it can be filled and rolled, cut horizontally down length of beef, about $^1/_2$ inch from top of beef, to within $^1/_2$ inch of opposite side; open flat. Flip beef over. Repeat with other side of beef, open flat.

2. In 10-inch skillet, melt 1 tablespoon butter over medium-high heat. Cook mushrooms in butter, stirring occasionally, until tender and liquid has evaporated. Cool 5 minutes. Add bread crumbs, cheese and parsley; toss to combine.

3. Sprinkle bread crumb mixture over beef to within 1 inch of edges. Tightly roll up beef, beginning with long side. Turn small end of beef under about 6 inches, so it cooks evenly. Tie beef with kitchen string at about 1$^1/_2$-inch intervals. In shallow roasting pan, place beef, seam side down, on rack. Brush with oil; sprinkle with salt. Insert ovenproof meat thermometer so tip is in center of thickest part of beef.

4. Bake uncovered 30 to 40 minutes or until thermometer reads at least 140°. Cover beef loosely with aluminum foil and let stand about 15 minutes or until

thermometer reads 145°. (Temperature will continue to rise about 5°, and beef will be easier to carve.)

5. Meanwhile, in 1-quart saucepan, heat all sauce ingredients to boiling, stirring occasionally; reduce heat to low. Simmer uncovered 35 to 40 minutes, stirring occasionally, until sauce is slightly reduced and syrupy. Remove string from beef before carving. Serve beef with sauce.

8 servings.
1 Serving: Calories 350 (Calories from Fat 155); Fat 17g (Saturated 8g); Cholesterol 95mg; Sodium 380mg; Carbohydrate 16g (Dietary Fiber 1g); Protein 33g
% Daily Value: Vitamin A 8%; Vitamin C 2%; Calcium 8%; Iron 18%
Exchanges: 1 Other Carbohydrate, 4$^1/_2$ Lean Meat, 1 Fat
Carbohydrate Choices: 1

Cut down length of beef, about $^1/_2$ inch from top, to within $^1/_2$ inch of opposite side; open flat.

Flip beef over; cut down length of beef to within $^1/_2$ inch of opposite edge; open flat.

Gorgonzola- and Mushroom-Stuffed Beef Tenderloin with Merlot Sauce

Beef Tenderloin with Pear-Cranberry Chutney

Prep Time: 40 min Start to Finish: 40 min

$^1/_2$ large red onion, thinly sliced
  2 cloves garlic, finely chopped
  2 tablespoons dry red wine or grape juice
  2 firm ripe pears, peeled, diced
$^1/_2$ cup fresh or frozen cranberries
  2 tablespoons packed brown sugar
$^1/_2$ teaspoon pumpkin pie spice
  4 beef tenderloin steaks, about 1 inch thick
    (1 pound)

1. Heat 12-inch nonstick skillet over medium-high heat. Cook onion, garlic and wine in skillet about 5 minutes, stirring frequently, until onion is tender but not brown.

2. Stir in pears, cranberries, brown sugar and pumpkin pie spice; reduce heat. Simmer uncovered about 10 minutes, stirring frequently, until cranberries burst. Place chutney in small bowl; set aside.

3. In same skillet, cook beef over medium heat about 8 minutes for medium doneness, turning once. Serve with chutney.

4 servings.
1 Serving: Calories 260 (Calories from Fat 80); Fat 8g (Saturated 3g); Cholesterol 65mg; Sodium 60mg; Carbohydrate 23g (Dietary Fiber 4g); Protein 25g
% Daily Value: Vitamin A 2%; Vitamin C 6%; Calcium 4%; Iron 15%
Exchanges: 1 Fruit, $^1/_2$ Other Carbohydrate, $3^1/_2$ Lean Meat
Carbohydrate Choices: $1^1/_2$

BETTY'S TIPS

⊗ **Kitchen Tip**
By selecting small portions of lean red meat cuts (round tip, eye of round, top round, top loin, tenderloin and sirloin), you can enjoy meat as part of a healthy diet.

Beef Tenderloin with Pear-Cranberry Chutney

Garlic and Mushroom Beef Roast

Prep Time: 10 min Start to Finish: 11 hr 10 min

3- to 4- pound beef boneless rump or tip roast
1 teaspoon salt
2 cloves garlic, finely chopped
8 ounces small whole fresh mushrooms
1/2 cup sun-dried tomatoes in oil, drained and chopped
1/2 cup light Italian dressing

1. Spray 12-inch nonstick skillet with cooking spray. If roast beef comes in netting or is tied, do not remove. Sprinkle beef with salt and garlic. Cook beef in skillet over medium-high heat 5 to 6 minutes, turning occasionally, until brown on all sides.

2. Spray 4- to 5-quart slow cooker with cooking spray. Place mushrooms in cooker. Place beef on mushrooms. Spread tomatoes over beef. Pour dressing over mixture in cooker.

3. Cover and cook on Low heat setting 9 to 11 hours.

4. Place beef on cutting board; remove netting or strings. Slice beef. Serve mushrooms and juices with beef.

6 servings.
1 Serving: Calories 305 (Calories from Fat 100); Fat 11g (Saturated 3g); Cholesterol 120mg; Sodium 640mg; Carbohydrate 5g (Dietary Fiber 1g); Protein 47g
% Daily Value: Vitamin A 4%; Vitamin C 8%; Calcium 2%; Iron 26%
Exchanges: 1 Vegetable, 6 Very Lean Meat, 1 1/2 Fat
Carbohydrate Choices: 0

Garlic and Mushroom Beef Roast

BETTY'S TIPS

⚙ **Serve-With**
This roast is scrumptious with roasted red potato quarters sprinkled with rosemary or thyme. Round out the meal with a salad of baby spinach with herbed vinaigrette dressing.

⚙ **Variation**
For wonderful comfort food, use this beef for hot roast beef sandwiches. Or serve it thinly sliced on hearty bread with mayo, Dijon mustard, sliced red onion and lettuce.

⚙ **Special Touch**
Arrange the meat on a platter, spoon the mushrooms around it and then tuck sprigs of fresh rosemary or basil around the food for a splash of color.

Beer-Marinated Rump Roast

Prep Time: 20 min Start to Finish: 10 hr 35 min

2 tablespoons olive or vegetable oil

1 medium onion, chopped ($^1/_2$ cup)

1 clove garlic, finely chopped

$^1/_2$ cup chili sauce

$^1/_2$ teaspoon salt

$^1/_4$ teaspoon pepper

1 can or bottle (12 ounces) regular or nonalcoholic beer

$3^1/_2$- to 4- pound beef rolled rump roast

2 cups hickory wood chips

1. Heat oil in 1-quart saucepan over medium-high heat. Cook onion and garlic in oil, stirring frequently, until onion is tender; remove from heat. Stir in chili sauce, salt, pepper and beer.

2. Place beef in shallow glass or plastic dish or resealable plastic food-storage bag. Pour beer mixture over beef; turn beef to coat. Cover dish or seal bag and refrigerate, turning beef occasionally, at least 8 hours but no longer than 24 hours.

3. Cover wood chips with water in small bowl; soak 30 minutes. If using charcoal grill, place drip pan directly under grilling area, and arrange coals around edge of firebox. Heat coals or gas grill for indirect heat.

4. Remove beef from marinade; reserve marinade. Insert spit rod lengthwise through center of beef; hold firmly in place with adjustable holding forks. Insert barbecue meat thermometer so tip is near center of beef but not touching spit rod. Drain wood chips. Add about $^1/_2$ cup wood chips to medium-low coals or lava rock.

5. Cover and grill beef on rotisserie over drip pan or over unheated side of gas grill over medium-low heat about 2 hours for medium doneness (160°), brushing occasionally with marinade and adding $^1/_2$ cup wood chips to coals or rock every 30 minutes. Remove spit rod, holding forks and thermometer. Discard any remaining marinade. Cover beef with aluminum foil and let stand 15 minutes before slicing.

Beer-Marinated Rump Roast

8 servings.
1 Serving: Calories 260 (Calories from Fat 80); Fat 9g (Saturated 2g); Cholesterol 105mg; Sodium 310mg; Carbohydrate 4g (Dietary Fiber 0g); Protein 40g
% Daily Value: Vitamin A 4%; Vitamin C 2%; Calcium 0%; Iron 20%
Exchanges: 5 Very Lean Meat
Carbohydrate Choices: 0

BETTY'S TIPS

⊘ **Substitution**
If you prefer not to use alcoholic beer, use nonalcoholic beer in the marinade. You can also substitute apple juice for the beer.

⊘ **Success Hint**
If you don't have a rotisserie for the roast, place it right on the grill over the drip pan or on the unheated side of a gas grill, and grill as directed.

Grilled Tequila-Lime Steak

Prep Time: 40 min Start to Finish: 6 hr 40 min

2 pounds beef boneless top round steak, about 1 inch thick
Tequila Marinade (right)
1 cup Old El Paso Thick 'n Chunky salsa

1. Pierce beef with fork several times on both sides. Make Tequilla Marinade in shallow glass or plastic dish or resealable plastic food-storage bag. Add beef; turn to coat. Cover dish or seal bag and refrigerate, turning beef occasionally, at least 6 hours but not longer than 24 hours.

2. Heat coals or gas grill for direct heat. Remove beef from marinade; reserve marinade. Cover and grill beef over medium heat 20 to 25 minutes for medium doneness, brushing occasionally with marinade and turning once. Discard any remaining marinade.

3. Cut beef across grain into thin slices. Serve with salsa.

8 servings.

Tequila Marinade
1/4 cup lime juice
2 tablespoons olive or vegetable oil
2 tablespoons tequila
1/2 teaspoon salt
1/2 teaspoon ground cumin
1/2 teaspoon ground red pepper (cayenne)
2 cloves garlic, finely chopped

Mix all ingredients.

1 Serving: Calories 155 (Calories from Fat 65); Fat 7g (Saturated 2g); Cholesterol 55mg; Sodium 250mg; Carbohydrate 3g (Dietary Fiber 1g); Protein 21g
% Daily Value: Vitamin A 2%; Vitamin C 10%; Calcium 0%; Iron 12%
Exchanges: 3 Lean Meat
Carbohydrate Choices: 0

BETTY'S TIPS

⚙ **Substitution**
If you don't have any tequila on hand, you can use lime juice instead.

⚙ **Success Hint**
Although round steak is a very flavorful cut of beef, it is very lean, so it benefits from an overnight marinating to help tenderize it.

⚙ **Did You Know?**
Piercing the meat with the tines of a fork helps the marinade penetrate the meat.

Grilled Tequila-Lime Steak

Italian Steak and Vegetables

Prep Time: 25 min Start to Finish: 40 min
(Photo on page 183)

1/2 cup balsamic vinaigrette dressing
1/4 cup chopped fresh basil leaves
1 1/2 teaspoons peppered seasoned salt
2 beef boneless New York strip steaks, about 1 inch thick (8 to 10 ounces each)
1 pound asparagus spears, cut into 2-inch pieces
1 medium red onion, cut into thin wedges
1 yellow bell pepper, cut into 8 pieces

1. Mix 2 tablespoons of the dressing, 2 tablespoons of the basil and 3/4 teaspoon of the peppered seasoned salt in large bowl; set aside for vegetables. Mix remaining dressing, basil and peppered seasoned salt in shallow glass or plastic dish or resealable plastic food-storage bag; add beef. Cover dish or seal bag and refrigerate 15 minutes.

2. Heat coals or gas grill for direct heat. Add asparagus, onion and bell pepper to reserved dressing mixture; toss to coat. Place in disposable 8-inch square foil pan or grill basket (grill "wok"). Reserve dressing in bowl.

3. Remove beef from marinade; reserve marinade. Cover and grill pan of vegetables 4 to 6 inches from medium heat 5 minutes. Add beef to grill next to pan. Cover and grill beef and vegetables 10 to 12 minutes, turning beef once and stirring vegetables occasionally, until beef is desired doneness and vegetables are tender. Brush beef with reserved marinade during last 5 minutes of cooking.

4. Add vegetables to bowl with reserved dressing; toss to coat. Cut beef into thin slices. Discard any remaining marinade. Serve vegetables with beef. Drizzle with additional dressing if desired.

4 servings.
1 Serving: Calories 210 (Calories from Fat 70); Fat 8g (Saturated 3g); Cholesterol 65mg; Sodium 400mg; Carbohydrate 8g (Dietary Fiber 2g); Protein 27g
% Daily Value: Vitamin A 16%; Vitamin C 58%; Calcium 2%; Iron 16%
Exchanges: 1 Vegetable, 3 1/2 Lean Meat
Carbohydrate Choices: 1/2

BETTY'S TIPS

⊘ **Substitution**
Experiment with different colors of bell peppers, such as red, green or orange, or use a combination of colors. Whole mushrooms are tasty in the vegetable mix too.

⊘ **Success Hint**
When handling the steak, use tongs or a spatula instead of a fork so you don't pierce the meat and release the juices during cooking.

⊘ **Special Touch**
Arrange the sliced steak on a small platter and sprinkle with chopped fresh basil, or tuck some basil sprigs between the slices.

Steak Marsala

Prep Time: 20 min Start to Finish: 20 min

4 beef tenderloin steaks, $3/4$ inch thick
(about 1 pound)
$1/2$ teaspoon salt
$1/4$ teaspoon pepper
2 cloves garlic, crushed
1 tablespoon capers, drained
$1/2$ cup Marsala wine or nonalcoholic red wine

1. Sprinkle both sides of each beef steak with salt and pepper. Rub with garlic. Spray 10-inch skillet with cooking spray; heat over medium-high heat. Add beef; cook 6 to 8 minutes, turning once, until desired doneness. Remove beef from skillet; cover to keep warm.

2. Add capers and wine to skillet. Heat to boiling over high heat. Cook uncovered 3 to 4 minutes, stirring frequently, until liquid is slightly reduced. Serve sauce over beef.

4 servings.
1 Serving: Calories 225 (Calories from Fat 110); Fat 12g (Saturated 3g); Cholesterol 65mg; Sodium 410mg; Carbohydrate 4g (Dietary Fiber 0g); Protein 25g
% Daily Value: Vitamin A 2%; Vitamin C 0%; Calcium 0%; Iron 12%
Exchanges: $3^1/2$ Lean Meat, $1/2$ Fat
Carbohydrate Choices: 0

BETTY'S TIPS

⚙ **Kitchen Tip**
Wondering what to serve with these saucy steaks? Try them with New Potatoes and Spring Vegetables, page 216.

Steak Marsala

Garlic Cube Steaks

Prep Time: 15 min Start to Finish: 45 min

1/3 cup fat-free egg product

2 large cloves garlic, crushed

15 fat-free saltine crackers, crushed (1/2 cup)

4 beef boneless cube steaks (about 1 pound)

1/4 teaspoon salt

1/4 teaspoon garlic pepper

2 tablespoons vegetable oil

1 medium onion, sliced

3/4 cup 50%-less-sodium beef broth

2 teaspoons cornstarch

2 tablespoons chopped parsley, if desired

1. In shallow dish, mix egg product and garlic. In another shallow dish, place cracker crumbs. Sprinkle both sides of beef steaks with salt and garlic pepper. Dip both sides of each steak into egg product mixture, then coat with cracker crumbs.

2. In 12-inch nonstick skillet, heat 1 tablespoon of oil over medium-high heat. Add beef; cook about 2 minutes or until brown. Turn beef, adding some of the remaining 1 tablespoon oil under each steak. Cook about 2 minutes longer or until brown. Add onion.

Reduce heat to low. Cover and cook about 30 minutes or until beef is tender. Remove beef from skillet; cover to keep warm.

3. Meanwhile, in small bowl, mix broth and cornstarch. Add to skillet; heat to boiling; stirring constantly. Serve sauce over beef; sprinkle with parsley.

4 servings.

1 Serving: Calories 260 (Calories from Fat 100); Fat 11g (Saturated 2g); Cholesterol 60mg; Sodium 430mg; Carbohydrate 13g (Dietary Fiber 1g); Protein 27g
% Daily Value: Vitamin A 6%; Vitamin C 4%; Calcium 2%; Iron 18%
Exchanges: 1 Starch, 3 1/2 Lean Meat
Carbohydrate Choices: 1

BETTY'S TIPS

✪ Kitchen Tip

Baked potatoes topped with fat-free sour cream and chopped onions are a hearty side with this meaty main dish.

To crush the crackers, place them in a resealable plastic food-storage bag and roll them with a rolling pin. Or you can pulse them in a food processor.

Garlic Cube Steaks

Herbed Salisbury Mushroom Steaks

Prep Time: 25 min Start to Finish: 35 min

1 package (8 ounces) sliced fresh mushrooms (3 cups)

1 pound extra-lean (at least 90%) ground beef

1/4 cup Progresso® plain bread crumbs

1/4 cup fat-free egg product

1/4 cup fat-free (skim) milk

3/4 teaspoon dried thyme leaves

3 tablespoons ketchup

2 teaspoons vegetable oil

1 jar (12 ounces) fat-free beef gravy

1. Finely chop 1 cup of the mushrooms. In medium bowl, mix chopped mushrooms, beef, bread crumbs, egg product, milk, thyme and 1 tablespoon of the ketchup. Shape mixture into 5 oval patties, 1/2 inch thick.

2. Heat oil in 12-inch nonstick skillet over medium-high heat. Add patties; cook about 5 minutes, turning once, until browned.

3. Add remaining sliced mushrooms, 2 tablespoons ketchup and the gravy. Heat to boiling; reduce heat to low. Cover and cook 5 to 10 minutes or until meat thermometer inserted in center of patties reads 160° and patties are no longer pink in center.

5 servings.

1 Serving: Calories 235 (Calories from Fat 80); Fat 9g (Saturated 3g); Cholesterol 50mg; Sodium 630mg; Carbohydrate 13g (Dietary Fiber 1g); Protein 25g
% Daily Value: Vitamin A 4%; Vitamin C 2%; Calcium 4%; Iron 16%
Exchanges: 1 Starch, 3 Lean Meat
Carbohydrate Choices: 1

BETTY'S TIPS

⊘ **Kitchen Tip**
Round out this homey meal with a side of steamed green beans and a simple mixed-greens salad.

Garnish with a sprig of fresh thyme for a splash of color and flavor.

Herbed Salisbury Mushroom Steaks

Chicken Fried Steak with Country Gravy

Chicken Fried Steak with Country Gravy

Prep Time: 40 min Start to Finish: 40 min

- 1/4 cup Gold Medal all-purpose flour
- 1/2 teaspoon seasoned salt
- 1/2 teaspoon pepper
- 2 eggs
- 2 tablespoons milk
- 18 saltine crackers, finely crushed (3/4 cup)
- 4 beef round steaks (cube steaks), 4 to 6 ounces each
- 1/4 cup vegetable oil
- 1 cup Country Gravy (right) or gravy made from a package

1. Heat oven to 225°. In shallow dish, mix flour, seasoned salt and pepper. In another shallow dish, beat eggs and milk with fork. Place cracker crumbs on a sheet of waxed paper.

2. Dip beef steaks in flour mixture, coating well; shake off excess. Dip floured beef in egg mixture, then in cracker crumbs, turning to coat completely; shake off excess.

3. In 12-inch skillet, heat oil over medium heat until hot. Cook beef in oil 12 to 14 minutes, turning once, until golden brown. Remove from skillet to wire rack placed on 15 x 10-inch pan with sides. Keep steaks warm in oven while making gravy.

4. Make Country Gravy. Spoon 1/4 cup gravy over each steak.

4 servings.
1 Serving: Calories 405 (Calories from Fat 205); Fat 23g (Saturated 5g); Cholesterol 160mg; Sodium 580mg; Carbohydrate 20g (Dietary Fiber 1g); Protein 30g
% Daily Value: Vitamin A 6%; Vitamin C 0%; Calcium 12%; Iron 18%
Exchanges: 1 Starch, 4 Medium-Fat Meat, 1/2 Fat
Carbohydrate Choices: 1

BETTY'S TIPS

⊘ **Kitchen Tip**
Pair this easy supper with a bagged salad tossed with a tangy dressing such as raspberry vinaigrette, or serve with a fresh fruit salad.

Quick & Low-Fat
Country Gravy

Prep Time: 15 min Start to Finish: 15 min

- 1 tablespoon vegetable oil
- 2 tablespoons Gold Medal all-purpose flour
- 1 cup milk
- 1/4 teaspoon salt
- 1/4 teaspoon pepper

1. After removing cooked meat from skillet or pan, add oil to drippings in skillet. Stir in flour, scraping up brown particles. Cook over medium-high heat 2 to 3 minutes, stirring constantly, until mixture is light golden brown.

2. Stir in milk. Heat over medium-high heat, stirring constantly, until mixture is boiling and thickened. If gravy is too thick, stir in more milk, 1 tablespoon at a time, until desired consistency. Stir in salt and pepper.

1 cup gravy.
1 Tablespoon: Calories 35 (Calories from Fat 20); Fat 2g (Saturated 1g); Cholesterol 0mg; Sodium 90mg; Carbohydrate 3g (Dietary Fiber 0g); Protein 1g
% Daily Value: Vitamin A 0%; Vitamin C 0%; Calcium 4%; Iron 0%
Exchanges: 1/2 Fat
Carbohydrate Choices: 0

Stir in flour, scraping up brown particles.

Spicy Beef Stir-Fry

Prep Time: 25 min Start to Finish: 55 min

1 pound beef boneless eye of round steak, trimmed of fat

1/4 cup citrus vinaigrette dressing

1/4 teaspoon ground red pepper (cayenne)

2 tablespoons reduced-sodium soy sauce

4 ounces uncooked fettuccine

1 can (8 ounces) bamboo shoots, drained

1 medium red bell pepper, cut into 1-inch pieces

1 cup 50%-less-sodium beef broth

1 tablespoon cornstarch

1. Cut beef diagonally across grain into thin bite-size strips. In large resealable plastic food-storage bag, mix dressing, ground red pepper and soy sauce; add beef. Seal bag; turn to coat. Refrigerate at least 30 minutes but no longer than 24 hours.

2. Cook and drain fettuccine as directed on package. Meanwhile, spray 10-inch skillet with cooking spray; heat over medium-high heat. Add beef mixture; cook about 5 minutes, stirring occasionally, until beef is browned. Add bamboo shoots and bell pepper; cook about 2 minutes, stirring occasionally, until bell pepper is tender.

3. In small bowl, mix broth and cornstarch. Add to skillet. Heat to boiling; boil and stir about 1 minute or until thickened. Serve over fettuccine.

4 servings (1 cup each).
1 Serving: Calories 330 (Calories from Fat 90); Fat 10g (Saturated 2g); Cholesterol 60mg; Sodium 450mg; Carbohydrate 3`g (Dietary Fiber 4g); Protein 29g
% Daily Value: Vitamin A 36%; Vitamin C 48%; Calcium 2%; Iron 20%
Exchanges: 2 Starch, 3 Lean Meat
Carbohydrate Choices: 2

BETTY'S TIPS

⚙ **Kitchen Tip**
Freezing the steak for about 30 minutes will make it easier to slice. For the tenderest meat, slice it at a diagonal across the grain.

If you have Asian dressing on hand, you can use it instead of the citrus vinaigrette.

Spicy Beef Stir-Fry

Low Fat

Sichuan Beef and Bean Sprouts

Prep Time: 10 min Start to Finish: 35 min

  1 pound beef boneless eye of round steak, trimmed of fat
 1/4 cup 33%-less-sodium chicken broth
  1 tablespoon soy sauce
  1 tablespoon Sichuan (or Szechuan) sauce
 1/8 teaspoon crushed red pepper flakes
  4 roma (plum) tomatoes, cut into eighths
  2 cups fresh bean sprouts (4 ounces)
  1 tablespoon chopped fresh cilantro

1. Cut beef with grain into 2-inch strips; cut strips across grain into 1/8-inch slices. (Beef is easier to cut if partially frozen, 30 to 60 minutes.) In medium bowl, mix broth, soy sauce, Sichuan sauce and red pepper. Stir in beef. Let stand 10 minutes.

2. Drain beef; reserve marinade. Heat 12-inch nonstick skillet over medium-high heat. Add half of beef to skillet; stir-fry 2 to 3 minutes or until brown. Remove beef from skillet. Repeat with remaining beef. Return all beef to skillet.

3. Add reserved marinade, tomatoes and bean sprouts to beef in skillet; stir-fry about 1 minute or until vegetables are warm. Sprinkle with cilantro.

4 servings (1 1/4 cups each).
1 Serving: Calories 185 (Calories from Fat 55); Fat 6g (Saturated 2g); Cholesterol 60mg; Sodium 420mg; Carbohydrate 6g (Dietary Fiber 1g); Protein 27g
% Daily Value: Vitamin A 10%; Vitamin C 12%; Calcium 2%; Iron 16%
Exchanges: 1 Vegetable, 3 1/2 Very Lean Meat, 1 Fat
Carbohydrate Choices: 1/2

BETTY'S TIPS

⚙ **Kitchen Tip**
If fresh bean sprouts are not available, a 14-ounce can of bean sprouts can be substituted. Drain the sprouts and rinse to freshen them.

Many stir-fries are high fat because the foods are cooked in hot oil. Using a nonstick skillet keeps the food from sticking and eliminates the fat.

Sichuan Beef and Bean Sprouts

Low Fat

Philly Cheese Steak Casserole

Prep Time: 25 min Start to Finish: 1 hr 15 min

3 cups uncooked dumpling or wide egg noodles (6 ounces)

1 pound beef boneless sirloin steak, about $3/4$ inch thick

$1/4$ teaspoon pepper

2 medium onions, chopped (1 cup)

1 small green bell pepper, chopped ($1/2$ cup)

1 can (14 ounces) fat-free beef broth

$1/4$ cup Gold Medal all-purpose flour

$1/2$ cup fat-free half-and-half

1 tablespoon Dijon mustard

$3/4$ cup shredded reduced-fat Cheddar cheese (3 ounces)

1. Heat oven to 350°. Spray 11 x 7-inch (2-quart) baking dish with cooking spray. Cook and drain noodles as directed on package.

2. Meanwhile, remove fat from beef. Cut beef into $3/4$-inch pieces. Heat 12-inch nonstick skillet over medium heat. Cook beef and pepper in skillet 2 to 3 minutes, stirring occasionally, until beef is brown. Stir in onions and bell pepper. Cook 2 minutes, stirring occasionally. Spoon into baking dish.

3. In medium bowl, beat broth and flour with wire whisk until smooth. Add to skillet; heat to boiling. Cook, stirring constantly, until mixture thickens; remove from heat. Stir in half-and-half and mustard. Spoon over beef mixture. Stir in cooked noodles.

4. Cover and bake 40 minutes. Sprinkle with cheese. Bake uncovered about 10 minutes longer or until cheese is melted and casserole is bubbly.

6 servings ($1^1/_3$ cups each).
1 Serving: Calories 260 (Calories from Fat 45); Fat 5g (Saturated 2g); Cholesterol 65mg; Sodium 540mg; Carbohydrate 30g (Dietary Fiber 2g); Protein 24g
% Daily Value: Vitamin A 4%; Vitamin C 10%; Calcium 12%; Iron 16%
Exchanges: 2 Starch, $2^1/_2$ Very Lean Meat, $1/2$ Fat
Carbohydrate Choices: 2

BETTY'S TIPS

❂ **Kitchen Tip**
To test pasta for doneness, run a piece under cold water, then bite into it. It's done if it's still slightly firm.

Spraying the baking dish with cooking spray allows the food to release easily and makes cleanup a snap.

Philly Cheese Steak Casserole

Italian-Style Shepherd's Pie

Prep Time: 20 min Start to Finish: 50 min

1 pound beef boneless sirloin, trimmed of fat, cut into 1-inch cubes

1 cup sliced onions (about 1 medium)

2 medium carrots, sliced (1 cup)

$1/2$ teaspoon seasoned salt

$1/4$ teaspoon pepper

$1^1/2$ cups sliced fresh mushrooms

1 jar (14 ounces) tomato pasta sauce (any variety) ($1^1/2$ cups)

$1/2$ package (7.2-ounce size) Betty Crocker® roasted garlic mashed potatoes (1 pouch)

1 cup hot water

$2/3$ cup milk

2 tablespoons butter or margarine

2 tablespoons shredded fresh Parmesan cheese

1. Heat oven to 375°. Spray 2-quart casserole or 11 x 7-inch baking dish with cooking spray. Heat 12-inch nonstick skillet over medium-high heat. Add beef, onions and carrots to skillet; sprinkle with seasoned salt and pepper. Cook 3 to 5 minutes, stirring frequently, until beef is brown.

2. Stir in mushrooms and pasta sauce. Heat to boiling. Cook over medium heat 5 minutes, stirring occasionally. Spread in casserole.

3. Make potatoes as directed on package for 4 servings, using 1 pouch Potatoes and Seasoning, water, milk and butter. Spoon into 8 mounds around edge of hot beef mixture. Sprinkle cheese over all.

4. Bake uncovered 25 to 30 minutes or until bubbly and potatoes are light golden brown.

4 servings ($1^1/2$ cups each).
1 Serving: Calories 425 (Calories from Fat 135); Fat 15g (Saturated 6g); Cholesterol 80mg; Sodium 860mg; Carbohydrate 48g (Dietary Fiber 5g); Protein 30g
% Daily Value: Vitamin A 100%; Vitamin C 34%; Calcium 14%; Iron 20%
Exchanges: $2^1/2$ Starch, 2 Vegetable, 3 Lean Meat
Carbohydrate Choices: 3

BETTY'S TIPS

⊕ **Kitchen Tip**
Add a dash of color by sprinkling the top of this casserole with about 2 tablespoons of chopped parsley before serving.

Italian-Style Shepherd's Pie

Plum Barbecue Short Ribs

Prep Time: 35 min Start to Finish: 6 hr 15 min

- 2 tablespoons vegetable oil
- 4 pounds beef short ribs
- 1 large sweet onion (such as Bermuda, Maui or Spanish), cut in half and sliced
- 1 bottle (12 ounces) chili sauce
- $^3/_4$ cup plum preserves
- 2 tablespoons packed brown sugar
- 2 tablespoons Dijon mustard
- 2 tablespoons red wine vinegar
- 2 tablespoons Worcestershire sauce
- $^1/_4$ teaspoon ground cloves

1. Heat oil in 12-inch skillet over medium-high heat. Cook ribs in oil, in batches if necessary, 8 to 10 minutes, turning occasionally, until brown on all sides.

2. Place ribs and onion in 5- to 6-quart slow cooker. Cover and cook on Low heat setting 4 hours 30 minutes to 5 hours 30 minutes.

3. About 30 minutes before ribs are done, cook remaining ingredients in 2-quart saucepan over medium heat 15 to 20 minutes, stirring frequently, until sauce has thickened.

4. Drain excess liquid from cooker. Pour sauce over ribs. Increase heat setting to High. Cover and cook 25 to 35 minutes or until hot.

6 servings.
1 Serving: Calories 500 (Calories from Fat 190); Fat 21g (Saturated 7g); Cholesterol 70mg; Sodium 1,050mg; Carbohydrate 54g (Dietary Fiber 2g); Protein 24g
% Daily Value: Vitamin A 18%; Vitamin C 12%; Calcium 4%; Iron 16%
Exchanges: 1 Fruit, 2$^1/_2$ Other Carbohydrate, 3 Medium-Fat Meat, 1$^1/_2$ Fat
Carbohydrate Choices: 3$^1/_2$

BETTY'S TIPS

⊕ **Do-Ahead**
Make the sauce up to 2 days ahead of your get-together, and store covered in the fridge. Reheat the sauce before pouring it over the ribs as directed in step 4.

⊕ **Special Touch**
Serve these ribs arranged on a pretty platter garnished with orange or lemon slices.

⊕ **Did You Know?**
Barbecue sauce traditionally is made with tomatoes, onion, mustard, garlic, brown sugar and vinegar. Adding the plum preserves lends a touch of sweetness to this sauce.

Plum Barbecue Short Ribs

Tex-Mex Meat Loaf

Prep Time: 10 min Start to Finish: 1 hr 10 min

1½ pounds extra-lean (at least 90%) ground beef

1 can (10 ounces) diced tomatoes and green chilies, undrained

¼ cup fat-free egg product

¼ cup Progresso plain bread crumbs

1 teaspoon salt-free garlic-and-herb seasoning

1 teaspoon chili powder

1 teaspoon ground cumin

Old El Paso Thick 'n Chunky salsa, if desired

1. Heat oven to 375°. In large bowl, mix all ingredients except salsa. Spoon mixture into 11 x 7-inch (2-quart) baking dish; or pat into 9 x 5-inch loaf.

2. Bake uncovered about 1 hour or until meat thermometer inserted in center reads 160°. Drain any liquid before slicing. Serve with salsa.

6 servings.

1 Serving: Calories 200 (Calories from Fat 70); Fat 8g (Saturated 3g); Cholesterol 65mg; Sodium 190mg; Carbohydrate 6g (Dietary Fiber 1g); Protein 26g
% Daily Value: Vitamin A 4%; Vitamin C 4%; Calcium 2%; Iron 16%
Exchanges: 1 Vegetable, 3½ Very Lean Meat, 1 Fat
Carbohydrate Choices: ½

BETTY'S TIPS

⚙ **Kitchen Tip**
You can make this meat loaf in a 9 x 5-inch loaf pan, but patting it into a loaf in a slightly larger pan allows a nice brown surface to form on the top and sides.

Tex-Mex Meat Loaf

Quick
Ground Beef Chow Mein

Prep Time: 25 min Start to Finish: 25 min

1   pound lean (at least 80%) ground beef
2   cups thinly sliced celery (3$^1/_2$ medium ribs)
1   medium red bell pepper, coarsely chopped (1 cup)
1   can (8 ounces) sliced water chestnuts, drained
1   bottle (12 ounces) teriyaki baste and glaze
2   cups coleslaw mix (shredded cabbage and carrots)
3   cups chow mein noodles

1. In 12-inch nonstick skillet, cook beef over medium-high heat 5 to 7 minutes, stirring frequently, until beef is cooked through and no pink remains. Stir in celery and bell pepper. Cook 3 to 4 minutes, stirring frequently, until vegetables are crisp-tender; drain.

2. Stir water chestnuts and teriyaki glaze into beef mixture. Cook about 2 minutes, stirring frequently, until hot and bubbly. Remove from heat.

3. Stir in coleslaw mix. Serve over noodles.

6 servings (1$^1/_4$ cups each).
1 Serving: Calories 380 (Calories from Fat 160); Fat 18g (Saturated 5g); Cholesterol 45mg; Sodium 1,460mg; Carbohydrate 34g (Dietary Fiber 4g); Protein 21g
% Daily Value: Vitamin A 60%; Vitamin C 42%; Calcium 6%; Iron 22%
Exchanges: 1$^1/_2$ Starch, 2 Vegetable, 2 Medium-Fat Meat, 1$^1/_2$ Fat
Carbohydrate Choices: 2

BETTY'S TIPS

❂ **Kitchen Tip**
The fat from the ground beef is just enough to cook the vegetables evenly. That's why it's drained off after the vegetables are cooked.

Add an Asian flair with hot cooked rice and a salad of sliced kiwifruit and chunks of fresh pineapple.

Deluxe Pizza Goulash

Prep Time: 40 min Start to Finish: 40 min

2   cups uncooked elbow macaroni (8 ounces)
$^1/_2$ pound lean (at least 80%) ground beef
1   small onion, chopped ($^1/_4$ cup)
1   package (3.5 ounces) sliced pepperoni
1   jar (4.5 ounces) Green Giant sliced mushrooms, drained
2   cans (15 ounces each) pizza sauce
1   cup shredded mozzarella cheese (4 ounces)

1. Cook and drain macaroni as directed on package.

2. Meanwhile, in 12-inch skillet, cook beef and onion over medium-high heat 5 to 7 minutes, stirring frequently, until beef is brown; drain. Stir in macaroni, pepperoni, mushrooms and pizza sauce.

3. Cover and cook over medium heat 8 to 10 minutes, stirring occasionally, until hot. Remove from heat. Sprinkle with cheese. Cover and let stand 2 to 3 minutes or until cheese is melted.

6 servings (1$^1/_3$ cups each).
1 Serving: Calories 465 (Calories from Fat 200); Fat 22g (Saturated 8g); Cholesterol 45mg; Sodium 1,160mg; Carbohydrate 42g (Dietary Fiber 4g); Protein 23g
% Daily Value: Vitamin A 16%; Vitamin C 24%; Calcium 20%; Iron 20%
Exchanges: 2$^1/_2$ Starch, 1 Vegetable, 2 Medium-Fat Meat, 2 Fat
Carbohydrate Choices: 3

BETTY'S TIPS

❂ **Kitchen Tip**
Don't have pizza sauce on hand? Use a 26-ounce jar of tomato pasta sauce instead. You can spice up the flavor with a pinch of dried oregano.

Deluxe Pizza Goulash

Ground Beef Chow Mein

Ground Beef Shepherd's Pie with Cheesy Garlic Mashed Potatoes

Prep Time: 25 min Start to Finish: 1 hr 5 min
(Photo on page 183)

1 pouch Betty Crocker roasted garlic mashed potato mix (from 7.2-ounce package)

$1^1/_4$ cups hot water

$^2/_3$ cup milk

2 tablespoons butter or margarine

1 pound lean (at least 80%) ground beef

1 medium onion, chopped ($^1/_2$ cup)

1 can ($10^3/_4$ ounces) condensed golden mushroom soup

2 cups Green Giant frozen mixed vegetables (from 1-pound bag), thawed and drained

$1^1/_2$ cups shredded American-Cheddar cheese blend (6 ounces)

1. Heat oven to 400°. Spray 2-quart casserole with cooking spray. Make potato mix as directed on package for 4 servings, using hot water, milk and butter.

2. In 10-inch nonstick skillet, cook beef and onion over medium-high heat 5 to 7 minutes, stirring frequently, until beef is brown; drain. Stir in soup, vegetables and 1 cup of cheese until cheese is melted.

3. Spoon beef mixture into casserole. Spoon potatoes around edge of beef mixture. Sprinkle remaining $^1/_2$ cup cheese over potatoes.

4. Bake uncovered 35 to 40 minutes or until mixture is heated through, potatoes are beginning to brown and cheese is melted.

6 servings ($1^1/_2$ cups each).
1 Serving: Calories 440 (Calories from Fat 250); Fat 28g (Saturated 14g); Cholesterol 85mg; Sodium 630mg; Carbohydrate 22g (Dietary Fiber 3g); Protein 25g
% Daily Value: Vitamin A 30%; Vitamin C 22%; Calcium 22%; Iron 12%
Exchanges: 1 Starch, 1 Vegetable, 3 Medium-Fat Meat, $2^1/_2$ Fat
Carbohydrate Choices: $1^1/_2$

BETTY'S TIPS

⌖ **Kitchen Tip**
Leftover roast beef? Chop 2 cups for this recipe instead of cooking the ground beef. Cook the onions in 1 tablespoon vegetable oil.

Cheesy Tomato-Beef Bake

Prep Time: 15 min Start to Finish: 45 min

1 pound lean ground beef
1 teaspoon chili powder
1 cup sour cream
$^2/_3$ cup mayonnaise or salad dressing
1 cup shredded sharp Cheddar cheese (4 ounces)
2 tablespoons finely chopped onion
2 cups Original Bisquick mix
$^1/_2$ cup cold water
2 to 3 medium tomatoes, thinly sliced
$^3/_4$ cup chopped green bell pepper

1. Heat oven to 375°. Spray 13 x 9-inch pan with cooking spray.

2. In 10-inch skillet, cook beef and chili powder over medium-high heat 6 to 8 minutes; stirring occasionally, until brown; drain and set aside.

3. In small bowl, stir sour cream, mayonnaise, cheese and onion until well mixed; set aside.

4. In medium bowl, stir Bisquick mix and cold water with fork until soft dough forms. Press dough in bottom and $^1/_2$ inch up sides of pan, using fingers dipped in Bisquick mix. Layer beef, tomatoes and bell pepper on dough. Spoon sour cream mixture over top; spread evenly over vegetables to cover. Bake uncovered 25 to 30 minutes or until edges of dough are light brown.

10 servings.
1 Serving: Calories 400 (Calories from Fat 270); Fat 30g (Saturated 10g); Cholesterol 60mg; Sodium 530mg; Carbohydrate 18g (Dietary Fiber 1g); Protein 14g
% Daily Value: Vitamin A 12%; Vitamin C 12%; Calcium 12%; Iron 10%
Exchanges: 1 Starch, 1 Vegetable, 1$^1/_2$ High-Fat Meat, 3 Fat
Carbohydrate Choices: 1

BETTY'S TIPS

☺ **Success Hint**
This recipe can easily be cut in half to serve five. Use an 8-inch square baking dish and bake as directed.

☺ **Serve-With**
Steamed green beans make a nice but simple side dish.
Offer a buffet of your favorite taco toppers, so guests can top their servings as they like.

☺ **Variation**
For a chicken version of this Mexican bake, use 2 cups diced cooked chicken in place of the ground beef. You can omit step 2 and just toss the chicken with the chili powder.

Cheesy Tomato-Beef Bake

Impossibly Easy Cheesy Meatball Pie

Prep Time: 10 min Start to Finish: 55 min

1½ cups refrigerated shredded hash brown
     potatoes (from 1-pound 4-ounce bag)
 ½ teaspoon salt
 ¼ teaspoon pepper
 ¾ cup Green Giant frozen sweet peas (from
     1-pound bag), thawed and drained
 12 frozen meatballs (from 16-ounce bag),
     thawed and cut in half
  1 cup shredded Cheddar cheese (4 ounces)
 ½ cup Original Bisquick mix
  1 cup milk
  2 eggs

1. Heat oven to 400°. Spray 9-inch glass pie plate or
   deep-dish pie plate with cooking spray.

2. In small bowl, toss potatoes with salt and pepper.
   Layer potatoes, peas, meatballs and cheese in pie
   plate.

3. In medium bowl, stir Bisquick mix, milk and eggs with
   fork or wire whisk until blended. Pour into pie plate.

4. Bake 30 to 40 minutes or until center is set and top
   is golden brown. Let stand 5 minutes before cutting.

6 servings.

1 Serving: Calories 390 (Calories from Fat 180); Fat 20g (Saturated 9g);
Cholesterol 155mg; Sodium 840mg; Carbohydrate 30g (Dietary Fiber
2g); Protein 22g
% Daily Value: Vitamin A 10%; Vitamin C 6%; Calcium 22%; Iron 14%
Exchanges: 2 Starch, 2 Medium-Fat Meat, 2 Fat
Carbohydrate Choices: 2

BETTY'S TIPS

⚙ **Substitution**
Frozen meatballs are available in a variety of flavors.
Plain meatballs are used in this pie, but Swedish meatballs with subtle spices or Italian meatballs with a
heartier flavor can be used.

⚙ **Success Hint**
Thaw the meatballs overnight in the refrigerator, or use
the Defrost setting on your microwave to quickly thaw
them.

The standing time for this pie, like many egg-based
dishes, allows the pie to set up before being cut.

Impossibly Easy Cheesy Meatball Pie

Taco Casserole

Prep Time: 30 min Start to Finish: 8 hr 30 min

1 1/2 pounds lean ground beef

1 can (14.5 ounces) diced tomatoes with green chilies, undrained

1 can (10.75 ounces) condensed cream of onion soup

1 envelope (1.25 ounces) Old El Paso taco seasoning mix

1/2 cup water

6 corn tortillas (5 or 6 inches in diameter, cut into 1/2-inch strips)

1 cup shredded Cheddar cheese (4 ounces)

3 medium green onions, sliced (3 tablespoons)

1/2 cup sour cream

1. Cook beef in 10-inch skillet over medium heat 8 to 10 minutes, stirring occasionally, until brown; drain.

2. Mix beef, tomatoes, soup, seasoning mix (dry) and water in 3 1/2- to 5-quart slow cooker. Gently stir in tortilla strips.

3. Cover and cook on Low heat setting 7 to 8 hours.

4. Sprinkle cheese over casserole; cover and let stand about 5 minutes or until cheese is melted. Sprinkle with onions; serve with sour cream.

6 servings.
1 Serving: Calories 475 (Calories from Fat 260); Fat 29g (Saturated 14g); Cholesterol 105mg; Sodium 960mg; Carbohydrate 24g (Dietary Fiber 3g); Protein 29g
% Daily Value: Vitamin A 26%; Vitamin C 14%; Calcium 26%; Iron 18%
Exchanges: 1 1/2 Starch, 3 1/2 Medium-Fat Meat, 2 Fat
Carbohydrate Choices: 1 1/2

BETTY'S TIPS

✿ **Substitution**
Try this recipe with lean ground turkey instead of the beef.

To make your own diced tomatoes and green chilies, combine a 14.5-ounce can of plain diced tomatoes with an undrained 4.5-ounce can of Old El Paso chopped green chilies.

✿ **Health Twist**
Using reduced-sodium taco seasoning mix would lower the sodium in this recipe to 820 milligrams per serving.

Taco Casserole

Corn Bread–Topped Black Bean Chili Casserole

Prep Time: 20 min Start to Finish: 45 min

- 1 pound lean (at least 80%) ground beef
- 1 medium onion, chopped ($^1/_2$ cup)
- 1 can (15 ounces) black beans with cumin and chili seasonings, undrained
- $1^1/_2$ cups Green Giant frozen mixed vegetables (from 1-pound bag)
- $1^1/_2$ cups Old El Paso Thick 'n Chunky salsa
- 1 pouch (6.5 ounces) Betty Crocker golden corn muffin mix
- 2 tablespoons milk
- 2 tablespoons butter or margarine, melted
- 1 egg

1. Heat oven to 375°. In 12-inch nonstick skillet, cook beef and onion over medium-high heat 5 to 7 minutes, stirring occasionally, until beef is brown; drain. Stir in black beans, mixed vegetables and salsa. Heat to boiling; cook over medium heat 5 minutes, stirring occasionally.

2. In ungreased 2-quart casserole or 8-inch square baking dish, spread beef mixture. Make muffin mix as directed on pouch, using 2 tablespoons milk, 2 tablespoons butter and egg. Drop batter by 8 spoonfuls onto chili mixture.

3. Bake uncovered 20 to 25 minutes or until topping is golden brown.

4 servings ($1^1/_2$ cups each).
1 Serving: Calories 680 (Calories from Fat 270); Fat 30g (Saturated 12g); Cholesterol 135mg; Sodium 1,480mg; Carbohydrate 78g (Dietary Fiber 15g); Protein 39g
% Daily Value: Vitamin A 82%; Vitamin C 14%; Calcium 18%; Iron 42%
Exchanges: $4^1/_2$ Starch, 2 Vegetable, 3 Medium-Fat Meat, 1 Fat
Carbohydrate Choices: 5

BETTY'S TIPS

⚙ **Kitchen Tip**
Substitute a can of chili beans for the black beans, if you like.

Make sure the chili mixture is hot before adding the batter so that the topping cooks all the way through.

Corn Bread–Topped Black Bean Chili Casserole

Quick

Reuben Casserole

Prep Time: 10 min Start to Finish: 30 min

3 cups hot water

1 cup milk

$^{1}/_{4}$ cup butter or margarine

1 tablespoon yellow mustard

1 package (7.2 ounces) Betty Crocker roasted garlic mashed potatoes (2 pouches)

1 package (6 ounces) sliced corned beef, cut into $^{1}/_{2}$-inch pieces

1 can (14.5 ounces) sauerkraut, well rinsed, drained

2 cups shredded Swiss cheese (8 ounces)

1 tablespoon caraway seed, if desired

1. Heat oven to 350°. Spray 8-inch square (2-quart) baking dish with cooking spray.

2. In 3-quart saucepan, heat water, milk and butter to a rapid boil; remove from heat. Stir in mustard. Stir in both pouches of Potatoes and Seasoning just until moistened. Let stand about 1 minute or until liquid is absorbed. Whip with fork until smooth.

3. Spread $1^{1}/_{2}$ cups of potatoes in baking dish. Top with corned beef. Spread sauerkraut over corned beef. Spoon remaining potatoes over top; spread gently. Sprinkle with cheese and caraway seed.

4. Bake uncovered 20 minutes.

Reuben Casserole

9 servings.
1 Serving: Calories 290 (Calories from Fat 160); Fat 18g (Saturated 9g); Cholesterol 60mg; Sodium 920mg; Carbohydrate 20g (Dietary Fiber 2g); Protein 14g
% Daily Value: Vitamin A 10%; Vitamin C 0%; Calcium 25%; Iron 8%
Exchanges: $1^{1}/_{2}$ Starch, $1^{1}/_{2}$ High-Fat Meat, $1^{1}/_{2}$ Fat
Carbohydrate Choices: $1^{1}/_{2}$

BETTY'S TIPS

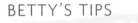

⚙ **Kitchen Tip**
Shredded Havarti cheese with caraway seed can be used in place of the Swiss cheese and the caraway seed.

On the
Side

Accompaniments for Every Meal

Gorgonzola Twice-Baked Potatoes with Bacon (page 218)

Spring Rice Pilaf (page 224)

Sweet Potato and Pepper Packet

Prep Time: 15 min Start to Finish: 35 min

2 medium dark-orange sweet potatoes, peeled and cut into 1-inch pieces

1 medium yellow bell pepper, cut into 1-inch pieces

2 tablespoons butter or margarine, melted

1 tablespoon honey

1/2 teaspoon seasoned salt

1 tablespoon chopped fresh chives

1. Heat coals or gas grill for direct heat. Cut 18 x 18-inch piece of heavy-duty aluminum foil. Spray with cooking spray. Place sweet potatoes and bell pepper on center of foil.

2. Mix butter, honey and seasoned salt in small bowl. Drizzle over potato mixture; stir to mix. Fold foil over vegetables so edges meet. Seal edges, making tight 1/2-inch fold; fold again. Allow space on sides for circulation and expansion.

3. Cover and grill packet 4 to 5 inches from medium heat 15 to 20 minutes or until sweet potatoes are tender. Place packet on serving platter. Cut large X across top of packet; unfold foil. Sprinkle with chives.

4 servings.
1 Serving: Calories 160 (Calories from Fat 55); Fat 6g (Saturated 4g); Cholesterol 15mg; Sodium 220mg; Carbohydrate 25g (Dietary Fiber 3g); Protein 2g
% Daily Value: Vitamin A 100%; Vitamin C 60%; Calcium 2%; Iron 2%
Exchanges: 1 Starch, 1 Vegetable, 1 Fat
Carbohydrate Choices: 1 1/2

BETTY'S TIPS

⊙ **Success Hint**

For the best flavor, buy sweet potatoes that are dark orange in color. Because they don't store well, keep them in a cool, dry, dark place for up to 1 week. They shouldn't be refrigerated.

For easy preparation, make these sweet potatoes in a disposable foil pan. Just cover with foil, then grill according to the recipe.

⊙ **Health Twist**

Sweet potatoes are an excellent source of beta-carotene, an antioxidant thought to reduce cancer risk.

Sweet Potato and Pepper Packet

Quick

Sweet Potatoes with Coconut-Ginger Topping

Prep Time: 10 min Start to Finish: 30 min

4 medium dark-orange sweet potatoes
(2 pounds) peeled and cut into 2-inch pieces

2 cloves garlic, finely chopped

1/2 cup water

1/2 teaspoon salt

1 tablespoon butter or margarine, melted

1/2 cup flaked coconut

1 tablespoon grated fresh ginger

3 tablespoons butter or margarine, softened

1. In 3-quart saucepan, place sweet potatoes, garlic, water and salt. Cover and heat to boiling; reduce heat to low. Simmer covered 15 to 20 minutes or until tender (do not drain).

2. Heat oven to 350°. In small bowl, mix 1 tablespoon melted butter, coconut and ginger; spread on ungreased cookie sheet. Bake 6 to 8 minutes, stirring frequently, until golden brown.

3. Mash potatoes, cooking liquid and 3 tablespoons butter with potato masher or electric mixer on low speed until no lumps remain. Spoon into ungreased casserole or serving dish. Sprinkle with coconut mixture.

8 servings.
1 Serving: Calories 130 (Calories from Fat 65); Fat 7g (Saturated 5g); Cholesterol 15mg; Sodium 200mg; Carbohydrate 16g (Dietary Fiber 2g); Protein 1g
% Daily Value: Vitamin A 100%; Vitamin C 12%; Calcium 2%; Iron 2%
Exchanges: 1/2 Starch, 1/2 Other Carbohydrate, 1 1/2 Fat
Carbohydrate Choices: 1

Sweet Potatoes with Coconut-Ginger Topping

BETTY'S TIPS

❂ **Substitution**
Instead of coconut, try chopped pecans as a topping for the potatoes.

❂ **Success Hint**
The moistness of sweet potatoes varies by color. Lighter sweet potatoes have a drier texture, so you may need to add milk or water when mashing them.

❂ **Do-Ahead**
Put the mashed potatoes in a microwavable dish, cover and refrigerate. Make the topping and store at room temperature. To serve, microwave the potatoes, loosely covered, on High for 10 to 12 minutes, stirring several times, then sprinkle with the topping.

Low Fat
Pineapple-Topped Sweet Potatoes

Prep Time: 5 min Start to Finish: 1 hr 15 min

2 medium dark-orange sweet potatoes
1/4 cup drained crushed pineapple in juice (from 8-ounce can)
1 tablespoon sunflower nuts
2 tablespoons packed brown sugar

1. Heat oven to 375°. Scrub potatoes; prick all over with fork. Place in shallow baking pan or pie pan (do not use glass). Bake 55 to 65 minutes or until tender.

2. Set oven control to broil. Cut potatoes lengthwise in half. Mash cut sides slightly with fork. Spoon pineapple over cut sides of potatoes. Top with sunflower nuts and brown sugar.

3. Broil with tops 4 to 6 inches from heat 2 to 3 minutes or until brown sugar is bubbly.

4 servings.
1 Serving: Calories 110 (Calories from Fat 10); Fat 1g (Saturated 0g); Cholesterol 0mg; Sodium 10mg; Carbohydrate 23g (Dietary Fiber 3g); Protein 2g
% Daily Value: Vitamin A 100%; Vitamin C 12%; Calcium 2%; Iron 2%
Exchanges: 1 Starch, 1/2 Fruit
Carbohydrate Choices: 1 1/2

BETTY'S TIPS

✿ **Kitchen Tip**
Place the sweet potatoes in a pan before you bake them so any syrup that leaks out won't create a mess in your oven.

Streusel-Topped Squash

Prep Time: 20 min Start to Finish: 1 hr 5 min

1 butternut squash (2 to 2 1/2 pounds), peeled, seeded and cut into 1/2-inch cubes (about 4 1/2 cups)
1/4 cup water
1/2 teaspoon salt
1/3 cup Gold Medal all-purpose flour
1/4 cup packed brown sugar
1/4 cup chopped pecans
2 tablespoons butter or margarine, softened
1/2 teaspoon pumpkin pie spice

1. Heat oven to 350°. In 11 x 7-inch microwavable dish, spread squash cubes. Add water; sprinkle with salt. Cover with plastic wrap, folding back one edge or corner 1/4 inch to vent steam. Microwave on High about 5 minutes or until squash is crisp-tender.

2. Meanwhile, in medium bowl, mix remaining ingredients with spoon. Sprinkle evenly over squash.

3. Bake uncovered 40 to 45 minutes or until streusel is brown.

8 servings (1/2 cup each).
1 Serving: Calories 140 (Calories from Fat 55); Fat 6g (Saturated 2g); Cholesterol 5mg; Sodium 170mg; Carbohydrate 20g (Dietary Fiber 2g); Protein 2g
% Daily Value: Vitamin A 100%; Vitamin C 10%; Calcium 4%; Iron 4%
Exchanges: 1 Other Carbohydrate, 1 Vegetable, 1 Fat
Carbohydrate Choices: 1

BETTY'S TIPS

✿ **Kitchen Tip**
If your microwave has a turntable you can't turn off, try cooking the squash in batches in a round microwavable dish.

Just before topping the squash with streusel, sprinkle a cup of dried cranberries over the squash.

Pineapple-Topped Sweet Potatoes

Streusel-Topped Squash

New Potatoes and Spring Vegetables

Prep Time: 20 min Start to Finish: 6 hr 40 min

  2   pounds small new potatoes
  2   cups baby-cut carrots, cut lengthwise in half
  1   large sweet onion (such as Bermuda, Maui, Spanish or Walla Walla), cut in half and thinly sliced
  1   teaspoon salt
  1   pound asparagus spears, cut into 2-inch pieces
 1/4 cup olive or vegetable oil
  6   tablespoons chopped fresh dillweed
1 to 2 teaspoons grated lemon peel
  2   tablespoons Dijon mustard
  1   teaspoon salt

New Potatoes and Spring Vegetables

1. Cut large potatoes in half as needed to make similar-size pieces. Place carrots in 5- to 6-quart slow cooker. Top with onion and potatoes; sprinkle with 1 teaspoon salt.

2. Cover and cook on Low heat setting 5 to 6 hours.

3. Add asparagus to cooker. Increase heat setting to High. Cover and cook 15 to 20 minutes or until asparagus is crisp-tender.

4. Mix oil, dillweed, lemon peel, mustard and 1 teaspoon salt in small bowl. Pour over vegetables in cooker; stir to coat. Vegetables will hold on Low heat setting up to 2 hours; stir occasionally.

18 servings (1/2 cup each).
1 Serving: Calories 85 (Calories from Fat 25); Fat 3g (Saturated 0g); Cholesterol 0mg; Sodium 310mg; Carbohydrate 13g (Dietary Fiber 2g); Protein 2g
% Daily Value: Vitamin A 66%; Vitamin C 8%; Calcium 0%; Iron 4%
Exchanges: 1/2 Starch, 1 Vegetable, 1/2 Fat
Carbohydrate Choices: 1

BETTY'S TIPS

⚙ **Success Hint**
Snap larger pieces of asparagus into smaller pieces by holding the stalk between your hands and bending it.

⚙ **Serve-With**
This delicately herbed vegetable dish complements the stronger flavors and textures of Garlic-Spiked Turkey Breast with Fresh Basil Mayonnaise (page 160).

⚙ **Special Touch**
Arrange these spring vegetables on a platter, or spoon them into a serving bowl. Tuck sprigs of fresh dillweed around the edge of the veggies.

Quick

Garlic and Cumin Potatoes

Prep Time: 10 min Start to Finish: 25 min

12	unpeeled small red potatoes, cut into quarters
2	tablespoons butter or margarine, melted
1/2	teaspoon garlic powder
1/2	teaspoon ground cumin
1/2	teaspoon ground paprika
1/2	teaspoon peppered seasoned salt
1/4	cup chopped fresh cilantro

1. Heat coals or gas grill for direct heat. Place potatoes in large bowl. Add remaining ingredients except cilantro; toss to coat. Place in grill basket (grill "wok").

2. Cover and grill potatoes 4 to 6 inches from medium heat 10 to 15 minutes, shaking basket or stirring potatoes frequently, until tender.

3. Sprinkle potatoes with cilantro; toss to coat.

4 servings.
1 Serving: Calories 185 (Calories from Fat 55); Fat 6g (Saturated 4g); Cholesterol 15mg; Sodium 220mg; Carbohydrate 30g (Dietary Fiber 3g); Protein 3g
% Daily Value: Vitamin A 6%; Vitamin C 12%; Calcium 2%; Iron 8%
Exchanges: 1 Starch, 1 Other Carbohydrate, 1 Fat
Carbohydrate Choices: 2

BETTY'S TIPS

⊗ **Substitution**
Using olive oil will change the flavor a little, but it's an excellent substitution for the butter.

If you don't have small red potatoes, cut unpeeled russets into 1 1/2-inch pieces; you'll need about 3 cups.

⊗ **Success Hint**
Shake the grill basket often to "stir" the potatoes, so they cook evenly and don't burn.

Garlic and Cumin Potatoes

Gorgonzola Twice-Baked Potatoes with Bacon

Prep Time: 15 min Start to Finish: 1 hr 35 min
(Photo on page 211)

4	large baking potatoes (8 to 10 ounces each)
4	slices bacon
$^2/_3$	cup milk
2	tablespoons butter or margarine
$^1/_2$	cup crumbled Gorgonzola or Roquefort cheese
4	medium green onions, sliced ($^1/_4$ cup)
$^1/_2$	teaspoon salt

1. Heat oven to 375°. Gently scrub potatoes, but do not peel. Pierce potatoes several times with fork. Place on oven rack. Bake 1 hour to 1 hour 15 minutes or until tender when pierced in center with fork. Let stand until cool enough to handle.

2. Meanwhile, in 12-inch skillet, cook bacon over medium heat 5 to 6 minutes, turning occasionally, until crisp; drain on paper towel.

3. Cut each potato lengthwise in half; scoop out inside, leaving a thin shell. In medium bowl, mash potatoes, milk and butter with potato masher or electric mixer on low speed until no lumps remain (amount of milk needed will vary depending upon type of potato used). Stir in cheese, green onions and salt. Fill potato shells with mashed potato mixture. Place on ungreased cookie sheet. Crumble bacon onto potatoes.

4. Bake about 20 minutes or until hot. Garnish with additional sliced green onion tops if desired.

8 servings.
1 Serving: Calories 160 (Calories from Fat 70); Fat 8g (Saturated 4g); Cholesterol 20mg; Sodium 390mg; Carbohydrate 17g (Dietary Fiber 1g); Protein 5g
% Daily Value: Vitamin A 6%; Vitamin C 8%; Calcium 8%; Iron 2%
Exchanges: 1 Starch, $1^1/_2$ Fat
Carbohydrate Choices: 1

BETTY'S TIPS

✿ **Success Hint**
A grapefruit spoon is super for scraping the potato from the shell.

✿ **Time-Saver**
You can cut down the baking time for the potatoes to about 30 minutes if you microwave them first for 6 minutes before putting them in the oven.

✿ **Do-Ahead**
Assemble the potatoes up to 12 hours ahead, cover with plastic wrap or aluminum foil and put in the fridge. Then bake as directed in step 4.

Béarnaise Corn and Potato Packets

Prep Time: 15 min Start to Finish: 50 min

1 package (20 ounces) refrigerated diced potatoes with onions

2 ears corn, husks removed and ears cut in half

¹/₄ cup butter or margarine, melted

2 tablespoons Dijon mustard

¹/₂ teaspoon salt

¹/₂ teaspoon garlic pepper

¹/₄ teaspoon dried tarragon leaves

2 tablespoons chopped fresh chives

1. Heat coals or gas grill for direct heat. Cut four 18 x 10-inch pieces of heavy-duty aluminum foil. Spray with cooking spray. Place potatoes and 1 piece corn on each foil piece. Mix remaining ingredients except chives in small bowl; drizzle over potatoes and corn. Turn corn to coat and gently stir potatoes.

2. Fold foil over potatoes and corn so edges meet. Seal edges, making tight ¹/₂-inch fold; fold again. Allow space on sides for circulation and expansion.

3. Cover and grill packets 4 to 6 inches from medium heat 25 to 35 minutes or until potatoes and corn are tender. Place packets on plates. Cut large X across top of each packet; unfold foil. Sprinkle with chives.

4 servings.
1 Serving: Calories 300 (Calories from Fat 115); Fat 13g (Saturated 7g); Cholesterol 30mg; Sodium 570mg; Carbohydrate 41g (Dietary Fiber 4g); Protein 5g
% Daily Value: Vitamin A 12%; Vitamin C 12%; Calcium 2%; Iron 4%
Exchanges: 2 Starch, 1 Other Carbohydrate, 2 Fat
Carbohydrate Choices: 3

BETTY'S TIPS

⊗ **Substitution**
Try this recipe with dried basil, thyme or Italian seasoning instead of the tarragon. Because the flavor of tarragon is more potent, use ¹/₂ teaspoon of the other herbs.

⊗ **Success Hint**
Grill these tasty packets alongside meat or poultry. Coordinate the cooking times in the recipes to make sure all the food will be done at the same time.

⊗ **Time-Saver**
Make these packets up to 2 hours ahead, then put them in the fridge until it's time to grill.

Bèarnaise Corn and Potato Packets

Tips from the Betty Crocker Kitchens

Comfort Foods

Piping-hot mashed potatoes, fork-tender meat loaf, smooth and rich gravy—these time-honored foods are the cornerstone of family cooking. They comfort us and create meal-time memories.

Making them perfect is easy with these few simple tricks.

Mashed Potatoes

Mashed potatoes should be light and fluffy with little or no potato lumps. You want to avoid sticky or gummy potatoes.

▶ Cut potatoes into pieces of the same size before cooking.

▶ When potatoes are fork-tender, drain them right away. Return to the same pan, and cook over low heat about 1 minute to remove excess water and to dry the potatoes, shaking the pan frequently to keep the potatoes from burning.

▶ Be sure to heat the milk to prevent potatoes from getting sticky.

▶ Beat potatoes only until light and fluffy. Overbeating will cause potatoes to become gummy. If you use an electric mixer, be especially careful not to overbeat.

BONUS TIP

Round red potatoes, white potatoes and yellow varieties are best for boiling and mashing.

Marvelous Meat Loaf

Meat loaf should be moist and tender with a firm, but not compact, texture.

▶ For moister meat loaf that is more tender, use a coarser grind of meat and soft, rather than dried, bread crumbs.

▶ Use a bulb baster or a large spoon to remove excess fat from around the meat loaf.

▶ Keep food safety in mind and check doneness. This also ensures a moist meat loaf. Meat loaf should reach 160° in the center; this is the required temperature for food safety and also ensures a moist meat loaf.

BONUS TIP

Boost the nutrition (and taste) of your meat loaf by mixing in 1 cup shredded zucchini, potato or carrot per pound of ground meat.

Goodness Gravy

Gravy should be smooth with no lumps and be free of excess fat.

▶ The most flavorful gravy starts with meat drippings and broth. If you're making turkey gravy, use turkey broth. If it's beef gravy, use beef broth.

▶ Let meat drippings stand for 5 minutes to allow the fat to come to the top. Then skim and remove the excess fat with a spoon or gravy separator.

▶ When using flour to thicken the gravy, use equal

amounts of fat and flour. Use 2 tablespoons of flour per cup of liquid. Remember, gravy will continue to thicken slightly after it is removed from the heat.

▶ Stir constantly with a wire whisk to avoid lumps.

BONUS TIP

If you don't have broth, you can also use water or another liquid for the gravy. Try apple cider or wine.

Home-Style Pot Roast

A pot roast should be tender but not dry.

- ▶ Browning the meat improves its appearance and flavor. Be sure to season the meat with salt and pepper (or other seasonings) before browning it to enhance the flavor.

- ▶ A pot roast should always be cooked with moist heat, so adding liquid is important. Vary the cooking liquid. Instead of water, try beef broth, tomato juice or even carbonated cola.

- ▶ Wait until the oven is completely preheated before placing the pot roast in it.

- ▶ Allow the roast to stand for 15 to 20 minutes after cooking to make carving easier. Cut the pot roast meat across the grain for best eating.

BONUS TIP

Add vegetables to the pot roast for the last hour of cooking for an easy all-in-one meal.

Comfort Macaroni and Cheese

- ▶ For even cooking, always cook pasta at a fast and continuous boil. Stir frequently to prevent the pasta from sticking.

- ▶ Do not rinse the cooked pasta after draining because the sauce will have trouble clinging to the macaroni.

- ▶ Natural cheeses tend to separate and curdle more than processed cheese, which will give a smooth sauce. Although this will not affect taste, it may affect appearance. If you like, consider a combination of cheeses.

BONUS TIP

Macaroni and cheese can be baked and served directly from the saucepan. If you're going to bake the macaroni and cheese, slightly undercook the pasta. As it bakes, the macaroni will continue to soak up sauce and become tenderer.

Super Stuffing

Great stuffing is moist—not too wet and not too dry.

- ▶ Use day-old, dry bread. If the bread is not dry, leave it out overnight. Firm bread is better than softer bread. It's easier to cut and retains more texture.

- ▶ When chopping vegetables, be sure the pieces are not too big. Keep them in proportion with the bread cubes. Cook just until soft.

- ▶ Using the right amount of liquid is important. Too much liquid will make the stuffing soggy; not enough liquid, and it will be dry. Follow the recipe and taste. If you're stuffing poultry, use less liquid because the stuffing will absorb the juices of the bird.

BONUS TIP

The bread will determine the flavor of the stuffing. Create a variety of stuffing by using corn bread, whole-grain breads, sourdough and herb breads.

Sausage and Cranberry Baked Stuffing

Prep Time: 10 min Start to Finish: 8 hr 55 min

8 cups lightly packed $^3/_4$-inch cubes French bread

1 pound bulk spicy pork sausage

2 ribs celery (with leaves), chopped (1$^1/_2$ cups)

1 medium onion, chopped ($^1/_2$ cup)

$^1/_2$ teaspoon dried sage leaves

$^1/_2$ cup dried cranberries

1 cup chicken broth

1 cup milk

2 eggs, beaten

1. Heat oven to 350°. Spray 13 x 9-inch baking dish with cooking spray. Place bread cubes in baking dish.

2. In 10-inch skillet, cook sausage, celery and onion over medium heat, stirring occasionally, until sausage is no longer pink and vegetables are tender; drain.

3. Add sausage mixture, sage and cranberries to baking dish; mix lightly with bread cubes. In medium bowl, beat broth, milk and eggs with fork or wire whisk until well mixed; pour over bread and stir gently to soak all bread cubes in milk mixture. Cover and re-frigerate at least 8 hours but no longer than 12 hours.

4. Bake uncovered 35 to 40 minutes or until knife in-serted in center comes out clean and top is golden brown.

12 servings.
1 Serving: Calories 175 (Calories from Fat 70); Fat 8g (Saturated 3g); Cholesterol 50mg; Sodium 480mg; Carbohydrate 18g (Dietary Fiber 1g); Protein 8g
% Daily Value: Vitamin A 2%; Vitamin C 2%; Calcium 6%; Iron 6%
Exchanges: 1 Starch, $^1/_2$ Vegetable, $^1/_2$ High-Fat Meat, 1 Fat
Carbohydrate Choices: 1

Sausage and Cranberry Baked Stuffing

BETTY'S TIPS

☺ **Success Hint**
Spicy sausage comes in both 12-ounce and 16-ounce packages. Either size will work well in this recipe.

☺ **Serve-With**
This dish is the perfect side for an unstuffed bird or turkey breast. Add green beans and a fruit salad for an easy holiday meal.

☺ **Special Touch**
Just before serving, sprinkle the casserole with a few dried cranberries or tuck sprigs of parsley or sage leaves around the edge of the dish.

Spring Rice Pilaf

Prep Time: 20 min Start to Finish: 3 hr 10 min

3 tablespoons butter or margarine

2 cups uncooked regular long-grain rice

$1/3$ cup finely chopped onion

$1/2$ teaspoon salt

2 cans (14 ounces each) reduced-sodium chicken broth

$1/2$ cup water

1 cup julienne strips (matchstick-size) carrots

$1/2$ cup Green Giant Select LeSueur frozen baby sweet peas (from 1-pound bag), thawed

$1/2$ cup finely chopped red bell pepper

$1/3$ cup slivered almonds, toasted

2 tablespoons chopped parsley

1. Melt butter in 12-inch skillet over medium-high heat. Cook rice, onion and salt in butter 8 to 10 minutes, stirring frequently, until rice is lightly golden brown. Stir in broth and water. Heat to boiling; remove from heat.

2. Spray inside of 3- to 4-quart slow cooker with cooking spray. Pour rice mixture into cooker. Stir in carrots. Make sure all rice is under liquid and not sticking to side of cooker.

3. Cover and cook on Low heat setting 2 hours to 2 hours 30 minutes.

4. Stir in peas and bell pepper. Increase heat setting to High. Cover and cook 15 to 20 minutes or until hot. Sprinkle with almonds and parsley. Rice will hold on Low heat setting up to 2 hours; stir occasionally.

16 servings ($1/2$ cup each).
1 Serving: Calories 140 (Calories from Fat 35); Fat 4g (Saturated 2g); Cholesterol 5mg; Sodium 200mg; Carbohydrate 22g (Dietary Fiber 1g); Protein 4g
% Daily Value: Vitamin A 28%; Vitamin C 4%; Calcium 2%; Iron 6%
Exchanges: $1^{1}/_{2}$ Starch, $1/2$ Fat
Carbohydrate Choices: $1^{1}/_{2}$

Spring Rice Pilaf

BETTY'S TIPS

⊛ **Serve-With**
Pair this pretty rice with any of the crowd-size meat recipes in this book, such as Plum Barbecue Short Ribs (page 200).

⊛ **Variation**
Transform this recipe into a tasty main dish by adding 1 cup chopped cooked ham along with the peas.

⊛ **Special Touch**
Use aromatic jasmine rice with its slightly flowery flavor to enhance the taste of this springy side dish.

Parmesan Rice and Peas with Bacon

Prep Time: 20 min Start to Finish: 40 min

2   slices bacon, chopped
1   medium onion, chopped ($^1/_2$ cup)
1   cup uncooked long-grain regular rice
1   can (14 ounces) chicken broth
$^1/_2$ cup water
1   cup Green Giant Select LeSueur frozen baby sweet peas (from 1-pound bag), thawed
$^3/_4$ cup grated Parmesan cheese
$^1/_8$ teaspoon pepper

1. In 2-quart saucepan, cook bacon over medium heat 3 to 4 minutes, stirring occasionally, until crisp. Stir in onion. Cook about 1 minute, stirring occasionally, until onion is tender.

2. Stir in rice until well coated with bacon fat. Stir in broth and water. Heat to boiling; reduce heat to low. Cover and simmer about 20 minutes or until rice is tender and broth is absorbed.

3. Gently stir in peas. Cover and cook 1 to 2 minutes or until peas are hot. Remove from heat. Stir in cheese and pepper.

8 servings.
1 Serving: Calories 165 (Calories from Fat 35); Fat 4g (Saturated 2g); Cholesterol 10mg; Sodium 440mg; Carbohydrate 24g (Dietary Fiber 1g); Protein 8g
% Daily Value: Vitamin A 2%; Vitamin C 2%; Calcium 14%; Iron 8%
Exchanges: 1$^1/_2$ Starch, $^1/_2$ High-Fat Meat
Carbohydrate Choices: 1$^1/_2$

BETTY'S TIPS

⚙ **Kitchen Tip**
For best results, use plain long-grain rice rather than converted or instant rice.

Parmesan Rice and Peas with Bacon

Low Fat

Mexican Beans

Prep Time: 10 min Start to Finish: 8 hr 10 min

1   package (16 ounces) dried navy beans, sorted and rinsed

10   cups water

1   can (28 ounces) diced tomatoes, undrained

1   can (15 ounces) black beans, rinsed and drained

1   can (11 ounces) Green Giant Mexicorn whole kernel corn, red and green peppers, drained

1   envelope (1.25 ounces) Old El Paso taco seasoning mix

1/2 cup frozen small whole onions (from 1-pound bag)

1   teaspoon chili powder

1. Heat beans and water to boiling in 4-quart Dutch oven; reduce heat to low. Cover and simmer 1 hour; drain.

2. Mix beans and remaining ingredients in 3 1/2- to 4-quart slow cooker.

3. Cover and cook on Low heat setting 6 to 7 hours. Beans will hold on Low heat setting up to 2 hours; stir occasionally.

17 servings (1/2 cup each).
1 Serving: Calories 135 (Calories from Fat 10); Fat 1g (Saturated 0g); Cholesterol 0mg; Sodium 300mg; Carbohydrate 30g (Dietary Fiber 7g); Protein 9g
% Daily Value: Vitamin A 6%; Vitamin C 8%; Calcium 8%; Iron 14%
Exchanges: 2 Starch
Carbohydrate Choices: 2

BETTY'S TIPS

⊗ **Substitution**
Instead of black beans, try pinto, navy or red beans to give this recipe different color and texture.

⊗ **Success Hint**
Rinse canned beans thoroughly to remove the starchy liquid and excess salt, then drain completely.

The dried beans in this recipe are precooked to make sure they'll be tender after cooking in the slow cooker

Mexican Beans

Make Ahead to Take Along

Something Sweet for Every Event

Toasted Coconut-Almond Biscotti (page 228)

Triple Chocolate-Cherry Bars (page 235)

Toasted Coconut-Almond Biscotti

Prep Time: 15 min Start to Finish: 2 hr 15 min
(Photo on page 227)

1 package Betty Crocker SuperMoist® white cake mix

1 tablespoon vegetable oil

2 eggs

1 cup flaked coconut, toasted*

$^1/_2$ cup chopped slivered almonds, toasted*

1 bag (6 ounces) semisweet chocolate chips (1 cup)

1 tablespoon shortening

1. Heat oven to 350°. In large bowl, mix cake mix, oil and eggs with spoon until dough forms (some dry mix will remain). Stir in coconut and almonds, using hands if necessary.

2. On ungreased cookie sheet, shape dough into 15 x 4-inch rectangle with greased hands. Bake 20 to 25 minutes or until golden brown. Cool on cookie sheet on wire rack 15 minutes.

3. Cut rectangle crosswise into $^1/_2$-inch slices. Place slices, cut sides down, on cookie sheet. Bake 10 to 12 minutes or until edges are deep golden brown. Cool 5 minutes; remove from cookie sheet or wire rack. Cool completely, about 30 minutes.

4. In 1-quart saucepan, heat chocolate chips and shortening over low heat, stirring constantly, until chocolate is melted. Drizzle chocolate over cookies, or dip one end of each cookie into chocolate. Let stand about 30 minutes or until chocolate is set.

2 dozen cookies.

Note: *To toast coconut and almonds, spread in an ungreased shallow pan. Bake uncovered in a 350° oven 5 to 8 minutes, stirring occasionally, until coconut is golden brown and almonds are toasted. Cool completely, about 15 minutes.

1 Cookie: Calories 170 (Calories from Fat 70); Total Fat 8g (Saturated Fat 3.5g); Cholesterol 20mg; Sodium 160mg; Total Carbohydrate 23g (Dietary Fiber 1g); Protein 2g
% Daily Value: Vitamin A 0%; Vitamin C 0%; Calcium 4%; Iron 4%
Exchanges: $^1/_2$ Starch, 1 Other Carbohydrate, $1^1/_2$ Fat
Carbohydrate Choices: $1^1/_2$

BETTY'S TIPS

⚙ **Kitchen Tip**
If using almonds that have been frozen, make sure they are room temperature before toasting so that the coconut and almonds toast evenly.

Old-Fashioned Peanut Butter Cookies

Prep Time: 1 hr 5 min Start to Finish: 1 hr 5 min

1 package Betty Crocker SuperMoist yellow or butter recipe yellow cake mix

$^1/_3$ cup water

1 cup creamy peanut butter

2 eggs

2 tablespoons sugar

1. Heat oven to 375°. In large bowl, beat half of cake mix, water, peanut butter and eggs with electric mixer on medium speed until smooth, or mix with spoon. Stir in remaining cake mix.

2. On ungreased cookie sheet, drop dough by rounded tablespoonfuls about 2 inches apart. Flatten in criss-cross pattern with fork dipped in sugar.

3. Bake 10 to 12 minutes or until golden brown. Cool 1 minute; remove from cookie sheet to wire rack.

About 4$^1/_2$ dozen cookies.
1 Cookie: Calories 70 (Calories from Fat 30); Total Fat 3.5g (Saturated Fat 1g); Cholesterol 10mg; Sodium 85mg; Total Carbohydrate 9g (Dietary Fiber 0g); Protein 2g
% Daily Value: Vitamin A 0%; Vitamin C 0%; Calcium 0%; Iron 0%
Exchanges: $^1/_2$ Starch, $^1/_2$ Fat
Carbohydrate Choices: $^1/_2$

BETTY'S TIPS

⚙ Kitchen Tip
Give a new look to these cookies by pressing the bottom of a cut-crystal glass, a potato masher or cookie stamp into the dough before baking.

Old-Fashioned Peanut Butter Cookies

Lemon Cookies

Chocolate Cookies

Lemon Cookies

Prep Time: 50 min Start to Finish: 50 min

- 1 package Betty Crocker SuperMoist lemon cake mix
- $1/2$ cup vegetable oil
- 2 eggs
- 1 tub (12 ounces) Betty Crocker Whipped lemon frosting or 1 tub (1 pound) Rich & Creamy lemon frosting

1. Heat oven to 350°. Grease cookie sheet with shortening or spray with cooking spray. In large bowl, mix cake mix, oil and eggs with spoon until dough forms.

2. On cookie sheet, drop dough by teaspoonfuls. Bake about 8 minutes or until set. Remove from cookie sheet to wire rack. Cool completely, about 30 minutes. Spread with frosting.

About 4 dozen cookies.
1 Cookie: Calories 100 (Calories from Fat 40); Total Fat 4.5g (Saturated Fat 1.5g); Cholesterol 10mg; Sodium 70mg; Total Carbohydrate 14g (Dietary Fiber 0g); Protein 0g
% Daily Value: Vitamin A 0%; Vitamin C 0%; Calcium 2%; Iron 0%
Exchanges: 1 Other Carbohydrate
Carbohydrate Choices: 1

BETTY'S TIPS

✿ **Kitchen Tip**
For Double-Lemon Cookies, place 2 tablespoons lemon juice in measuring cup and add enough vegetable oil to measure $1/2$ cup; use instead of the $1/2$ cup oil.

Low Fat
Chocolate Cookies

Prep Time: 55 min Start to Finish: 55 min

- 1 package Betty Crocker SuperMoist devil's food cake mix
- $1/2$ cup vegetable oil
- 2 eggs
- $1/4$ cup sugar

1. Heat oven to 350°. In large bowl, mix cake mix, oil and eggs with spoon until dough forms.

2. Shape dough into 1-inch balls; roll in sugar. On ungreased cookie sheet, place balls about 2 inches apart.

3. Bake 8 to 10 minutes or until set. Remove from cookie sheet to wire rack.

About 4 dozen cookies.
1 Cookie: Calories 60 (Calories from Fat 20); Total Fat 2.5g (Saturated Fat 0.5g); Cholesterol 10mg; Sodium 85mg; Total Carbohydrate 10g (Dietary Fiber 0g); Protein 0g
% Daily Value: Vitamin A 0%; Vitamin C 0%; Calcium 0%; Iron 2%
Exchanges: $1/2$ Other Carbohydrate, $1/2$ Fat
Carbohydrate Choices: $1/2$

BETTY'S TIPS

✿ **Kitchen Tip**
To make Chocolate-Chip Chocolate Cookies, stir $2/3$ cup miniature semisweet chocolate chips into the dough.

Chocolate-Raspberry Cheesecake Bars

Prep Time: 20 min Start to Finish: 3 hr 10 min

1   package Betty Crocker SuperMoist chocolate fudge cake mix

$^1/_2$ cup butter or margarine, softened

2   packages (8 ounces each) cream cheese, softened

1   container (6 ounces) Yoplait Original red raspberry yogurt ($^2/_3$ cup)

1   tub (1 pound) Betty Crocker Rich & Creamy chocolate frosting

3   eggs

$^1/_2$ cup raspberry pie filling

1. Heat oven to 325°. Lightly grease bottom only of 13 x 9-inch pan with shortening, or spray bottom with cooking spray. In large bowl, beat cake mix and butter with electric mixer on low speed until crumbly; reserve 1 cup. Press remaining crumbly mixture, using floured fingers, in bottom of pan.

2. In same bowl, beat cream cheese, yogurt and frosting on medium speed until smooth. Beat in eggs until blended. Pour over mixture into pan. Sprinkle with reserved crumbly mixture.

3. Bake about 48 minutes or until center is set. Refrigerate uncovered at least 2 hours before serving. For bars, cut into 6 rows by 4 rows. Serve bars with a dollop of pie filling. Store covered in refrigerator.

24 bars.

1 Bar: Calories 310 (Calories from Fat 150); Total Fat 17g (Saturated Fat 11g); Cholesterol 60mg; Sodium 260mg; Total Carbohydrate 35g (Dietary Fiber 1g); Protein 4g
% Daily Value: Vitamin A 10%; Vitamin C 0%; Calcium 6%; Iron 6%
Exchanges: 1 Starch, 1$^1/_2$ Other Carbohydrate, 3 Fat
Carbohydrate Choices: 2

BETTY'S TIPS

☺ **Kitchen Tip**
Cheesecakes are baked at low temperatures to prevent excess shrinkage. They are easier to cut if you use a wet knife, cleaning it after each cut.

Chocolate-Raspberry Cheesecake Bars

Cherries Jubilee Cheesecake Bars

Prep Time: 20 min   Start to Finish: 4 hr 5 min

1 package Betty Crocker SuperMoist cherry chip cake mix

$1/2$ cup butter or margarine, softened

2 packages (8 ounces each) cream cheese, softened

1 tub (1 pound) Betty Crocker Rich & Creamy cherry frosting

3 eggs

1. Heat oven to 325°. In large bowl, beat cake mix and butter with electric mixer on low speed until crumbly; reserve 1 cup. Press remaining crumbly mixture in bottom of ungreased 13 x 9-inch pan.

2. In same bowl, beat cream cheese and frosting on medium speed until smooth. Beat in eggs until blended; pour over crust. Sprinkle with reserved crumbly mixture.

3. Bake about 45 minutes or until set. Cool completely, about 1 hour. Cover and refrigerate at least 2 hours. For bars, cut into 6 rows by 6 rows. Store covered in refrigerator.

36 bars.

1 Bar: Calories 190 (Calories from Fat 90); Total Fat 11g (Saturated Fat 6g); Cholesterol 40mg; Sodium 150mg; Total Carbohydrate 21g (Dietary Fiber 0g); Protein 2g
% Daily Value: Vitamin A 6%; Vitamin C 0%; Calcium 4%; Iron 2%
Exchanges: $1/2$ Starch, 1 Other Carbohydrate, 2 Fat
Carbohydrate Choices: $1^1/2$

BETTY'S TIPS

✿ **Kitchen Tip**
A dollop of cherry yogurt mixed with whipped topping gives these yummy bars a special finish!

Cherries Jubilee Cheesecake Bars

Peanut Butter–Toffee Bars

Peanut Butter-Toffee Bars

Prep Time: 20 min Start to Finish: 1 hr 50 min

- 1 package Betty Crocker SuperMoist yellow cake mix
- 1 cup crunchy peanut butter
- 1/2 cup water
- 2 eggs
- 1 bag (10 ounces) almond toffee bits or milk chocolate toffee bits (1³/₄ cups)
- 1 bag (12 ounces) semisweet chocolate chips (2 cups)

1. Heat oven to 350°. Grease bottom and sides of 15 x 10 x 1-inch pan with shortening, or spray with cooking spray; lightly flour. In large bowl, mix cake mix, peanut butter, water and eggs with spoon. Stir in toffee bits. Spread evenly in pan.

2. Bake 20 to 25 minutes or until golden brown. Immediately sprinkle chocolate chips over hot bars. Let stand about 5 minutes or until chips are melted; spread evenly. Cool completely, about 1 hour. For bars, cut into 10 rows by 6 rows.

60 bars.
1 Bar: Calories 120 (Calories from Fat 60); Total Fat 6g (Saturated Fat 3g); Cholesterol 5mg; Sodium 85mg; Total Carbohydrate 15g (Dietary Fiber 0g); Protein 2g
% Daily Value: Vitamin A 0%; Vitamin C 0%; Calcium 2%; Iron 2%
Exchanges: 1/2 Starch, 1/2 Other Carbohydrate, 1 Fat
Carbohydrate Choices: 1

BETTY'S TIPS

❁ **Kitchen Tip**
Almond toffee bits can become rancid, so be sure to do a "taste-test" before adding them to your recipe. Store toffee bits in the freezer to prevent this.

Triple Chocolate-Cherry Bars

Prep Time: 15 min Start to Finish: 2 hr
(Photo on page 227)

- 1 package Betty Crocker SuperMoist chocolate fudge cake mix
- 1 can (21 ounces) cherry pie filling
- 2 eggs, beaten
- 1 cup miniature semisweet chocolate chips
- 1 tub (12 ounces) Betty Crocker Whipped chocolate frosting

1. Heat oven to 350°. Grease bottom and sides of 15 x 10 x 1-inch pan with shortening, or spray with cooking spray. In large bowl, mix cake mix, pie filling, eggs and chocolate chips with spoon. Pour into pan.

2. Bake 28 to 38 minutes or until toothpick inserted in center comes out clean. Cool completely, about 1 hour. Spread with frosting. For bars, cut into 8 rows by 6 rows.

48 bars.
1 Bar: Calories 110 (Calories from Fat 35); Total Fat 3.5g (Saturated Fat 2.5g); Cholesterol 10mg; Sodium 90mg; Total Carbohydrate 18g (Dietary Fiber 0g); Protein 0g
% Daily Value: Vitamin A 0%; Vitamin C 0%; Calcium 0%; Iron 2%
Exchanges: 1 Other Carbohydrate, 1 Fat
Carbohydrate Choices: 1

BETTY'S TIPS

❁ **Kitchen Tip**
Make Triple Chocolate-Strawberry Bars by using strawberry pie filling instead of the cherry.

Truffle Lover's Cupcakes

Prep Time: 35 min Start to Finish: 2 hr 10 min

Cupcakes

1	package Betty Crocker SuperMoist chocolate fudge cake mix
1⅓	cups water
½	cup vegetable oil
3	eggs
¼	cup miniature semisweet chocolate chips
⅓	cup hazelnuts (filberts), toasted, skins removed and ground
1	teaspoon grated orange peel
4	teaspoons hazelnut-flavored liqueur
4	teaspoons orange-flavored liqueur

Ganache

⅓	cup whipping (heavy) cream
½	cup semisweet chocolate chips
	Miniature semisweet chocolate chips
	Additional grated orange peel

Truffle Lover's Cupcakes

1. Heat oven to 375°. Place paper baking cup in each of 24 regular-size muffin cups (use 8 each of 3 different colors).

2. In large bowl, beat cake mix, water, oil and eggs with electric mixer on low speed 1 minute, scraping bowl constantly. Divide batter among three small bowls (1½ cups batter in each). Stir ¼ cup miniature chocolate chips into batter in one bowl; spoon into 8 muffin cups of same color.

3. Reserve 2 tablespoons ground hazelnuts for topping. Stir remaining hazelnut into batter in second bowl; spoon into 8 muffin cups of second color. Stir 1 teaspoon grated orange peel into remaining batter; spoon into remaining 8 muffin cups of remaining color.

4. Bake 21 to 26 minutes or until toothpick inserted in center comes out clean. Cool 10 minutes; remove from pan to wire rack. Prick holes in tops of hazelnut and orange cupcakes with toothpick. Brush ½ teaspoon hazelnut liqueur over each hazelnut cupcake; brush ½ teaspoon orange liqueur over each orange cup cake. Cool completely, about 30 minutes.

5. In heavy 1-quart saucepan, heat whipping cream over medium-high heat until hot but not boiling; remove from heat. Stir in ½ cup chocolate chips until

melted. Let stand 5 minutes. Dip tops of cupcakes into ganache. Top hazelnut cupcakes with reserved ground hazelnuts, top chocolate chip cupcakes with miniature chocolate chips and top orange cupcakes with orange peel. Refrigerate at least 10 minutes before serving. Store loosely covered in refrigerator.

24 cupcakes.

1 Cupcake: Calories 200 (Calories from Fat 100); Total Fat 11g (Saturated Fat 4g); Cholesterol 30mg; Sodium 180mg; Total Carbohydrate 24g (Dietary Fiber 1g); Protein 2g
% Daily Value: Vitamin A 0%; Vitamin C 0%; Calcium 4%; Iron 6%
Exchanges: 1 Starch, ½ Other Carbohydrate, 2 Fat
Carbohydrate Choices: 1½

BETTY'S TIPS

⚙ **Kitchen Tip**
To toast hazelnuts, bake uncovered in ungreased shallow pan in a 350° oven 6 to 10 minutes, stirring occasionally, until light brown.

Rub the nuts with a towel to remove skins. Place nuts in food processor or blender; cover and process until ground.

Double-Coconut Cupcakes

Prep Time: 35 min Start to Finish: 1 hr 45 min

- 2 cups flaked coconut
- $^1/_2$ cup sweetened condensed milk (from 14-ounce can)
- 1 package Betty Crocker SuperMoist yellow cake mix
- $1^1/_4$ cups water
- $^1/_3$ cup vegetable oil
- 3 eggs

  Coconut Cream Frosting (right) or 1 tub (1 pound) Betty Crocker Rich & Creamy vanilla frosting
- 1 cup flaked coconut, toasted

1. Heat oven to 375°. Place paper baking cup in each of 24 regular-size muffin cups.

2. In medium bowl, stir 2 cups coconut and the milk; set aside.

3. In large bowl, beat cake mix, water, oil and eggs with electric mixer on low speed 30 seconds. Beat on medium speed 2 minutes, scraping bowl occasionally. Divide batter evenly among muffin cups ($^3/_4$ full). Top each with about 1 tablespoon coconut mixture.

4. Bake 15 to 22 minutes or until top springs back when lightly touched. Cool 5 minutes; remove pan to wire rack. Cool completely, about 30 minutes.

5. Make Coconut Cream Frosting; immediately frost cupcakes. Dip tops of cupcakes in toasted coconut. Store loosely covered at room temperature.

24 cupcakes
1 Cupcake: Calories 280 (Calories from Fat 110); Total Fat 12g (Saturated Fat 6g); Cholesterol 35mg; Sodium 220mg; Total Carbohydrate 40g (Dietary Fiber 0g); Protein 2g
% Daily Value: Vitamin A 4%; Vitamin C 0%; Calcium 6%; Iron 4%
Exchanges: 1 Starch, 2 Other Carbohydrate, 2 Fat
Carbohydrate Choices: $2^1/_2$

BETTY'S TIPS

✿ **Kitchen Tip**
To toast the coconut, bake in a shallow pan at 350° for 5 to 7 minutes, stirring occasionally, until golden brown.

Quick & Low Fat
Coconut Cream Frosting

Prep Time: 10 min Start to Finish: 10 min

- 3 cups powdered sugar
- $^1/_3$ cup butter or margarine, softened
- $^1/_4$ teaspoon salt
- 1 teaspoon coconut extract
- 1 to 3 tablespoons milk

1. In medium bowl, beat powdered sugar, butter and salt with spoon or with electric mixer on low speed until well blended.

2. Beat in coconut extract and 1 tablespoon milk. Gradually beat in just enough remaining milk to make frosting smooth and spreadable.

24 servings (about 2 tablespoons each).
1 Serving: Calories 80 (Calories from Fat 25); Total Fat 2.5g (Saturated Fat 1.5g); Cholesterol 5mg; Sodium 40mg; Total Carbohydrate 15g (Dietary Fiber 0g); Protein 0g
% Daily Value: Vitamin A 0%; Vitamin C 0%; Calcium 0%; Iron 0%
Exchanges: 1 Other Carbohydrate, $^1/_2$ Fat
Carbohydrate Choices: 1

Double-Coconut Cupcakes

Black and White Rum Cakes

Prep Time: 55 min Start to Finish; 2 hr

Cupcakes

- 1 package Betty Crocker SuperMoist white cake mix
- 1¼ cups water
- ⅓ cup vegetable oil
- 3 eggs
- 3 ounces unsweetened baking chocolate, melted, cooled
- 2 teaspoons rum extract

Rum Frosting

- 2 egg whites
- ½ cup sugar
- ¼ cup light corn syrup
- 2 tablespoons water
- 2 teaspoons rum extract

Decoration

Betty Crocker Decors chocolate shot, if desired

Black and White Rum Cakes

1. Heat oven to 375°. Place paper baking cup in each of 24 regular-size muffin cups.

2. In large bowl, beat cake mix, 1¼ cups water, oil and 3 eggs with electric mixer on low speed 30 seconds. Beat on medium speed 2 minutes, scraping bowl occasionally. Place 2 cups of batter in small bowl; stir in chocolate. Into remaining batter, stir 2 teaspoons run extract.

3. Spoon about 1½ tablespoons chocolate batter into bottom of each muffin cup. Top each with about 1½ tablespoons rum batter.

4. Bake 15 to 20 minutes or until toothpick inserted in center comes out clean. Cool 10 minutes; remove from pan to wire rack. Cool completely, about 30 minutes.

5. In medium bowl, beat 2 egg whites with electric mixer on high speed just until stiff peaks form; set aside.

6. In 1-quart saucepan, stir sugar, corn syrup and 2 tablespoons water until well mixed. Cover and heat to rolling boil over medium heat. Uncover and boil 4 to 8 minutes, without stirring, to 242° on candy thermometer or until small amount of mixture dropped into cup of very cold water forms a firm ball that holds its shape until pressed. For an accurate temperature reading, tilt the saucepan slightly so mixture is deep enough for thermometer.

7. Pour hot syrup very slowly in thin stream into egg whites, beating constantly on medium speed. Add 2 teaspoons rum extract. Beat on high speed about 10 minutes or until stiff peaks form. Immediately spread frosting on cupcakes. Sprinkle with chocolate shot. Store loosely covered in refrigerator.

24 cupcakes.

1 Cupcake: Calories 170 (Calories from Fat 70); Total Fat 8g (Saturated Fat 2.5g); Cholesterol 25mg; Sodium 160mg; Total Carbohydrate 25g (Dietary Fiber 0g); Protein 2g
% Daily Value: Vitamin A 0%; Vitamin C 0%; Calcium 4%; Iron 4%
Exchanges: ½ Starch, 1 Other Carbohydrate, 1½ Fat
Carbohydrate Choices: 1½

BETTY'S TIPS

✪ Kitchen Tip

Punch up these rum-flavored treats with a scoop of rum-raisin ice cream.

In a rush? Instead of the cooked frosting, substitute Betty Crocker fluffy white frosting mix with the rum extract.

Spring Polka Dot Cupcakes

Prep Time: 40 min Start to Finish: 1 hr 45 min

Cupcakes

- 1 package Betty Crocker SuperMoist white cake mix
- 1¼ cups water
- ⅓ cup vegetable oil
- 1 box (4-serving size) orange-flavored gelatin
- 3 egg whites

Bright Buttercream Frosting

- 3 cups powdered sugar
- ⅓ cup butter or margarine, softened
- 1 teaspoon vanilla
- 2 to 3 tablespoons milk
  Yellow, red and blue food colors
- ⅓ cup white baking chips

1. Heat oven to 375°. Place paper baking cup in each of 24 regular-size muffin cups.

2. In large bowl, beat cake mix, water, oil, gelatin and egg whites with electric mixer on low speed 30 seconds. Beat on medium speed 2 minutes, scraping bowl occasionally. Divide batter evenly among muffin cups (about ⅔ full).

3. Bake 15 to 20 minutes or until toothpick inserted in center comes out clean. Cool 10 minutes; remove from pan to wire rack. Cool completely, about 30 minutes.

4. Meanwhile, in medium bowl, beat powdered sugar and butter with spoon or electric mixer on low speed until well blended. Beat in vanilla and 2 tablespoons milk. Gradually beat in just enough of remaining milk to make frosting smooth and spreadable. Divide frosting among 4 small bowls. Stir 6 drops yellow food color into frosting in one bowl. Stir 4 drops red food coloring into frosting in second bowl. Stir 6 to 8 drops blue food color into frosting in third bowl. Stir 4 drops yellow and 2 drops red food color into frosting in fourth bowl.

5. Frost 6 cupcakes with each color of frosting. Poke 4 or 5 white baking chips, flat side up, into frosting on each cupcake to resemble polka dots. Store loosely covered at room temperature.

24 cupcakes.
1 Cupcake: Calories 240 (Calories from Fat 80); Total Fat 9g (Saturated Fat 3g); Cholesterol 5mg; Sodium 190mg; Total Carbohydrate 37g (Dietary Fiber 0g); Protein 2g
% Daily Value: Vitamin A 0%; Vitamin C 0%; Calcium 4%; Iron 2%
Exchanges: 1 Starch, ½ Other Carbohydrate, 1½ Fat
Carbohydrate Choices: 2½

BETTY'S TIPS

✿ **Kitchen Tip**
Have fun making yellow cupcakes by using Betty Crocker SuperMoist white cake mix and lemon gelatin.

Spring Polka Dot Cupcakes

Ball Game Cupcakes

Prep Time: 35 min Start to Finish: 1 hr 55 min

1   package Betty Crocker SuperMoist yellow cake mix

1   cup water

1/3   cup vegetable oil

3   eggs

1   cup miniature semisweet chocolate chips

1   tub (1 pound) Betty Crocker Rich & Creamy vanilla frosting

Assorted colors Betty Crocker decorating icing (in 4.25-ounce tubes) or Betty Crocker Easy Flow decorating icing (in 6.4-ounce cans)

Assorted food colors

1. Heat oven to 375°. Place paper baking cup in each of 24 regular-size muffin cups.

2. In large bowl, beat cake mix, water, oil and eggs with electric mixer on low speed 30 seconds. Beat on medium speed 2 minutes, scraping bowl occasionally. Fold in chocolate chips. Divide batter evenly among muffin cups (2/3 full).

3. Bake 20 to 25 minutes or until toothpick inserted in center comes out clean. Cool 10 minutes; remove from pan to wire rack. Cool completely, about 30 minutes.

4. For soccer balls, frost cupcakes with vanilla frosting. With black icing, pipe a pentagon shape in the center of cupcake, piping a few rows of icing into center of pentagon. Pipe lines from pentagon to edge of cupcake to resemble seams. With toothpick or spatula, spread black icing in center of pentagon to fill in the entire shape.

For baseballs, frost cupcakes with vanilla frosting. With black, red or blue icing, pipe 2 arches on opposite sides of cupcakes, curing lines slightly toward center. Pipe small lines from each arch to resemble stitches on baseball.

For basketballs, color frosting with yellow and red food colors to make orange; frost cupcakes. With black icing, pipe line across center of cupcake. On either side, pipe an arch that curves slightly toward center line.

For tennis balls, color frosting with yellow and green food colors to make tennis-ball yellow; frost cupcakes. With white icing, pipe curved design to resemble tennis balls.

5. Store cupcakes loosely covered at room temperature.

24 cupcakes.

1 Cupcake: Calories 260 (Calories from Fat 100); Total Fat 11g (Saturated Fat 6g); Cholesterol 25mg; Sodium 150mg; Total Carbohydrate 39g (Dietary Fiber 0g); Protein 2g
% Daily Value: Vitamin A 0%; Vitamin C 0%; Calcium 4%; Iron 4%
Exchanges: 1 Starch, 1 1/2 Other Carbohydrate, 2 Fat
Carbohydrate Choices: 2 1/2

BETTY'S TIPS

✿ Kitchen Tip

Choose any flavor cake mix for these sporty cupcakes. Follow package directions for the amounts of water, oil and eggs, and fold chocolate chips into the batter.

Arrange cupcakes on green grass. To make grass, shake 1 cup coconut and 3 drops green food coloring in tightly covered jar until evenly tinted.

Ball Game Cupcakes

PB & J Cupcakes

Prep Time: 30 min Start to Finish: 1 hr 40 min

Cupcakes

- 1 package Betty Crocker SuperMoist yellow cake mix
- 1 1/4 cups water
- 3/4 cup creamy peanut butter
- 1/4 cup vegetable oil
- 3 eggs

PB & J Frosting

- 1 tub (12 ounces) Betty Crocker Whipped vanilla frosting
- 1/2 cup creamy peanut butter
- 2 to 4 tablespoons grape jelly

1. Heat oven to 375°. Place paper baking cup in each of 24 regular-size muffin cups.

2. In large bowl, beat cake mix, water, 3/4 cup peanut butter, oil and eggs with electric mixer on low speed 30 seconds. Beat on medium speed 1 minute 30 seconds, scraping bowl occasionally. Divide batter evenly among muffin cups (about 2/3 full).

3. Bake 15 to 20 minutes or until toothpick inserted in center comes out clean. Cool 10 minutes; remove from pan to wire rack. Cool completely, about 30 minutes.

4. In medium bowl, mix frosting and peanut butter. Frost cupcakes with frosting. Make a small indentation in center of frosting on each cupcake with back of spoon. Just before serving, spoon 1/4 to 1/2 teaspoon jelly into each indentation.

24 cupcakes.
1 Cupcake: Calories 270 (Calories from Fat 120); Total Fat 13g (Saturated Fat 4.5g); Cholesterol 25mg; Sodium 210mg; Total Carbohydrate 32g (Dietary Fiber 1g); Protein 5g
% Daily Value: Vitamin A 0%; Vitamin C 0%; Calcium 4%; Iron 4%
Exchanges: 2 Starch, 2 1/2 Fat
Carbohydrate Choices: 2

BETTY'S TIPS

⊛ **Kitchen Tip**
No grape jelly on the shelf? Substitute your favorite flavor of jam, preserves or jelly.

PB & J Cupcakes

Low Fat
Almond Baby Cakes

Prep Time: 1 hr 50 min Start to Finish: 1 hr 50 min

Cakes

1	package Betty Crocker SuperMoist white cake mix
1¼	cups water
⅓	cup vegetable oil
1	teaspoon almond extract
3	egg whites

Almond Glaze

1	bag (2 pounds) powdered sugar
½	cup water
½	cup corn syrup
2	teaspoons almond extract
1 to 3	teaspoons hot water

Decoration

Assorted colors Betty Crocker decorating icing (in 4.25-ounce tubes)

Almond Baby Cakes

1. Heat oven to 375°. Grease bottoms only of about 60 mini muffin cups with shortening, or spray bottoms with cooking spray.

2. In large bowl, beat cake mix, 1¼ cups water, oil, 1 teaspoon almond extract and egg whites with electric mixer on low speed 30 seconds. Beat on medium speed 2 minutes, scraping bowl occasionally. Divide batter evenly among muffin cups (about ½ full). (If using one pan, refrigerate batter while baking other cakes; wash pan before filling with additional batter.)

3. Bake 10 to 15 minutes or until toothpick inserted in center comes out clear. Cool 5 minutes; remove from pan to wire rack. Cool completely, about 30 minutes.

4. Place wire rack on cookie sheet or waxed paper to catch glaze drips. In 3-quart saucepan, stir powdered sugar, ½ cup water, corn syrup and 2 teaspoons almond extract. Heat over low heat, stirring frequently, until sugar is dissolved; remove from heat. Stir in hot water, 1 teaspoon at a time, until glaze is pourable. Turn each baby cake on wire rack so top side is down. Pour about 1 tablespoon glaze over each baby cake, letting glaze coat the sides. Let stand 15 minutes.

5. With decorating icing, pipe designs on cakes in shapes of letters, animals, safety pins, booties, rattles or bottles. Store loosely covered at room temperature.

About 60 baby cakes.

1 Baby Cake: Calories 120 (Calories from Fat 20); Total Fat 2.5g (Saturated Fat 0.5g); Cholesterol 0mg; Sodium 65mg; Total Carbohydrate 25g (Dietary Fiber 0g); Protein 0g
% Daily Value: Vitamin A 0%; Vitamin C 0%; Calcium 0%; Iron 0%
Exchanges: 1½ Other Carbohydrate, ½ Fat
Carbohydrate Choices: 1½

BETTY'S TIPS

❀ **Kitchen Tip**

Baby cakes aren't just for showers. They're great for other themed parties too. Pipe letters on the cakes to spell out "Congratulations" or "Bon Voyage."

Bake the baby cakes up to 2 weeks ahead of time. Freeze, then add the glaze when it's time for the party.

Praline Mini Bundt Cakes

Prep Time: 20 min Start to Finish: 1 hr 20 min

Cakes

1	package Betty Crocker SuperMoist yellow cake mix
1¹/₄	cups water
¹/₃	cup vegetable oil
3	eggs
¹/₂	cup chopped pecans
¹/₂	cup English toffee bits

Brown Sugar Glaze

¹/₄	cup butter (do not use margarine)
¹/₂	cup packed brown sugar
2	tablespoons corn syrup
2	tablespoons milk
1	cup powdered sugar
1	teaspoon vanilla
¹/₄	cup English toffee bits

1. Heat oven to 350°. Generously grease 12 mini fluted tube cake pans or 12 jumbo muffin cups with shortening (do not spray with cooking spray); lightly flour.

2. In large bowl, beat cake mix, water, oil and eggs with electric mixer on low speed 30 seconds. Beat on medium speed 2 minutes, scraping bowl occasionally. Fold in pecans and ¹/₂ cup toffee bits. Divide batter evenly among mini pans.

3. Bake 18 to 23 minutes or until toothpick inserted in center comes out clean. Cool 10 minutes; remove from pans to wire rack. Cool completely, about 1 hour.

4. In 1-quart saucepan, melt butter over medium-high heat. Stir in brown sugar, corn syrup and milk. Heat to rolling boil over medium-high heat, stirring frequently; remove from heat. Immediately beat in powdered sugar and vanilla with wire whisk until smooth. Immediately drizzle about 1 teaspoon glaze over each cake, sprinkle each with 1 teaspoon toffee bits. Store loosely covered at room temperature.

Praline Mini Bundt Cakes

12 mini cakes.
1 Mini Cake: Calories 460 (Calories from Fat 190); Total Fat 21g (Saturated Fat 7g); Cholesterol 65mg; Sodium 360mg; Total Carbohydrate 64g (Dietary Fiber 0g); Protein 4g
% Daily Value: Vitamin A 6%; Vitamin C 0%; Calcium 10%; Iron 6%
Exchanges: 1 Starch, 3¹/₂ Other Carbohydrate, 4 Fat
Carbohydrate Choices: 4

BETTY'S TIPS

✿ **Kitchen Tip**
Almond lovers can get a nut fix by substituting almonds for the pecans and almond extract for the vanilla.

To keep the cake from sticking to the cake pans, be sure to grease and flour the pans generously.

Honey-Rhubarb Cake

Prep Time: 20 min Start to Finish: 2 hr 20 min

Cake

- ¼ cup butter or margarine
- 4 cups chopped fresh or frozen rhubarb, thawed if frozen
- ½ cup honey
- ½ cup granulated sugar
- 1 package Betty Crocker SuperMoist yellow cake mix
- 1¼ cups water
- ⅓ cup vegetable oil
- 3 eggs

Sweetened Whipped Cream

- 1 cup whipping (heavy) cream
- 3 tablespoons powdered sugar
- ½ teaspoon vanilla

1. Heat oven to 350°. In 13 x 9-inch pan, melt butter in oven. Remove pan from oven; turn pan so butter evenly coats bottom of pan. Spread rhubarb evenly in pan. Drizzle with honey and granulated sugar.

2. In large bowl, beat cake mix, water, oil and eggs with electric mixer on low speed 30 seconds. Beat on medium speed 2 minutes, scraping bowl occasionally. Pour over rhubarb mixture.

3. Bake 50 to 57 minutes or until toothpick inserted in center comes out clean. Cool completely, about 1 hour.

4. In chilled medium bowl, beat whipping cream, powdered sugar and vanilla on high speed until soft peaks form. Frost cake with whipped cream. Store loosely covered in refrigerator.

15 servings.
1 Serving: Calories 350 (Calories from Fat 160); Total Fat 17g (Saturated Fat 7g); Cholesterol 70mg; Sodium 260mg; Total Carbohydrate 47g (Dietary Fiber 0g); Protein 3g
% Daily Value: Vitamin A 8%; Vitamin C 0%; Calcium 15%; Iron 4%
Exchanges: 1 Starch, 2 Other Carbohydrate, 3 Fat
Carbohydrate Choices: 3

BETTY'S TIPS

❂ **Kitchen Tip**
For easiest serving, use a metal spatula.

Whipped topping can be used instead of making Sweetened Whipped Cream.

Honey-Rhubarb Cake

Strawberry-Filled Take-Along Cake with Brown Sugar Frosting

Prep Time: 40 min Start to Finish: 3 hr

Cake
$1/2$ cup butter (do not use margarine)

1 package Betty Crocker SuperMoist butter recipe yellow cake mix

$1^1/4$ cups water

3 eggs

$1/2$ cup strawberry jam or preserves

Brown Sugar Frosting
$1/2$ cup butter

1 cup packed brown sugar

$1/4$ cup milk

$2^1/2$ cups powdered sugar

Strawberry-Filled Take-Along Cake with Brown Sugar Frosting

1. In heavy 1-quart saucepan, heat $1/2$ cup butter over medium heat, moving and turning pan occasionally, just until butter is light brown. (Watch carefully; butter can brown and then burn quickly.) Cool 15 minutes.

2. Heat oven to 350°. Grease bottom only of 13 x 9-inch pan with shortening, or spray bottom with cooking spray.

3. In large bowl, beat browned butter, cake mix, water and eggs with electric mixer on low speed 30 seconds. Beat on medium speed 2 minutes, scraping bowl occasionally. Pour into pan.

4. Bake 34 to 39 minutes or until toothpick inserted in center comes out clean. Cool completely, about 1 hour.

5. Spread jam evenly over top of cake. Freeze at least 15 minutes or until jam is set.

6. Meanwhile, in 2-quart saucepan, melt $1/2$ cup butter over medium heat. Stir in brown sugar. Heat to boiling, stirring constantly; reduce heat to low. Boil and stir 2 minutes; remove from heat. Stir in milk. Heat to boiling over medium heat, stirring constantly. Cool to lukewarm, about 20 minutes.

7. Gradually stir powdered sugar into brown sugar mixture. If frosting becomes too stiff, stir in additional milk, 1 teaspoon at a time, or heat over low heat, stirring constantly. Spread frosting over jam. Store loosely covered at room temperature.

15 servings.
1 Serving: Calories 430 (Calories from Fat 140); Total Fat 15g (Saturated Fat 7g); Cholesterol 75mg; Sodium 330mg; Total Carbohydrate 70g (Dietary Fiber 0g); Protein 3g
% Daily Value: Vitamin A 10%; Vitamin C 0%; Calcium 8%; Iron 6%
Exchanges: 1 Starch, $3^1/2$ Other Carbohydrate, 3 Fat
Carbohydrate Choices: $4^1/2$

BETTY'S TIPS

⊗ **Kitchen Tip**
So that it spreads easily, stir the jam before spreading it on the cake.

In a rush? Use 1 tub Betty Crocker Rich & Creamy dulce de leche (caramel) frosting instead of the Brown Sugar Frosting.

S'mores Cake

Prep Time: 15 min Start to Finish: 3 hr 15 min

- 1 package Betty Crocker SuperMoist yellow cake mix
- 1 cup graham cracker crumbs (14 squares)
- 1 1/4 cups water
- 1/3 cup vegetable oil
- 3 eggs
- 1 jar (16 to 17 ounces) hot fudge or chocolate topping
- 1 jar (7 ounces) marshmallow creme

1. Heat oven to 350°. Grease bottom only of 13 x 9-inch pan with shortening, or spray bottom with cooking spray.

2. In large bowl, beat cake mix, cracker crumbs, water, oil and eggs with electric mixer on low speed 30 seconds. Beat on medium speed 2 minutes. Pour into pan.

3. Reserve 1/4 cup hot fudge topping. Drop remaining hot fudge topping by generous tablespoonfuls randomly in 12 to 14 mounds onto batter in pan.

4. Bake 40 to 45 minutes or until toothpick inserted in center comes out clean. Run knife around side of pan to loosen cake. Cool 15 minutes.

5. Spoon teaspoonfuls of marshmallow creme onto warm cake; carefully spread with knife dipped in hot water. Drop small dollops of reserved hot fudge topping randomly over marshmallow creme. Swirl topping through marshmallow creme with knife for marbled design. Cool 2 hours. Store uncovered at room temperature. (Once cut, store cake in the pan, uncovered, with plastic wrap pressed against cut sides.)

15 servings.
1 Serving: Calories 370 (Calories from Fat 110); Total Fat 12g (Saturated Fat 3.5g); Cholesterol 45mg; Sodium 380mg; Total Carbohydrate 62g (Dietary Fiber 1g); Protein 4g
% Daily Value: Vitamin A 0%; Vitamin C 0%; Calcium 10%; Iron 8%
Exchanges: 1 Starch, 3 Other Carbohydrate, 2 Fat
Carbohydrate Choices: 4

BETTY'S TIPS

✪ Kitchen Tip

Buy graham cracker crumbs instead of crushing graham crackers. Look for the crumbs in the baking section of the grocery store.

To easily cut the cake, use a serrated knife and dip it in hot water before cutting each piece, to keep the frosting from sticking.

S'mores Cake

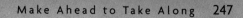

Peppermint Pattie Poke Cake

Prep Time: 25 min Start to Finish: 3 hr 10 min

Cake

1 package Betty Crocker SuperMoist triple chocolate fudge cake mix

1¼ cups water

⅓ cup vegetable oil

3 eggs

Filling

1 box (4-serving size) white chocolate instant pudding and pie filling mix

2 cups milk

½ teaspoon peppermint extract

Frosting

¼ teaspoon peppermint extract

1 tub (12 ounces) Betty Crocker Whipped milk chocolate frosting

¾ cup coarsely chopped chocolate-covered peppermint patties (8 candies)

1. Heat oven to 350°. Grease bottom only of 13 x 9-inch pan with shortening, or spray bottom with cooking spray.

2. In large bowl, beat cake mix, water, oil and eggs with electric mixer on low speed 30 seconds. Beat on medium speed 2 minutes, scraping bowl occasionally. Pour into pan.

3. Bake 32 to 37 minutes or until toothpick inserted in center comes out clean. Cool 15 minutes. Poke top of warm cake every ½ inch with handle of wooden spoon.

4. In medium bowl, beat pudding mix, milk and ½ teaspoon peppermint extract with wire whisk about 2 minutes. Immediately pour pudding evenly into holes in cake. Cover loosely and refrigerate about 2 hours or until chilled.

5. Stir ¼ teaspoon peppermint extract into frosting. Spread frosting over top of cake. Sprinkle with peppermint patties. Store loosely covered in refrigerator.

15 servings.
1 Serving: Calories 370 (Calories from Fat 140); Total Fat 16g (Saturated Fat 4.5g); Cholesterol 45mg; Sodium 430mg; Total Carbohydrate 53g (Dietary Fiber 2g); Protein 5g
% Daily Value: Vitamin A 2%; Vitamin C 0%; Calcium 8%; Iron 10%
Exchanges: 1½ Starch, 2 Other Carbohydrate, 3 Fat
Carbohydrate Choices: 3½

BETTY'S TIPS

⚙ **Kitchen Tip**
To keep candies from sticking together, sprinkle 1 tablespoon sugar over the cutting board. As you cut the candies, toss them with the sugar.

Peppermint Pattie Poke Cake

Easy Tiramisu Cake

Prep Time: 25 min Start to Finish: 2 hr 10 min

Cake

- 1 package Betty Crocker SuperMoist white cake mix
- 1 cup water
- $1/3$ cup vegetable oil
- $1/4$ cup brandy
- 3 egg whites

Espresso Syrup

- 4 tablespoons instant espresso coffee (dry)
- $1/2$ cup boiling water
- 2 tablespoons corn syrup

Topping

- 1 package (8 ounces) cream cheese, softened
- $1/2$ cup powdered sugar
- 2 cups whipping (heavy) cream
- 1 tablespoon baking cocoa, if desired

1. Heat oven to 350°. Grease bottom only of 13 x 9-inch pan with shortening, or spray bottom with cooking spray.

2. In large bowl, beat cake mix, 1 cup water, oil, brandy and egg whites with electric mixer on low speed 30 seconds. Beat on medium speed 2 minutes, scraping bowl occasionally. Pour into pan.

3. Bake 28 to 33 minutes or until toothpick inserted in center comes out clean. Cool 15 minutes.

4. In small bowl, stir dry espresso and $1/2$ cup boiling water until mixed. Stir in corn syrup. Pierce top of cake every $1/2$ inch with long-tined fork. Brush top of cake with espresso syrup. Cool completely, about 1 hour.

5. In medium bowl, beat cream cheese and powdered sugar on low speed until mixed. Beat on high speed until smooth. Gradually beat in whipping cream, beating on high speed about 2 minutes until stiff peaks form. Spread cream mixture over top of cake; dust with baking cocoa. Store loosely covered in refrigerator.

Easy Tiramisu Cake

15 servings.
1 Serving: Calories 380 (Calories from Fat 220); Total Fat 25g (Saturated Fat 13g); Cholesterol 60mg; Sodium 300mg; Total Carbohydrate 35g (Dietary Fiber 0g); Protein 4g
% Daily Value: Vitamin A 15%; Vitamin C 0%; Calcium 8%; Iron 4%
Exchanges: 1 Starch, 1 Other Carbohydrate, 5 Fat
Carbohydrate Choices: 2

BETTY'S TIPS

⚙ **Kitchen Tip**
Instead of brandy, you can use $1\ 1/2$ teaspoons of brandy extract plus $1/4$ cup water.

Keep the topping smooth and creamy by adding the whipping cream gradually to the cream cheese mixture.

Tres Leches Cake

Tres Leches Cake

Prep Time: 15 min Start to Finish: 4 hr

Cake

1	package Betty Crocker SuperMoist yellow cake mix
1	cup water
$1/3$	cup vegetable oil
3	eggs
1	cup whipping (heavy) cream
1	cup whole milk
1	can (14 ounces) sweetened condensed milk
$1/3$	cup rum

Topping

1	cup whipping (heavy) cream
2	tablespoons rum or 1 teaspoon rum extract
$1/2$	teaspoon vanilla
1	cup flaked coconut, toasted
$1/2$	cup chopped pecans, toasted

1. Heat oven to 350°. Grease bottom only 13 x 9-inch pan with shortening, or spray bottom with cooking spray.

2. In large bowl, beat cake mix, water, oil and eggs with electric mixer on low speed 30 seconds. Beat on medium speed 2 minutes. Pour into pan.

3. Bake 33 to 38 minutes or until toothpick inserted in center comes out clean. Let stand 5 minutes. In large bowl, mix 1 cup whipping cream, whole milk, condensed milk and $1/3$ cup rum. Pierce top of hot cake every $1/2$ inch with long-tined fork, wiping fork occasionally to reduce sticking. Carefully pour whipping cream mixture evenly over top of cake. Cover and refrigerate about 3 hours or until chilled and most of whipping cream mixture has been absorbed into cake.

4. In chilled large bowl, beat 1 cup whipping cream, 2 tablespoons rum and vanilla on high speed until soft peaks form. Frost cake with whipped cream mixture. Sprinkle with coconut and pecans. Store covered in refrigerator.

15 servings.

1 Serving: Calories 450 (Calories from Fat 240); Total Fat 27g (Saturated Fat 13g); Cholesterol 95mg; Sodium 300mg; Total Carbohydrate 47g (Dietary Fiber 0g); Protein 6g
% Daily Value: Vitamin A 15%; Vitamin C 0%; Calcium 20%; Iron 6%
Exchanges: 2 Starch, 1 Other Carbohydrate, 5 Fat
Carbohydrate Choices: 3

BETTY'S TIPS

✿ **Kitchen Tip**

Instead of rum in the cake, use 1 tablespoon rum extract plus enough water to measure $1/3$ cup. In the topping, substitute 1 teaspoon rum extract for the rum.

In English, the Spanish words *tres leches* mean "three milks." The milk trio in this recipe is whipping cream, whole milk and sweetened condensed milk.

Orange–Poppy Seed Bundt Cake

Prep Time: 20 min Start to Finish: 3 hr 10 min

Cake

1	package Betty Crocker SuperMoist yellow cake mix
1	tablespoon grated orange peel
$^3/_4$	cup orange juice
$^1/_2$	cup water
$^1/_3$	cup vegetable oil
3	eggs
2	tablespoons poppy seed

Orange Glaze

1	cup powdered sugar
$^1/_4$	teaspoon grated orange peel
1 to 2	tablespoons orange juice
	Additional grated orange peel, if desired

1. Heat oven to 350°. Grease 12-cup fluted tube cake pan with shortening (do not spray with cooking spray); lightly flour.

2. In large bowl, beat cake mix, 1 tablespoon orange peel, $^3/_4$ cup orange juice, water, oil and eggs with electric mixer on low speed 30 seconds. Beat on medium speed 2 minutes, scraping bowl occasionally. Stir in poppy seed. Pour into pan.

3. Bake 40 to 45 minutes or until toothpick inserted in center comes out clean. Cool 10 minutes; remove from pan to wire rack or heatproof serving plate. Cool completely, about 2 hours.

4. In small bowl, mix powdered sugar, $^1/_4$ teaspoon orange peel and 1 tablespoon orange juice. Stir in additional orange juice, 1 teaspoon at a time, until glaze is smooth and consistency of thick syrup. Spread glaze over top of cake, allowing some to drizzle down sides. Garnish with additional orange peel. Store loosely covered at room temperature.

16 servings.
1 Serving: Calories 230 (Calories from Fat 80); Total Fat 8g (Saturated Fat 2g); Cholesterol 40mg; Sodium 220mg; Total Carbohydrate 36g (Dietary Fiber 0g); Protein 3g
% Daily Value: Vitamin A 0%; Vitamin C 4%; Calcium 8%; Iron 4%
Exchanges: 1 Starch, $1^1/_2$ Other Carbohydrate, $1^1/_2$ Fat
Carbohydrate Choices: $2^1/_2$

Orange–Poppy Seed Bundt Cake

BETTY'S TIPS

⚙ **Kitchen Tip**

The orange part of the peel packs the most flavor. So grate only the bright orange skin and avoid the bitter-tasting white layer.

In a rush? Microwave $^1/_2$ tub (1-pound size) Betty Crocker Rich & Creamy vanilla frosting with $^1/_4$ teaspoon grated orange peel on High 20 to 30 seconds. Stir, then pour over cake.

Dreamy Desserts

Amazing Endings to Wow the Crowd

Peanut Butter Silk Cake (page 263)

Peaches and Cream Cake (page 255)

Blueberry-Lemon Cake

Prep Time: 20 min   Start to Finish: 2 hr

- 1 package Betty Crocker SuperMoist white cake mix
- 1¼ cups water
- ⅓ cup vegetable oil
- 1 tablespoon grated lemon peel
- 3 eggs
- 1⅓ cups blueberry pie filling (from 21-ounce can)
- 1 tub (12 ounces) Betty Crocker Whipped vanilla frosting

1. Heat oven to 350°. Grease bottoms only of two 8-inch or 9-inch round pans with shortening, or spray bottoms with cooking spray; lightly flour.

2. In large bowl, beat cake mix, water, oil, lemon peel and eggs with electric mixer on low speed 30 seconds. Beat on medium speed 2 minutes, scraping bowl occasionally. Pour into pans.

3. Bake 8-inch rounds 27 to 32 minutes, 9-inch rounds 23 to 28 minutes, or until toothpick inserted in center comes out clean. Cool 10 minutes. Run knife around sides of pans to loosen cakes; remove from pans to wire racks. Cool completely, about 1 hour.

4. Place 1 cake layer, rounded side down, on serving plate. Spread ⅔ cup pie filling over layer. Top with second layer, rounded side up. Frost side with frosting, building up a slight edge at top of cake. Spread remaining pie filling over top of cake to frosted edge. Store loosely covered in refrigerator.

16 servings.
1 Serving: Calories 380 (Calories from Fat 120); Total Fat 13g (Saturated Fat 3g); Cholesterol 40mg; Sodium 260mg; Total Carbohydrate 64g (Dietary Fiber 0g); Protein 3g
% Daily Value: Vitamin A 0%; Vitamin C 4%; Calcium 6%; Iron 6%
Exchanges: 1 Starch, 3 Other Carbohydrate, 2½ Fat
Carbohydrate Choices: 4

BETTY'S TIPS

⚙ **Kitchen Tip**
You won't use the entire can of pie filling in this recipe. Try the leftover pie filling over ice cream or vanilla yogurt.

Blueberry-Lemon Cake

Peaches and Cream Cake

Prep Time: 30 min Start to Finish: 2 hr 25 min
(Photo on page 253)

1 bag (16 ounces) frozen sliced peaches, thawed
1 package Betty Crocker SuperMoist yellow cake mix
$1/3$ cup vegetable oil
$1/3$ cup whipping (heavy) cream
3 eggs
$1/4$ cup peach preserves
$3^1/4$ cups powdered sugar
$1/2$ cup butter, softened (do not use margarine)
2 tablespoons peach-flavored liqueur
2 to 4 tablespoons whipping (heavy) cream or milk
3 tablespoons peach preserves

1. Heat oven to 350°. Grease bottoms only of two 8-inch or 9-inch round pans with shortening, or spray bottoms with cooking spray.

2. Reserve 8 peach slices for garnish; cover and refrigerate. In blender or food processor, cover and blend remaining peaches until pureed. Reserve $1/4$ cup blended peaches for filling; cover and refrigerate.

3. In large bowl, beat remaining blended peaches, cake mix, oil, $1/3$ cup whipping cream and eggs with electric mixer on low speed 30 seconds. Beat on medium speed 2 minutes, scraping bowl occasionally. Pour into pans.

4. Bake 8-inch rounds 38 to 42 minutes, 9-inch rounds 28 to 33 minutes, or until toothpick inserted in center comes out clean. Cool 10 minutes. Run knife around side of pans to loosen cakes; carefully remove from pans to wire rack. Cool completely, about 1 hour.

5. In small bowl, stir together reserved $1/4$ cup blended peaches and $1/4$ cup peach preserves; set aside for filling.

6. In medium bowl, beat powdered sugar, butter, liqueur and just enough of the 2 to 4 tablespoons whipping cream with spoon or with electric mixer on low speed until smooth and spreadable.

7. Place 1 cake layer, rounded side down, on serving plate. Spread peach filling over layer to within $1/4$ inch of edge. Top with second layer, rounded side up. Frost side and top of cake with frosting. In small bowl, stir 3 tablespoons peach preserves; carefully spoon preserves around top edge of cake, allowing some to drizzle down side. Just before serving, cut reserved peach slices lengthwise in half and place on top of cake. Store loosely covered in refrigerator.

16 servings.
1 Serving: Calories 410 (Calories from Fat 150); Total Fat 17g (Saturated Fat 7g); Cholesterol 65mg; Sodium 270mg; Total Carbohydrate 64g (Dietary Fiber 0g); Protein 3g
% Daily Value: Vitamin A 10%; Vitamin C 25%; Calcium 8%; Iron 4%
Exchanges: 1 Starch, 3 Other Carbohydrate, 3 Fat
Carbohydrate Choices: 4

BETTY'S TIPS

⚙ **Kitchen Tip**
If you don't have peach liqueur, use $1^1/2$ teaspoons vanilla plus 2 tablespoons water.

Peach liqueur gives the frosting a burst of ultra-peachy flavor. Try it drizzled over fresh peach slices and vanilla ice cream for a super-easy summer dessert.

Citrus Cake with Lemon Whipped Cream Frosting

Prep Time: 30 min Start to Finish: 2 hr 10 min

1 package Betty Crocker SuperMoist lemon cake mix
$1/2$ cup water
$1/2$ cup orange juice
$1/3$ cup vegetable oil
3 eggs
2 cups whipping (heavy) cream
$1/4$ cup powdered sugar
1 can (15.75 ounces) lemon pie filling
2 teaspoons grated orange peel
Strips of lemon and orange peel

12 to 16 servings
1 Serving: Calories 440 (Calories from Fat 230); Total Fat 26g (Saturated Fat 12g); Cholesterol 110mg; Sodium 420mg; Total Carbohydrate 48g (Dietary Fiber 0g); Protein 5g
% Daily Value: Vitamin A 15%; Vitamin C 4%; Calcium 15%; Iron 6%
Exchanges: 1 Starch, 2 Other Carbohydrate, 5 Fat
Carbohydrate Choices: 3

BETTY'S TIPS

⊘ Kitchen Tip

Instead of pie filling, try lemon, lime or orange curd. Look for a 10-ounce jar near the jams and jellies at your supermarket.

For a refreshing lemon-lime version, omit the orange juice, add $1^1/4$ cups water and stir 1 teaspoon grated lime peel into the batter.

1. Heat oven to 350° (if using dark or nonstick pans, heat oven to 325°). Grease bottoms and sides of two 8-inch or 9-inch round pans with shortening, or spray with cooking spray; lightly flour.

2. In large bowl, beat cake mix, water, orange juice, oil and eggs with electric mixer on low speed 30 seconds. Beat on medium speed 2 minutes, scraping bowl occasionally. Pour into pans.

3. Bake 8-inch rounds 33 to 38 minutes, 9-inch rounds 28 to 33 minutes, or until toothpick inserted in center comes out clean. Cool 10 minutes. Run knife around sides of pans to loosen cakes; carefully remove from pans to wire rack. Cool completely, about 1 hour.

4. In chilled medium bowl, beat whipping cream and powdered sugar on high speed until stiff peaks form. Fold in $1/2$ cup pie filling and grated orange peel.

5. Place 1 cake layer, rounded side down, on serving plate. Spread remaining pie filling over layer to within $1/4$ inch of edge. Top with second layer, rounded side up. Spread whipped cream mixture over top and sides of cake. Garnish top of cake with strips of lemon and orange peel. Store loosely covered in refrigerator.

Citrus Cake with Lemon Whipped Cream Frosting

Lemon Cake with Raspberry Mousse

Prep Time: 20 min Start to Finish: 2 hr 10 min

1 package Betty Crocker SuperMoist lemon cake mix

1^1/$_3$ cups buttermilk

^{1}/$_3$ cup vegetable oil

1 teaspoon grated lemon peel

3 eggs

2 cups raspberry pie filling (from 21-ounce can)

1^1/$_2$ cups whipping (heavy) cream

Fresh raspberries, if desired

Mint leaves, if desired

1. Heat oven to 350°. Grease bottoms only of two 8-inch or 9-inch round pans with shortening, or spray bottoms with cooking spray.

2. In large bowl, beat cake mix, buttermilk, oil, lemon peel and eggs with electric mixer on low speed 30 seconds. Beat on medium speed 2 minutes, scraping bowl occasionally. Pour into pans.

3. Bake 8-inch rounds 33 to 38 minutes, 9-inch rounds 28 to 33 minutes, or until toothpick inserted in center comes out clean. Cool 10 minutes. Run knife around side of pans to loosen cakes; remove from pans to wire rack. Cool completely, about 1 hour.

4. Place 1 cake layer, rounded side down, on serving plate. Spread ^{3}/$_4$ cup pie filling to within ^{1}/$_4$ inch of edge. Top with second layer, rounded side up.

5. In chilled medium bowl, beat whipping cream on high speed until soft peaks form. Beat in remaining 1^1/$_4$ cups pie filling* on low speed just until blended. Frost side and top of cake with raspberry mousse. Garnish with fresh raspberries and mint leaves. Store loosely covered in refrigerator.

Note: *For a smooth mousse, strain the raspberry seeds out of the pie filling by placing the filling in a mesh strainer or sieve over a bowl and using the back of a spoon to press the filling through the sieve.

Lemon Cake with Raspberry Mousse

16 servings.
1 Serving: Calories 310 (Calories from Fat 150); Total Fat 16g (Saturated Fat 7g); Cholesterol 70mg; Sodium 250mg; Total Carbohydrate 37g (Dietary Fiber 0g); Protein 4g
% Daily Value: Vitamin A 8%; Vitamin C 0%; Calcium 10%; Iron 4%
Exchanges: 1 Starch, 1^1/$_2$ Other Carbohydrate, 3 Fat
Carbohydrate Choices: 2^1/$_2$

BETTY'S TIPS

⚙ Kitchen Tip
If you don't have buttermilk on hand, substitute 1^1/$_4$ cups water when making the cake mix. Add the grated lemon peel for a burst of fresh lemon flavor.

Confetti Celebration Cake

Prep Time: 20 min Start to Finish: 2 hr

- 1 package Betty Crocker SuperMoist white cake mix
- 1¼ cups water
- ⅓ cup vegetable oil
- 3 egg whites
- 1 bottle (1.75 ounces) Betty Crocker Decors rainbow mix candy sprinkles
- 1 tub (1 pound) Betty Crocker Rich and Creamy vanilla frosting
- 2 to 4 different colors Betty Crocker decorating icing (in 4.25-ounce tubes)

1. Heat oven to 350°. Grease bottoms only of two 8-inch or 9-inch round pans with shortening (do not spray with cooking spray).

2. In large bowl, beat cake mix, water, oil and egg whites with electric mixer on low speed 30 seconds. Beat on medium speed 2 minutes, scraping bowl occasionally. Reserve 1 tablespoon candy sprinkles for decoration. Stir remaining sprinkles into batter. Pour into pans.

3. Bake 8-inch rounds 27 to 32 minutes, 9-inch rounds 23 to 28 minutes, or until toothpick inserted in center comes out clean. Cool 10 minutes. Run knife around sides of pan to loosen cakes; remove from pans to wire rack. Cool completely, about 1 hour.

4. Place 1 cake layer, rounded side down, on serving plate. Spread ⅓ cup frosting over layer. Top with second layer, rounded side up. Frost side and top of cake with remaining frosting.

5. Decorate top edge of cake with decorating icing in randomly squiggly pattern, overlapping colors. Sprinkle reserved candy sprinkles over top of cake.

16 servings.

1 Serving: Calories 340 (Calories from Fat 140); Total Fat 16g (Saturated Fat 5g); Cholesterol 0mg; Sodium 290mg; Total Carbohydrate 47g (Dietary Fiber 1g); Protein 3g
% Daily Value: Vitamin A 0%; Vitamin C 0%; Calcium 4%; Iron 8%
Exchanges: 1 Starch, 2 Other Carbohydrate, 3 Fat
Carbohydrate Choices: 3

BETTY'S TIPS

✿ Kitchen Tip

Enclose a sprinkle of bright-colored confetti in your party invitation. Scatter the same confetti on your dining or serving table too.

Confetti Celebration Cake

Pumpkin Angel Food Cake with Ginger-Cream Filling

Prep Time: 10 min Start to Finish: 3 hr

Cake

1 package Betty Crocker white angel food cake mix

1 tablespoon Gold Medal all-purpose flour

1¹/₂ teaspoons pumpkin pie spice

³/₄ cup canned pumpkin (not pumpkin pie mix)

1 cup cold water

Ginger-Cream Filling

2 cups whipping (heavy) cream

¹/₄ cup powdered sugar

2 tablespoons finely chopped crystallized ginger

1. Move oven rack to lowest position. Heat oven to 350°. In extra-large glass or metal bowl, beat all cake ingredients with electric mixer on low speed 30 seconds. Beat on medium speed 1 minute. Pour into ungreased 10-inch angel food pan (tube pan).

2. Bake 37 to 47 minutes or until crust is dark golden brown and cracks are dry. Immediately turn pan upside down onto heatproof funnel or glass bottle. Let hang about 2 hours or until cake is completely cool. Loosen cake from side of pan with knife or long metal spatula. Turn cake upside down onto serving plate.

3. In chilled large bowl, beat whipping cream and powdered sugar with electric mixer on high speed until stiff. Fold in ginger. Cut cake horizontally in half to make 2 even layers. Spread half of the filling on bottom layer; replace top of cake. Spread remaining filling on top of cake. Sprinkle with additional pumpkin pie spice if desired.

12 servings.
1 Serving: Calories 275 (Calories from Fat 115); Fat 13g (Saturated 8g); Cholesterol 45mg; Sodium 270mg; Carbohydrate 36g (Dietary Fiber 1g); Protein 4g
% Daily Value: Vitamin A 56%; Vitamin C 0%; Calcium 6%; Iron 2%
Exchanges: 1 Starch, 1¹/₂ Other Carbohydrate, 2¹/₂ Fat
Carbohydrate Choices: 2¹/₂

Pumpkin Angel Food Cake with Ginger-Cream Filling

BETTY'S TIPS

⚙ **Substitution**
Don't have crystallized ginger? Mix 1 teaspoon ground ginger with the powdered sugar when making the filling.

⚙ **Success Hint**
A serrated or electric knife will help you cleanly cut the cake into 2 layers. Use these knives for slicing the cake as well.

⚙ **Time-Saver**
Save a step or two by just cutting the cake into slices and topping with the filling or with frozen (thawed) whipped topping and garnishing with the chopped crystallized ginger.

Banana Turtle Torte

Prep Time: 30 min Start to Finish: 5 hr 15 min

1 package Betty Crocker SuperMoist German chocolate cake mix

$1^1/_3$ cups water

$^1/_2$ cup vegetable oil

3 eggs

$1^1/_2$ cups whipping (heavy) cream

3 bananas

1 cup butterscotch caramel topping

6 tablespoons chopped pecans, toasted

1. Heat oven to 350°. Grease bottoms only of two 9-inch round pans with shortening, or spray bottoms with cooking spray.

2. In large bowl, beat cake mix, water, oil and eggs with electric mixer on low speed 30 seconds. Beat on medium speed 2 minutes, scraping bowl occasionally. Pour into pans.

3. Bake 28 to 33 minutes or until toothpick inserted in center comes out clean. Cool 10 minutes. Run knife around sides of pans to loosen cakes; remove from pans to wire rack. Cool completely, about 1 hour. Freeze uncovered about 1 hour for easier cutting and frosting if desired.

4. In chilled medium bowl, beat whipping cream on high speed until stiff peaks form.

5. Split each cake horizontally into 2 layers. Place top of 1 layer, cut side up, on serving plate. Spread $^2/_3$ cup whipped cream over layer to within $^1/_4$ inch of edge. Slice 1 banana; arrange on whipped cream, overlapping slices if necessary. Drizzle $^1/_4$ cup butterscotch caramel topping over banana, spreading to coat slices. Sprinkle with 2 tablespoons pecans. Top with bottom half of layer, cut side down.

6. Top layer with $^2/_3$ cup whipped cream, 1 sliced banana, $^1/_4$ cup butterscotch caramel topping and 2 tablespoons pecans. Top with bottom half of second cake, cut side up. Repeat filling. Top with top half of cake, cut side down. Frost top of cake with remaining whipped cream. Spoon remaining butterscotch caramel topping over whipped cream. Swirl caramel into whipping cream with tip of knife.

7. Cover and refrigerate about 2 hours or until ready to serve. For best results, serve cake the same day. Store covered in refrigerator.

16 servings.

1 Serving: Calories 380 (Calories from Fat 18); Total Fat 20(Saturated Fat 8); Cholesterol 7mg; Sodium 34g; Total Carbohydrate 46(Dietary Fiber 1); Protein 4
% Daily Value: Vitamin A 8%; Vitamin C 0%; Calcium 6%; Iron 6%
Exchanges: 1 Starch, 2 Other Carbohydrate, 4 Fat
Carbohydrate Choices: 3

BETTY'S TIPS

⚙ **Kitchen Tip**

To toast nuts, bake uncovered in an ungreased shallow pan in a 350° oven for 6 to 10 minutes, stirring occasionally, until golden brown.

For a jazzy presentation, drizzle caramel topping on each plate. Center the slice of torte, then place a dab of whipped cream topping with a pecan half next to it.

Banana Turtle Torte

Cashew Lover's Cake

Prep Time: 30 min Start to Finish: 4 hr

- 1 can (9.5 ounces) honey-roasted whole cashews
- 1 package Betty Crocker SuperMoist yellow cake mix
- $1^1/_4$ cups water
- $^1/_3$ cup vegetable oil
- 3 eggs
- 2 packages (3 ounces each) cream cheese, softened
- $^3/_4$ cup butterscotch caramel topping
- 2 cups whipping (heavy) cream

1. Heat oven to 350°. Grease bottom only of 15 x 10 x 1-inch pan with shortening, or spray bottom with cooking spray.

2. Reserve $^2/_3$ cup cashews for garnish. Place remaining cashews in food processor or blender; cover and process until finely ground.

3. In large bowl, beat cake mix, water, oil and eggs with electric mixer on low speed 30 seconds. Beat on medium speed 2 minutes, scraping bowl occasionally. Stir in ground cashews. Pour into pan.

4. Bake 22 to 28 minutes or until toothpick inserted in center comes out clean. Run knife around sides of pan to loosen cake. Cool completely in pan or wire rack, about 1 hour. Cut cake crosswise into 3 pieces, freeze pieces in pan 1 hour.

5. In medium bowl, beat cream cheese and butterscotch caramel topping on low speed until well blended. Gradually beat in whipping cream on low speed. Beat on high speed about 4 minutes or until mixture thickens and soft peaks form.

6. Remove 1 cake piece from pan, using wide spatula; place on serving plate. Spread $^3/_4$ cup caramel mixture over cake piece. Top with second cake piece; spread with $^3/_4$ cup caramel mixture. Top with third cake piece. Frost sides and top of cake with remaining caramel mixture. Sprinkle reserved whole cashews over top of cake. Cover and refrigerate about 1 hour or until ready to serve. Store covered in refrigerator.

Cashew Lover's Cake

20 servings.
1 Serving: Calories 370 (Calories from Fat 210); Total Fat 24g (Saturated Fat 10g); Cholesterol 75mg; Sodium 290mg; Total Carbohydrate 35g (Dietary Fiber 0g); Protein 5g
% Daily Value: Vitamin A 10%; Vitamin C 0%; Calcium 8%; Iron 8%
Exchanges: $1^1/_2$ Starch, 1 Other Carbohydrate, $4^1/_2$ Fat
Carbohydrate Choices: 2

BETTY'S TIPS

⚙ **Kitchen Tip**
The easiest way to cut this cake into 20 serving pieces is to slice it lengthwise in half with a sharp knife, then cut it crosswise 10 times to make 20 pieces.

Pecan lovers can use pecans instead of cashews.

Peanut Butter Silk Cake

Prep Time: 15 min Start to Finish: 2 hr 15 min
(Photo on page 253)

1	package Betty Crocker SuperMoist yellow cake mix
1 1/4	cups water
1/2	cup creamy peanut butter
1/3	cup vegetable oil
3	eggs
1/4	cup butter or margarine
1/4	cup packed brown sugar
1	cup whipping (heavy) cream
1/2	cup creamy peanut butter
1	tub (1 pound) Betty Crocker Rich & Creamy chocolate frosting
1	cup chopped pecans, if desired

1. Heat oven to 350°. Generously grease bottoms only of two 8-inch or 9-inch round pans with shortening, or spray bottoms with cooking spray.

2. In large bowl, beat cake mix, water, 1/2 cup peanut butter, oil and eggs with electric mixer on low speed 30 seconds. Beat on medium speed 2 minutes, scraping bowl occasionally. Pour into pans.

3. Bake 32 to 38 minutes or until toothpick inserted in center comes out clean. Cool 10 minutes. Run knife around sides of pans to loosen cakes; remove from pans to wire rack. Cool completely, about 1 hour.

4. In 2-quart saucepan, melt butter over medium heat; stir in brown sugar. Heat to boiling; boil and stir 1 minute. Remove from heat. Refrigerate 10 minutes.

5. In chilled medium bowl, beat whipping cream on high speed until soft peaks form; set aside. In another medium bowl, beat 1/2 cup peanut butter and the brown sugar mixture on medium speed until smooth and creamy. Add whipped cream to peanut butter mixture; beat on medium speed until mixture is smooth and creamy.

6. Split each cake layer horizontally to make 2 layers. Fill each layer with about 2/3 cup peanut butter mixture to within 1/2 inch of edge. Frost side and top of cake with frosting. Press pecans onto frosting on side of cake. Store covered in refrigerator.

12 to 16 servings.

1 Serving: Calories 750 (Calories from Fat 430); Total Fat 48g (Saturated Fat 19g); Cholesterol 90mg; Sodium 530mg; Total Carbohydrate 69g (Dietary Fiber 4g); Protein 13g
% Daily Value: Vitamin A 10%; Vitamin C 0%; Calcium 15%; Iron 10%
Exchanges: 2 Starch, 2 1/2 Other Carbohydrate, 1 High-Fat Meat, 8 Fat
Carbohydrate Choices: 4 1/2

BETTY'S TIPS

⚙ **Kitchen Tip**
To cut cake layers in half horizontally, place 6 toothpicks halfway down sides of each layer. Using the toothpicks as a guide, slice layer in half with a long knife.

For a fun garnish, top this cake with coarsely cut-up chocolate-covered peanut butter cups. Or dot the top with mini cups cut in half crosswise.

Ultimate Carrot Cake

Prep Time: 20 min Start to Finish: 2 hr 15 min

1 package Betty Crocker SuperMoist carrot cake mix

$1/2$ cup water

$1/2$ cup vegetable oil

4 eggs

1 can (8 ounces) crushed pineapple in juice, undrained

$1/2$ cup chopped nuts

$1/2$ cup shredded coconut

$1/2$ cup raisins

1 tub (1 pound) Betty Crocker Rich & Creamy cream cheese frosting

1. Heat oven to 350°. Grease bottoms only of two 8-inch or 9-inch round pans with shortening, or spray bottoms with cooking spray; lightly flour.

2. In large bowl, beat cake mix, water, oil, eggs and pineapple (with juice) with electric mixer on low speed 30 seconds. Beat on medium speed 2 minutes. Stir in nuts, coconut and raisins. Pour into pans.

3. Bake 8-inch rounds 40 to 45 minutes, 9-inch rounds 30 to 35 minutes, or until toothpick inserted in center comes out clean. Cool 10 minutes. Run knife around sides of pans to loosen cakes; remove from pans to wire rack. Cool completely, about 1 hour.

4. Fill layers and frost side and top of cake with frosting. Store covered in refrigerator.

12 servings.
1 Serving: Calories 370 (Calories from Fat 220); Total Fat 24g (Saturated Fat 7g); Cholesterol 80mg; Sodium 400mg; Total Carbohydrate 34g (Dietary Fiber 1g); Protein 5g
% Daily Value: Vitamin A 8%; Vitamin C 0%; Calcium 15%; Iron 8%
Exchanges: 1 Starch, $1^1/2$ Other Carbohydrate, $4^1/2$ Fat
Carbohydrate Choices: 2

BETTY'S TIPS

✹ **Kitchen Tip**
Select your favorite type of nuts for this fabulous cake—pecans, walnuts, almonds or hazelnuts work great!

Ultimate Carrot Cake

Chocolate-Cherry Ice-Cream Cake

Prep Time: 25 min Start to Finish: 9 hr 45 min

16   creme-filled chocolate sandwich cookies

$1/4$ cup butter or margarine

1   quart (4 cups) cherry or cherry vanilla ice cream, softened

8   creme-filled chocolate sandwich cookies, coarsely chopped

1   cup miniature semisweet chocolate chips

1   quart (4 cups) vanilla ice cream, softened

$1/2$ cup fudge ice-cream sauce
    Sweetened whipped cream, if desired

12   fresh cherries with stems

1. Heat oven to 350°. Place 16 cookies in food processor. Cover and process until finely ground. Add butter; cover and process until mixed. Press in springform pan, 9 x 3 inches. Bake 8 to 10 minutes or until firm. Cool completely, about 30 minutes.

2. Wrap outside of springform pan with aluminum foil. Spread cherry ice cream over cooled crust. Freeze 30 minutes.

3. Sprinkle chopped cookies and $1/2$ cup chocolate chips over cherry ice cream; press slightly. Spread vanilla ice cream over top. Drop fudge sauce over ice cream in small spoonfuls; swirl slightly into ice cream. Sprinkle with remaining $1/2$ cup chocolate chips; press slightly. Freeze about 8 hours until firm.

4. To serve, let stand at room temperature 5 to 10 minutes. Carefully remove side of pan. Cut dessert into wedges. Top each with whipped cream and cherry.

12 servings.
1 Serving: Calories 395 (Calories from Fat 190); Total Fat 21g (Saturated Fat 12g); Cholesterol 55mg; Sodium 165mg; Total Carbohydrate 46g (Dietary Fiber 2g); Protein 5g
% Daily Value: Vitamin A 10%; Vitamin C 2%; Calcium 14%; Iron 4%
Exchanges: 2 Starch, 1 Other Carbohydrate, 4 Fat
Carbohydrate Choices: 3

Chocolate-Cherry Ice-Cream Cake

BETTY'S TIPS

✪ Success Hint

Spray the back of a metal spoon with cooking spray, then use it to press the crumb mixture into the pan.

It's a snap to spread the fudge sauce over the ice cream. Just spoon the sauce into a resealable plastic food-storage bag, cut off a small tip from a corner and squeeze.

✪ Do-Ahead

This special dessert keeps well in the freezer for up to 2 weeks. Make the dessert, freeze until firm, then cover with aluminum foil to store.

Betty Crocker ON WHAT'S NEW

Parties That Take the Cake

Soak-Up-the-Sun

KIDS' BIRTHDAY PARTY

Invitations

Pick up postcards with summer scenes to use as invitations. Ask guests to dress in beachwear.

Continue the tropical theme with these games:

- ▶ Dance the limbo under a broom handle.

- ▶ Hold a squirt-bottle water fight.

- ▶ Bury pennies or pretty seashells in a sandbox, and let kids dig for "treasure" with sand shovels.

- ▶ Provide fabric paints, craft glue and sequins for kids to decorate their own T-shirts, visors or sunglasses.

Menu

- ▶ Giant submarine sandwiches
- ▶ Ants on a log
- ▶ Fruit kabobs and dip
- ▶ Snack mix with fish-shaped crackers
- ▶ Lemonade
- ▶ *Birthday Cake:*

Confetti Celebration Cake, page 258

Set the Mood

Turn your backyard or deck into a tropical paradise with colorful beach towels, beach balls, and if you have one, a beach umbrella. Buy inexpensive plastic leis for the guests. Use sand pails and shovels as the centerpiece. Look for tropical-themed plates and napkins, or mix and match them in a bright assortment of colors.

BLAST-FROM-THE-PAST
ADULT BIRTHDAY PARTY

Set the Mood

Use photos, trophies and other memorabilia of the birthday honoree for the centerpiece or as decorations around the room. Put on music from the guest of honor's favorite era.

March 21 1955 — THE DAILY HERALD

EXTRA

Metro Edition

Amazing Baby Born In Local Hospital!

Jim's Birth Is Big News So Don't Miss The Celebration!

BIRTHDAY PARTY NEWS!
You are invited to the biggest bash of any year!

WHEN: March 21th
TIME: 7:00
WHERE: Our House
3022 Oak Street

OTHER NEWS OF 1955

Oscar Goes to *On the Waterfront* for Best Picture

Nobel Prize for Literature Goes to *Halldór Kiljan Laxness* (Iceland)

Federal Republic of West Germany becomes a sovereign state (May 5)

The Soviet Union and seven East European countries sign the Warsaw Pact, a mutual defense treaty (May 14)

Invitations

Design a "newspaper" invitation with a headline announcing the big event (the guest of honor's birth), followed by other news from the birth year and details about the party. Include a scrapbook page, and ask guests to write or design a memory of the birthday person. Give the completed scrapbook as a gift at the party.

Keep the party lively with these nostalgic games:

- Hold a hula hoop contest.
- Play charades.
- Go on a scavenger hunt.

Menu

- Martinis
- Cocktail wieners or glazed meatballs
- Cheese ball and crackers
- Rumaki
- Shrimp cocktail
- Mixed seasoned nuts
- *Birthday Cake:*

Citrus Cake with Lemon Whipped Cream Frosting, page 256

RECIPE

WEDDING SHOWER

Invitations

Fill out recipe cards with the party details. Tuck a blank recipe card in with the invitation, and ask guests to share their favorite recipe with the bride-to-be.

Set the Mood

Create a centerpiece with cookbooks, cooking utensils and a flower-filled vase placed in a chef's hat. Set out a pretty recipe box where guests can file their recipe cards for the guest of honor. Look for cooking-themed paper plates and napkins.

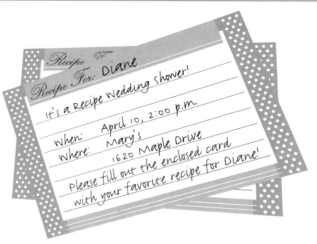

Recipe For: Diane

It's a Recipe Wedding shower!

When: April 10, 2:00 p.m.
Where: Mary's
1620 Maple Drive
Please fill out the enclosed card with your favorite recipe for Diane!

Wrap eating utensils in napkins, and use cookie cutters as napkin rings. (The cutters make nice favors for the guests too!)

Get the party cookin' with these activities:

▶ Buy a white apron for the bride, and have guests decorate it with fabric paints.

    ▶ Have each guest share a favorite cooking tip, success story or disaster story with the bride.

Menu

▶ Grilled chicken or shrimp Caesar salad

▶ Mixed olives

▶ Assorted breads

▶ Fresh fruit platter

▶ *Celebration Cake:*

Lemon Cake with Raspberry Mousse, page 257

CALENDAR
BABY SHOWER

Invitations

Using old calendars, tear out a month page for each guest and write the party information on the page. Ask guests to bring gifts for their month.

Set the Mood

Create a centerpiece of baby items, pacifiers, toys, bottles or baby shoes. Put gifts in a large laundry basket. Both the centerpiece and basket can go home with the new mom. Have your children (or others') color paper place mats. String a clothesline near the festivities, and clip the gifts (towels, cloths, etc.) to it for all to admire.

No shower is complete without games!

- ▶ Have each guest share with the new mom a song, poem, article or quote that pertains to parenthood.

- ▶ Play "Who's that baby?" Ask guests to bring a baby picture, and let everyone guess who's who.

- ▶ Buy a selection of jarred baby foods and remove the labels. Let guests guess the flavors by color and smell.

Menu

- ▶ Quiche or baked egg dish
- ▶ Purchased spinach salad
- ▶ Nut breads or warm dinner rolls
- ▶ Fruit iced tea or punch
- ▶ *Celebration Cake:*

Almond Baby Cakes, page 242

Cranberry-Orange Cheesecake

Prep Time: 15 min Start to Finish: 7 hr 30 min

$1^1/_2$ cups chocolate cookie crumbs

$^1/_4$ cup powdered sugar

$^1/_4$ cup butter or margarine, melted

3 packages (8 ounces each) cream cheese, softened

1 cup granulated sugar

4 eggs

1 container (8 ounces) sour cream (1 cup)

2 tablespoons grated orange peel

2 tablespoons orange-flavored liqueur, if desired

$1^1/_2$ cups Cranberry-Orange Sauce (page 271)

1. Heat oven to 300°. Wrap outside of 9- or 10-inch springform pan with aluminum foil. In small bowl, stir together cookie crumbs, powdered sugar and butter. Press in bottom of pan.

2. Beat cream cheese, granulated sugar, eggs, sour cream, orange peel and liqueur with electric mixer on medium speed until smooth. Pour over crust.

3. Bake 1 hour 20 minutes to 1 hour 30 minutes or until center is set. Cool 15 minutes; carefully run knife around side of pan to loosen cheesecake. Cool 1 hour. Cover and refrigerate at least 4 hours. Remove side of pan. Spoon Cranberry-Orange Sauce onto cheesecake just before serving.

12 servings.
1 Serving: Calories 590 (Calories from Fat 325); Fat 12g (Saturated 20g); Cholesterol 155mg; Sodium 350mg; Carbohydrate 58g (Dietary Fiber 1g); Protein 9g
% Daily Value: Vitamin A 24%; Vitamin C 12%; Calcium 8%; Iron 10%
Exchanges: 3 Starch, 1 Fruit, $6^1/_2$ Fat
Carbohydrate Choices: 4

BETTY'S TIPS

✪ **Success Hint**
Wrapping the springform pan in aluminum foil prevents any leaks during baking—and saves on oven cleanup!

✪ **Do-Ahead**
Make this cheesecake and the Cranberry-Orange Sauce up to 24 hours ahead. Cover each separately and refrigerate until you're ready to serve the dessert.

✪ **Special Touch**
Garnish with sugared cranberries, kumquats and lemon leaves. To sugar the cranberries, roll frozen cranberries in granulated sugar. For the lemon leaves, use a scissors to cut the leaves to resemble holly leaves.

Quick & Low Fat
Cranberry-Orange Sauce

Prep Time: 10 min Start to Finish: 25 min

2	cups fresh or frozen cranberries (8 ounces)
1/2	cup sugar
2	teaspoons cornstarch
1/2	cup water
1/2	cup orange marmalade

12 servings (2 tablespoons each).
1 Serving: Calories 60 (Calories from Fat 5); Fat 0g (Saturated 0g); Cholesterol 0mg; Sodium 5mg; Carbohydrate 15g (Dietary Fiber 2g); Protein 0g
% Daily Value: Vitamin A 0%; Vitamin C 0%; Calcium 0%; Iron 0%
Exchanges: 1 Fruit
Carbohydrate Choices: 1

1. Wash cranberries; remove blemished berries. In 2-quart saucepan, mix cranberries, sugar and cornstarch. Stir in water. Heat to boiling over medium-high heat, stirring occasionally. Simmer uncovered 5 to 8 minutes, stirring occasionally, until cranberries pop.

2. Stir in marmalade. Serve sauce warm or chilled.

Cranberry-Orange Cheesecake

Raspberry-Apple Crumb Pie

Raspberry-Apple Crumb Pie

Prep Time: 15 min Start to Finish: 1 hr 40 min

Pie

1 refrigerated pie crust (from 15-ounce package)

3 cups thinly sliced peeled cooking apples (3 medium)

$^1/_2$ cup sugar

2 tablespoons Gold Medal all-purpose flour

$^1/_2$ teaspoon ground cinnamon

2 cups frozen raspberries (from 1-pound bag), thawed

$^1/_2$ cup cubed or crumbled pure almond paste (from 7- or 8-ounce package)

Almond Crumb Topping

$^1/_2$ cup Gold Medal all-purpose flour

$^1/_4$ cup sugar

$^1/_4$ cup butter or margarine

$^1/_2$ cup sliced almonds

1. Heat oven to 350°. Place pie crust in 9-inch glass pie plate as directed on package for one-crust filled pie. In large bowl, stir together apples, $^1/_2$ cup sugar, 2 tablespoons flour and cinnamon. Spoon into crust-lined pie plate. Sprinkle with raspberries. Sprinkle almond paste over raspberries.

2. In medium bowl, mix $^1/_2$ cup flour and $^1/_4$ cup sugar. Cut in butter, using pastry blender or crisscrossing 2 knives, until particles are size of small peas. Stir in almonds. Sprinkle evenly over almond paste.

3. Bake 1 hour to 1 hour 20 minutes, covering edge of crust with aluminum foil after about 30 minutes, until apples are tender in center and surface is golden brown. Serve warm or cooled.

8 servings.
1 Serving: Calories 415 (Calories from Fat 160); Fat 18g (Saturated 5g); Cholesterol 15mg; Sodium 140mg; Carbohydrate 65g (Dietary Fiber 6g); Protein 5g
% Daily Value: Vitamin A 4%; Vitamin C 10%; Calcium 4%; Iron 10%
Exchanges: 2 Starch, 2 Fruit, 3 Fat
Carbohydrate Choices: 4

BETTY'S TIPS

⚙ **Success Hint**

Look for almond paste near the baking chocolate and nuts. Check the label to make sure it lists almonds as the first ingredient.

If pieces of the almond paste are sticking out, tuck them into the crumb topping so they don't brown too quickly.

⚙ **Serve-With**

This luscious pie is terrific with a scoop of vanilla ice cream.

⚙ **Do-Ahead**

You can make the pie several hours before serving. To warm it up, microwave pieces on individual microwavable plates on High for about 10 seconds.

Chocolate-Glazed Cherry-Pecan Pie

Prep Time: 15 min Start to Finish: 2 hr

$^2/_3$ cup dried cherries

3 tablespoons brandy

1 refrigerated pie crust (from 15-ounce package)

3 tablespoons butter or margarine, melted

$^3/_4$ cup sugar

$^3/_4$ cup light corn syrup

$^1/_2$ teaspoon almond extract

3 eggs

$1^1/_2$ cups broken pecans

$^1/_4$ cup semisweet chocolate chips

$^1/_2$ teaspoon vegetable oil

1. In small bowl, mix cherries and brandy. Let stand 15 minutes; do not drain.

2. Heat oven to 375°. Place pie crust in 9-inch glass pie plate as directed on package for one-crust filled pie. In large bowl, beat butter, sugar, corn syrup, almond extract and eggs with hand beater or wire whisk until well mixed. Stir in cherry mixture and pecans. Pour into crust-lined pie plate.

3. Bake 30 minutes, covering with aluminum foil after 15 minutes if pie is browning too quickly. Reduce oven temperature to 325°. Bake 12 to 15 minutes longer or until center is set and surface is deep golden brown. Cool 30 minutes.

4. In microwavable bowl, microwave chocolate chips and oil uncovered on High 1 minute; stir until smooth. Drizzle chocolate over pie. Cool completely, about 30 minutes.

Chocolate-Glazed Cherry-Pecan Pie

8 servings.
1 Serving: Calories 545 (Calories from Fat 260); Fat 29g (Saturated 7g); Cholesterol 90mg; Sodium 190mg; Carbohydrate 65g (Dietary Fiber 3g); Protein 6g
% Daily Value: Vitamin A 6%; Vitamin C 0%; Calcium 2%; Iron 8%
Exchanges: 2 Starch, 2 Other Carbohydrate, 6 Fat
Carbohydrate Choices: 4

BETTY'S TIPS

❂ **Substitution**
If you don't have brandy, soak the cherries in a mixture of $^1/_4$ cup water and 1 teaspoon brandy extract.

❂ **Success Hint**
Store custard-type pies like this in the fridge. But if you want to serve it warm, place slices on individual microwavable plates and microwave on High for about 10 seconds.

Caramel-Pecan Chocolate Dessert

Prep Time: 20 min Start to Finish: 5 hr 15 min

1 package (1 pound 3.8 ounces) Betty Crocker fudge brownie mix

¼ cup water

½ cup vegetable oil

2 eggs

1 cup milk chocolate chips

½ cup whipping (heavy) cream

20 caramels (from 14-ounce bag), unwrapped

1 egg, beaten

1 cup broken pecans

¾ cup whipping (heavy) cream

2 tablespoons powdered sugar

1. Heat oven to 350° (if using dark or nonstick pan, heat oven to 325°). Grease bottom and side of 10-inch springform pan with shortening. In medium bowl, stir brownie mix, water, oil and 2 eggs until well blended. Stir in chocolate chips. Spread in pan.

2. Bake 50 to 60 minutes or until puffed in center and toothpick inserted near center comes out clean. Cool completely, about 1 hour.

3. Meanwhile, in 1-quart saucepan, heat ½ cup whipping cream and caramels over medium heat, stirring frequently, until caramels are melted. Stir small amount of hot mixture into beaten egg, then stir egg back into remaining mixture in saucepan. Cook over medium heat 2 to 3 minutes, stirring constantly, until thickened. Stir in pecans. Spread over brownie. Refrigerate uncovered at least 3 hours until chilled.

4. Run metal spatula around side of pan to loosen dessert; remove side of pan. Transfer dessert on pan base to serving plate. In chilled small bowl, beat ¾ cup whipping cream and powdered sugar with electric mixer on high speed until stiff peaks form. Spoon whipped cream in 12 dollops around edge of dessert. Cut into wedges to serve. Store covered in refrigerator.

12 servings.
1 Serving: Calories 585 (Calories from Fat 310); Fat 34g (Saturated 13g); Cholesterol 90mg; Sodium 240mg; Carbohydrate 65g (Dietary Fiber 3g); Protein 6g
% Daily Value: Vitamin A 8%; Vitamin C 0%; Calcium 10%; Iron 10%
Exchanges: 2 Starch, 2 Other Carbohydrate, 7 Fat
Carbohydrate Choices: 2

BETTY'S TIPS

❂ **Success Hint**
Mark the top of the dessert with a knife where you'll cut, before adding the whipped cream garnish. That way, you'll know the whipped cream will be centered on each serving.

❂ **Time-Saver**
Whipped cream from a spray can works great for this recipe—and saves the time of whipping the cream.

❂ **Do-Ahead**
Make the dessert up to 24 hours ahead and refrigerate. Up to 2 hours before serving, beat the cream with the powdered sugar as directed.

Caramel-Pecan Chocolate Dessert

"Jamocha" Ice-Cream Pie

Prep Time: 20 min Start to Finish: 4 hr 20 min

Coffee Pat-in-Pan Pie Crust (below)

2 pints (4 cups) coffee ice cream, slightly softened

3/4 cup hot fudge topping

1 cup frozen (thawed) whipped topping, if desired

Coffee-flavored chocolate candies or chocolate-covered coffee beans, if desired

1. Make Coffee Pat-in-Pan Pie Crust.

2. Spread 1 pint of ice cream in pie crust. Cover and freeze about 1 hour or until firm.

3. Spread hot fudge topping over ice cream in pie crust. Carefully spread remaining pint of ice cream over topping. Cover and freeze at least 2 hours until firm but no longer than 2 weeks.

4. To serve, let stand at room temperature about 10 minutes before cutting. Garnish with whipped topping and candies just before serving.

8 servings.

Coffee Pat-in-Pan Pie Crust

1 cup Gold Medal all-purpose flour

1/2 cup butter or margarine, softened

2 teaspoons powdered instant coffee (dry)

Heat oven to 400°. Mix all ingredients in medium bowl with spoon until dough forms. Press firmly and evenly against bottom and side of pie plate, 9 x 1 1/4 inches. Bake 12 to 15 minutes or until light brown. Cool completely, about 45 minutes.

1 Serving: Calories 395 (Calories from Fat 190); Fat 21g (Saturated 13g); Cholesterol 60mg; Sodium 230mg; Carbohydrate 46g (Dietary Fiber 1g); Protein 5g
% Daily Value: Vitamin A 14%; Vitamin C 0%; Calcium 10%; Iron 6%
Exchanges: 2 Starch, 1 Other Carbohydrate, 4 Fat
Carbohydrate Choices: 3

BETTY'S TIPS

⊛ **Success Hint**
Frozen pies are easier to cut and serve if you let them stand a few minutes at room temperature.

⊛ **Time-Saver**
Instead of making the crust, buy a 9-inch ready-to-use chocolate or vanilla wafer cookie crust.

⊛ **Did You Know?**
Mocha refers to the yummy combination of chocolate and coffee.

"Jamocha" Ice-Cream Pie

Blueberry-Topped Lemon Ice-Cream Pie

Prep Time: 10 min Start to Finish: 5 hr 35 min

- 1 package (6 ounces) ready-to-use vanilla wafer cookie crust
- 1 pint (2 cups) vanilla ice cream, slightly softened
- 1 pint (2 cups) lemon sherbet, slightly softened
- 1/2 cup fresh blueberries
- 1/4 cup blueberry preserves
- 1 tablespoon lemon juice
  Grated lemon peel, if desired

1. Heat oven to 375°. Bake cookie crust 5 minutes. Cool completely, about 20 minutes. Spread 1 cup of vanilla ice cream over bottom of cooled crust. Freeze 30 minutes.

2. Spread lemon sherbet over ice cream. Freeze 30 minutes.

3. Spread remaining ice cream over sherbet. Freeze at least 4 hours until firm.

4. Mix blueberries, preserves and lemon juice in small bowl; refrigerate until serving. Serve 1 tablespoon blueberry mixture over each slice of pie. Garnish with lemon peel.

8 servings.
1 Serving: Calories 340 (Calories from Fat 135); Fat 15g (Saturated 6g); Cholesterol 15mg; Sodium 250mg; Carbohydrate 47g (Dietary Fiber 1g); Protein 4g
% Daily Value: Vitamin A 8%; Vitamin C 6%; Calcium 6%; Iron 6%
Exchanges: 1 Starch, 2 Other Carbohydrate, 3 Fat
Carbohydrate Choices: 3

Blueberry-Topped Lemon Ice-Cream Pie

BETTY'S TIPS

☺ **Substitution**

Make the switch to orange by using orange sherbet for the pie, orange juice for the topping and grated orange peel for the garnish.

Frozen blueberries work well in this recipe. Mix them with the preserves and lemon juice while they're still frozen.

☺ **Success Hint**

If the ice cream and sherbet begin to melt before you're done putting it all together, place them—along with the rest of the pie—in the freezer until slightly firm, about 15 minutes.

Ginger-Peach Dessert

Prep Time: 15 min Start to Finish: 5 hr 30 min

Gingersnap Crust (below)

2 quarts (8 cups) peach frozen yogurt, softened

1 container (8 ounces) frozen reduced-fat whipped topping, thawed

1/4 cup finely chopped pecans

2 medium peaches, cut into thin slices

1. Make Gingersnap Crust. Spread frozen yogurt over cooled crust. Freeze 30 minutes.

2. Spread whipped topping over frozen yogurt; sprinkle with pecans. Freeze about 4 hours or until firm.

3. To serve, let stand at room temperature 5 to 10 minutes. Cut dessert into squares. Top each square with 2 or 3 peach slices.

12 servings.

Gingersnap Crust

40 gingersnap cookies (about 1 1/2 inches in diameter)

1/2 cup pecan pieces

1/2 cup butter or margarine, melted

Heat oven to 350°. Place cookies and pecans in food processor. Cover and process until crushed. Add butter; process until mixed. Press evenly in rectangular pan, 13 x 9 x 2 inches. Bake 8 to 10 minutes or until center is set when lightly touched. Cool completely, about 25 minutes.

1 Serving: Calories 400 (Calories from Fat 170); Fat 19g (Saturated Fat 9g); Cholesterol 25mg; Sodium 270mg; Carbohydrate 49g (Dietary Fiber 2g); Protein 8g
% Daily Value: Vitamin A 10%; Vitamin C 0%; Calcium 22%; Iron 4%
Exchanges: 1 Starch, 1 Fruit, 4 Fat
Carbohydrate Choices: 3

BETTY'S TIPS

☺ **Substitution**
Try substituting peach ice cream for the frozen yogurt and walnuts for the pecans.

☺ **Success Hint**
The frozen yogurt needs to be just soft enough so you can scoop and spread it; soften it by placing in the fridge for 20 to 30 minutes. If you let it stand at room temperature, it will become too soft on the outside and still be too firm on the inside.

☺ **Special Touch**
Enhance the ginger flavor by sprinkling the peaches with chopped crystallized ginger just before serving.

Ginger-Peach Dessert

Lemon-Pear Gingerbread Trifle

Prep Time: 20 min Start to Finish: 13 hr 55 min

1 package Betty Crocker gingerbread cake and cookie mix

1 1/4 cups lukewarm water

1 egg

2 cans (15.25 ounces each) sliced pears

1 can (15.75 ounces) lemon pie filling

2 cups whipping (heavy) cream

1. Heat oven to 350°. Spray bottom only of 13 x 9-inch pan with cooking spray. In large bowl, stir gingerbread mix, water and egg with fork until blended. Stir vigorously about 2 minutes until well mixed. Pour into pan. Bake 18 to 20 minutes or until toothpick inserted in center comes out clean.

2. Meanwhile, drain pears into 2-cup glass measuring cup, reserving 3/4 cup pear liquid. Add 1/2 cup pie filling to pear liquid. Microwave uncovered on High 1 to 2 minutes or until heated; stir with wire whisk until smooth. Prick top of warm cake in several places with fork. Pour warm lemon sauce over cake; spread evenly. Refrigerate pears and remaining pie filling. Cool cake completely, about 1 hour.

3. Cut cake into 1 1/2-inch squares. In large bowl, beat whipping cream with electric mixer on high speed until thickened. Slowly beat in remaining pie filling; continue beating until thickened. Place 1/3 of cake cubes in bottom of 2-quart clear glass bowl. Spread with 1/3 of cream mixture. Arrange 1/3 of pears on cream mixture. Repeat layers twice with cake, cream mixture and pears. Cover and refrigerate at least 12 hours.

12 servings.
1 Serving: Calories 330 (Calories from Fat 155); Fat 17g (Saturated 9g); Cholesterol 55mg; Sodium 150mg; Carbohydrate 41g (Dietary Fiber 2g); Protein 3g
% Daily Value: Vitamin A 10%; Vitamin C 0%; Calcium 6%; Iron 8%
Exchanges: 1 Starch, 2 Fruit, 3 Fat
Carbohydrate Choices: 3

Lemon-Pear Gingerbread Trifle

BETTY'S TIPS

⊘ **Substitution**
Pear halves can be sliced and used in this recipe.

⊘ **Variation**
For a smaller trifle, cut only half of the gingerbread into pieces and use half the amount of pears, lemon filling and whipping cream. Freeze the remaining gingerbread.

⊘ **Special Touch**
Dot the top of the trifle with dollops of whipped cream. Sprinkle a little chopped crystallized ginger on each dollop.

Eggnog Pots de Crème

Prep Time: 15 min Start to Finish: 8 hr 15 min

1¹/₂ cups dairy eggnog
¹/₂ cup half-and-half
3 egg yolks
2 teaspoon cornstarch
¹/₂ teaspoon rum extract
   Ground nutmeg

6 servings.
1 Serving: Calories 80 (Calories from Fat 45); Fat 5g (Saturated 2g); Cholesterol 155mg; Sodium 45mg; Carbohydrate 4g (Dietary Fiber 0g); Protein 4g
% Daily Value: Vitamin A 4%; Vitamin C 0%; Calcium 8%; Iron 2%
Exchanges: ¹/₂ Milk, 1 Fat
Carbohydrate Choices: 0

1. In 2-quart saucepan, heat eggnog and half-and-half over medium-low heat, stirring occasionally, until hot.

2. In medium bowl, beat egg yolks, cornstarch and rum extract with wire whisk. Stir a small amount of hot eggnog mixture into egg mixture, then gradually stir egg mixture back into remaining eggnog mixture in saucepan. Continue cooking over medium-low heat, stirring constantly, until mixture just begins to boil and thicken. Immediately remove from heat.

3. Pour into 6 small serving dishes. Sprinkle with nutmeg. Refrigerate at least 8 hours until well chilled and set.

BETTY'S TIPS

⊛ **Success Hint**
Pots de Crème is a creamy, rich French custard served in small pot-shaped cups. Its consistency is slightly soft and not as firm as a traditional pudding.

⊛ **Do-Ahead**
You can make this dessert up to 24 hours ahead. Just cover each dish with plastic wrap and refrigerate.

⊛ **Special Touch**
Top each serving with a couple of raspberries and fresh mint leaves.

Eggnog Pots de Crème

Creamy Rice Pudding with Brandied Cherry Sauce

Prep Time: 15 min Start to Finish: 4 hr 20 min

Rice Pudding

4	cups milk
3/4	cup uncooked regular long-grain rice
1/3	cup sugar
1/4	teaspoon salt
2	eggs, beaten
1	cup whipping (heavy) cream
1	teaspoon vanilla

Brandied Cherry Sauce

1/2	cup sugar
1	tablespoon cornstarch
1/4	cup orange juice
1 1/2	cups frozen unsweetened tart red cherries (from 1-pound bag)
2	tablespoons brandy or orange juice

Creamy Rice Pudding with Brandied Cherry Sauce

1. In 2-quart saucepan, heat milk, rice, 1/3 cup sugar and salt to boiling over medium-high heat. Reduce heat to medium-low. Simmer uncovered 40 to 45 minutes, stirring frequently, until rice is tender and mixture is thickened.

2. Stir a small amount of hot rice mixture into eggs, then stir eggs back into remaining mixture in saucepan. Continue cooking over medium heat about 3 minutes, stirring constantly, until heated through. Cool 45 minutes, stirring occasionally.

3. In chilled large serving bowl, beat whipping cream and vanilla with electric mixer on high speed until thickened. Fold in cooled rice mixture. Cover and refrigerate at least 3 hours until well chilled.

4. In 1-quart saucepan, mix 1/2 cup sugar and cornstarch. Stir in orange juice and frozen cherries. Heat over medium-high heat, stirring frequently, until mixture boils and thickens slightly. Stir in brandy. Serve sauce warm or chilled with pudding.

BETTY'S TIPS

⊗ **Success Hint**
The rice should just barely bubble as it cooks. The milk may evaporate during cooking, so you may have to stir in a little hot water to keep the sauce-like consistency.

⊗ **Time-Saver**
Cool the pudding in a jiffy by placing the saucepan in a bowl of ice water. Stir frequently so the pudding cools evenly.

⊗ **Do-Ahead**
Up to 24 hours ahead, make the pudding and spoon it into individual serving dishes; cover and refrigerate. Refrigerate the sauce in a covered container.

8 servings.
1 Serving: Calories 345 (Calories from Fat 115); Fat 13g (Saturated 8g); Cholesterol 95mg; Sodium 160mg; Carbohydrate 49g (Dietary Fiber 1g); Protein 8g
% Daily Value: Vitamin A 14%; Vitamin C 4%; Calcium 18%; Iron 6%
Exchanges: 1 Starch, 1 Milk, 1 1/2 Other Carbohydrate, 2 Fat
Carbohydrate Choices: 3

Ice Cream with Marinated Strawberries

S'mores Chocolate Chip Ice-Cream Sandwiches

Ice Cream with Marinated Strawberries

Prep Time: 15 min Start to Finish: 2 hr 15 min

- 1 quart (4 cups) fresh strawberries
- $^1/_2$ cup powdered sugar
- $^1/_4$ cup orange-flavored liqueur or orange juice
- 1 quart strawberry or vanilla ice cream

1. Cut strawberries in half; place in large bowl. Sprinkle with powdered sugar and liqueur; stir gently. Cover and refrigerate about 2 hours.

2. Spoon strawberries over ice cream.

8 servings.
1 Serving: Calories 210 (Calories from Fat 70); Fat 8g (Saturated 5g); Cholesterol 30mg; Sodium 55mg; Carbohydrate 31g (Dietary Fiber 2g); Protein 3g
% Daily Value: Vitamin A 6%; Vitamin C 72%; Calcium 10%; Iron 2%
Exchanges: 1 Starch, 1 Fruit, $1^1/_2$ Fat
Carbohydrate Choices: 2

BETTY'S TIPS

✪ **Substitution**
Try this recipe with raspberries or frozen yogurt.

✪ **Success Hint**
Choose plump strawberries that are red all over, and wash them just before using.

✪ **Special Touch**
A mint leaf and orange-peel curls add a finishing touch to this summer dessert.

S'mores Chocolate Chip Ice-Cream Sandwiches

Prep Time: 15 min Start to Finish: 3 hr 15 min

- About 3 tablespoons marshmallow creme
- 16 fudge-covered graham cookies ($1^1/_2$ x $1^3/_4$ inches each)
- $^1/_2$ cup chocolate chip ice cream

1. Spoon about 1 teaspoon marshmallow creme on 1 cookie. Top with about $^1/_2$ tablespoon ice cream. Top with another cookie, pressing gently. Place in shallow pan; immediately place in freezer. Repeat for remaining sandwiches, placing each in freezer as made.

2. Freeze at least 3 hours until firm. Wrap individually in plastic wrap or waxed paper.

8 sandwiches.
1 Sandwich: Calories 90 (Calories from Fat 35); Fat 4g (Saturated 4g); Cholesterol 5mg; Sodium 50mg; Carbohydrate 13g (Dietary Fiber 0g); Protein 1g
% Daily Value: Vitamin A 0%; Vitamin C 0%; Calcium 0%; Iron 0%
Exchanges: 1 Other Carbohydrate, $^1/_2$ Fat
Carbohydrate Choices: 1

BETTY'S TIPS

✪ **Substitution**
Have fun choosing other ice ream flavors for these bite-size sandwiches!

✪ **Success Hint**
These frozen treats make a fun summer dessert. To serve a crowd, make a double or triple batch.

Quick

Orange Sorbet and Raspberry Parfaits

Prep Time: 15 min Start to Finish: 15 min

1   pint (2 cups) fresh raspberries
2   tablespoons sugar
2   tablespoons orange or raspberry liqueur
4   slices (about $^3/_4$ inch thick) frozen pound cake (from 10.25-ounce package), thawed
1   pint (2 cups) orange sorbet

1. Reserve about $^1/_4$ cup raspberries for garnish. Mix remaining raspberries, sugar and liqueur in medium bowl.

2. Cut pound cake into $^3/_4$-inch cubes. Layer half of cake, half of sorbet and half of raspberry mixture in each of 4 parfait glasses. Repeat layers. Sprinkle with reserved raspberries. Serve immediately.

4 servings.
1 Serving: Calories 405 (Calories from Fat 170); Fat 19g (Saturated 8g); Cholesterol 80mg; Sodium 60mg; Carbohydrate 60g (Dietary Fiber 6g); Protein 5g
% Daily Value: Vitamin A 2%; Vitamin C 32%; Calcium 4%; Iron 10%
Exchanges: 2 Starch, 2 Fruit, 1 Other Carbohydrate, 3 Fat
Carbohydrate Choices: 4

BETTY'S TIPS

⊕ **Substitution**
Angel food, sponge cake, ladyfingers or other cakes would be delicious in this recipe.

⊕ **Success Hint**
Buy plump, bright red raspberries with no signs of mold. They spoil quickly when damp, so don't rinse them until just before you're ready to use them. Store the berries uncovered in the fridge for no more than 2 days.

⊕ **Special Touch**
If you don't have parfait glasses, layer this dessert in champagne or wine goblets or fancy dessert dishes. Add a touch of color with a sprig of fresh mint.

Orange Sorbet and Raspberry Parfaits

helpful **nutrition** and **cooking** information

nutrition guidelines

We provide nutrition information for each recipe, which includes calories, fat, cholesterol, sodium, carbohydrate, fiber and protein. Individual food choices can be based on this information.

Recommended intake for a daily diet of 2,000 calories as set by the Food and Drug Administration

Total Fat	Less than 65g
Saturated Fat	Less than 20g
Cholesterol	Less than 300mg
Sodium	Less than 2,400mg
Total Carbohydrate	300g
Dietary Fiber	25g

criteria used for calculating nutrition information

- The first ingredient was used wherever a choice is given (such as ⅓ cup sour cream or plain yogurt).

- The first ingredient amount was used wherever a range is given (such as 3- to 3½-pound cut-up broiler-fryer chicken).

- The first serving number was used wherever a range is given (such as 4 to 6 servings).

- "If desired" ingredients and recipe variations were not included (such as, sprinkle with brown sugar, if desired).

- Only the amount of a marinade or frying oil that is estimated to be absorbed by the food during preparation or cooking was calculated.

ingredients used in recipe testing and nutrition calculations

- Ingredients used for testing represent those that the majority of consumers use in their homes: large eggs, 2% milk, 80%-lean ground beef, canned ready-to-use chicken broth and vegetable oil spread containing not less than 65 percent fat.

- Fat-free, low-fat or low-sodium products were not used, unless otherwise indicated.

- Solid vegetable shortening (not butter, margarine, nonstick cooking sprays or vegetable oil spread because they can cause sticking problems) was used to grease pans, unless otherwise indicated.

equipment used in recipe testing

We use equipment for testing that the majority of consumers use in their homes. If a specific piece of equipment (such as a wire whisk) is necessary for recipe success, it is listed in the recipe.

- Cookware and bakeware without nonstick coatings were used, unless otherwise indicated.

- No dark-colored, black or insulated bakeware was used.

- When a pan is specified in a recipe, a metal pan was used; a baking dish or pie plate means ovenproof glass was used.

- An electric hand mixer was used for mixing only when mixer speeds are specified in the recipe directions. When a mixer speed is not given, a spoon or fork was used.

cooking terms glossary

Beat: Mix ingredients vigorously with spoon, fork, wire whisk, hand beater or electric mixer until smooth and uniform.

Boil: Heat liquid until bubbles rise continuously and break on the surface and steam is given off. For a rolling boil, the bubbles form rapidly.

Chop: Cut into coarse or fine irregular pieces with a knife, food chopper, blender or food processor.

Cube: Cut into squares ½ inch or larger.

Dice: Cut into squares smaller than ½ inch.

Grate: Cut into tiny particles using small rough holes of grater (citrus peel or chocolate).

Grease: Rub the inside surface of a pan with shortening, using pastry brush, piece of waxed paper or paper towel, to prevent food from sticking during baking (as for some casseroles).

Julienne: Cut into thin, matchlike strips, using knife or food processor (vegetables, fruits, meats).

Mix: Combine ingredients in any way that distributes them evenly.

Sauté: Cook foods in hot oil or margarine over medium-high heat with frequent tossing and turning motion.

Shred: Cut into long thin pieces by rubbing food across the holes of a shredder, as for cheese, or by using a knife to slice very thinly, as for cabbage.

Simmer: Cook in liquid just below the boiling point on top of the stove; usually after reducing heat from a boil. Bubbles will rise slowly and break just below the surface.

Stir: Mix ingredients until consistency is uniform. Stir once in a while for stirring occasionally, often for stirring frequently and continuously for stirring constantly.

Toss: Tumble ingredients (such as green salad) lightly with a lifting motion, usually to coat evenly or mix with another food.

metric conversion chart

Volume

U.S. Units	Canadian Metric	Australian Metric
¼ teaspoon	1 mL	1 ml
½ teaspoon	2 mL	2 ml
1 teaspoon	5 mL	5 ml
1 tablespoon	15 mL	20 ml
¼ cup	50 mL	60 ml
⅓ cup	75 mL	80 ml
½ cup	125 mL	125 ml
⅔ cup	150 mL	170 ml
¾ cup	175 mL	190 ml
1 cup	250 mL	250 ml
1 quart	1 liter	1 liter
1½ quarts	1.5 liters	1.5 liters
2 quarts	2 liters	2 liters
2½ quarts	2.5 liters	2.5 liters
3 quarts	3 liters	3 liters
4 quarts	4 liters	4 liters

Weight

U.S. Units	Canadian Metric	Australian Metric
1 ounce	30 grams	30 grams
2 ounces	55 grams	60 grams
3 ounces	85 grams	90 grams
4 ounces (¼ pound)	115 grams	125 grams
8 ounces (½ pound)	225 grams	225 grams
16 ounces (1 pound)	455 grams	500 grams
1 pound	455 grams	½ kilogram

Measurements

Inches	Centimeters
1	2.5
2	5.0
3	7.5
4	10.0
5	12.5
6	15.0
7	17.5
8	20.5
9	23.0
10	25.5
11	28.0
12	30.5
13	33.0

Temperatures

Fahrenheit	Celsius
32°	0°
212°	100°
250°	120°
275°	140°
300°	150°
325°	160°
350°	180°
375°	190°
400°	200°
425°	220°
450°	230°
475°	240°
500°	260°

Note: The recipes in this cookbook have not been developed or tested using metric measures. When converting recipes to metric, some variations in quality may be noted.

Index

Note: Underscored page references indicate boxed text or tips. **Boldfaced** page references indicate photographs.